Forests and Tribal Livelihood

About the Authors

Lancy Lobo is a Doctorate in Sociology from the Delhi School of Economics, University of Delhi. He is now the Director, Centre for Culture and Development, Vadodara. Earlier, he served as Director, Centre for Social Studies, Surat. He has conducted extensive studies on *dalits*, tribals, OBCs and minorities in rural and urban Gujarat. He was an International Fellow at the Woodstock Centre, Georgetown University, Washington, D.C. during 1999-2000. He has authored and co-authored ten books.

Jayesh Shah is a Research Associate at the Centre for Culture and Development, Vadodara. He is a Doctorate in Management from The M.S. University of Baroda. He also holds post-graduate diplomas in Industrial Relations, Labour Laws, Organization Behaviour, Clinical Psychology and Computer Science. He has served as Chief Executive Officer in a leading international company for more than ten years. Earlier he worked as freelance Management Consultant for more than 10 years in Gujarat. He has conducted extensive studies on labour, employment and industry in his career. He has authored many articles in professional journals and co-authored four books.

FORESTS AND TRIBAL LIVELIHOOD
Changing Behaviours and Attitudes

Lancy Lobo
Jayesh Shah

CONCEPT PUBLISHING COMPANY PVT. LTD.
NEW DELHI-110059

ISBN-13: 978-93-5125-180-4

First Published 2017

Published and Printed by

Concept
Since 1974

Concept Publishing Company Pvt. Ltd.
Regd. Office:
A/15-16, Commercial Block, Mohan Garden,
New Delhi-110059 (INDIA)
Phones : 25351460, 25351794, *Fax* : 091-11-25357109
Email : publishing@conceptpub.com
Website: www.conceptpub.com

Editorial Office:
H-13, Bali Nagar, New Delhi-110 015, India.

Cataloging in Publication Data—DK Courtesy: D.K. Agencies (P) Ltd. <docinfo@dkagencies.com>

Lobo, Lancy *(Of Centre for Culture and Development)*, **author.**
Forests and tribal livelihood : changing behaviours and attitudes / Lancy Lobo, Jayesh Shah.
pages cm
Includes bibliographical references and index.
ISBN 9789351251804

1. Forests and forestry—Social aspects—India—Gujarat. 2. Forests and forestry—Economic aspects—India—Gujarat. 3. Gujarat (India)—Scheduled tribes. I. Shah, Jayesh (Research Associate), author. II. Title.

HD9766.I43G85 2016 DDC 338.17498095475 23

Preface

Mankind as a whole has entered a new phase in the history with reference to the environment. The quality and magnitude of exploitation of natural resources is a derivative of factors such as the level of contemporary technology, population, demand pattern, and socio-cultural attitudes of the society towards nature at different periods. Indian society has not been an exception to this. This book is about the changing behaviours of forests and tribals' livelihood since Independence. It attempts to analyse the changing character of forests in mainland Gujarat, the result of the changes in the forests on the tribal livelihood, impact of developmental activities on the lives of tribal people, interventions by the State and Central Government and the conflicts among the stakeholders of the forests.

Long-term policy implications focus on the national scenario, taking Gujarat as a case study. Review of various Acts regarding forests and tribals, which are neglected by the policy formulators, are the part of this book. The book also shows interesting facts that there are not many linkages between the changes in the forest and the migration of tribals. Increased migration has caused cultural diversification. This trend in recent times is due to the tribals largely not depending on the forest alone.

There is a widespread debate among the social activists working for the tribals that the tribals have the right to the forest land as they have been living there for centuries and have their own customary laws with reference to forest land. On the other hand, most of the land has been surveyed and settled by the state. In such a scenario, it is of utmost importance that these conflicting issues should be resolved amicably. The book throws light on this aspect through an outline of long-term policy implications.

Vadodara (Gujarat) **Lancy Lobo**
June 2015 **Jayesh Shah**

Acknowledgements

The initiative for this study came from JESA of Gujarat, who gave an outline of research questions and with whom we had interactions during the study. Dr. Biswaroop Das has been a great help in the peer review. Professor A.M. Shah took great interest in this study. To all of them we are grateful.

Our thanks are due to the following libraries and archives: Forest Library (Gandhinagar), CSS (Surat), Central Library (Vadodara), DILR (Vadodara) Maharashtra State Archives (Mumbai), and NRSA (Hyderabad).

Nirzar Lakhia processed the satellite imagery, and it was a pleasure to work with him. The study would not have been possible but for the cooperation of Forest bureaucracy: Principal Secretary, DCFs (except Godhra and Baria), and T.L. Patel, Joint Director (FRA). Leading NGOs like, Viksat, AKRSP, Sadguru Foundation, Development Support Centre were generous with their time. We are thankful to them. We also thank our respondents in 184 villages and our field investigators who collected the primary data.

We held two workshops: (l) of the ex-princely state Rajas and Ranis to learn from them about the status of forests and tribals before Independence, and (2) We shared the findings of our study with scholars, NGOs, forest bureaucrats working with forests and tribals. We sincerely thank them.

Chandrakant Upadhyaya and TRAI faculty, Noel D'Lima, Bindu Bhatt and Shashikant Kumar have spared their time for our study. Amit Mitra critically commented on the manuscript. The staff of CCD, especially M. Bachaspathimayum, deserves special mention for her deep commitment to this study. Amba Gamit and Soma Vartha have facilitated this study. We are grateful to them.

Finally, we thank ALBOAN for providing a grant to carry out this study.

Lancy Lobo
Jayesh Shah

Contents

List of Tables

List of Charts

Abbreviations

ACF	Assistant Conservator of Forests
AKRSP	Agakhan Rural Support Programmes
ARCH	Action Research in Community and Health
ARDA	Advanced Research and Development Agency
BAIF	Bharatiya Agro, Industries Foundation
BAMCEF	Backward and Minority Communities Employees' Federation
BRGF	Backward Regions Grant Fund
BSC	Behaviour Science Centre
BSNL	Bharat Sanchar Nigam Limited
CARE	Credit Analysis and Research Ltd
CBF	Central Board of Forestry
CDM	Clean Development Mechanism
CF	Conservator of Forests
CM	Chief Minister
CPR	Common Property Resources
CRZ	Coastal Regulation Zone
CWH	Critical Wildlife Habitats
DCF	Deputy Conservator of Forest
DISHA	Developing Initiatives for Social and Human Actions
DJ	Disc Jockeys
DLC	District Level Committee
DPCs	Direct Purchase Centres
EPA	Environment Protection Act
FAO	Food and Agriculture Organisation
FCA	Forest Conservation Act
FDAs	Forest Development Agency
FIR	First Investigation Report
FPF	Forest Protection Force
FRA	Forest Rights Act
FRC	Forest Rights Committees
GDP	Gross Domestic Product
GFDP	Gujarat Forestry Development Programme

GIS	Geographical Information System
GPS	Global Positioning System
GRs	Government Resolutions
GSFDC	Gujarat State Forest Development Corporation (Limited)
GVM	Gram Vikas Mandals
ICAR	Indian Council of Agricultural Research
IDDP	Integrated Dairy Development Projects
ITDA	Integrated Tribal Development Areas
ITDP	Integrated Tribal Development Projects
IWADP	Integrated Wadi and Agriculture Diversification Project
JFM	Joint Forest Management
JPC	Joint Parliamentary Committee
LCC	Land Capability Classification
MFP	Minor Forest Produce
MLA	Member of the Legislative Assembly
MoEF	Ministry of Environment and Forests
MoTA	Ministry of Tribal Affairs
NABARD	National Bank for Agricultural and Rural Development
NAC	National Agriculture Commission
NCA	National Commission of Agriculture
NDA	National Democratic Alliance
NFD	Nehru Foundation for Development
NFP	National Forest Policy
NGO	Non-Governmental Organization
NMSWDF	NM Sadguru Water and Development Foundation
NREGA	National Rural Employment Guarantee Act
NRHM	National Rural Health Mission
NRM	Natural Resource Management
NRSA	National Remote Sensing Agency
NSA	National Security Act
NTFPs	Non-Timber Forest Products,
NTP	National Tribal Policy
PCCF	Principal Chief Conservator of Forests
PESA	Panchayats Extension to the Scheduled Areas
POR	Proofs of Residence
PTG	Primitive Tribal Group
RFO	Range Forest Officer
RKVY	Rashtriya Krishi Vikas Yojana
ROVADAN	Rotary Vapi Dang Development Trust

RSSS	Rajpipla Social Service Society
RTO	Road Transport Office
SDLC	Sub-Divisional Level Committee
SHGs	Self-Help Groups
ST	Scheduled Tribe
SRI	System of Rice Intensification
SRP	State Reserve Police
TPP	Ten Point Programmes
TSP	Tribal Sub-Plan
UNFCC	United Nations Framework Convention on Climate Change
UPA	United Progressive Alliance
VFPC	Village Forest Protection Committee
VIKSAT	Vikram Sarabhai Centre for Development Interaction Nehru Foundation for Development
VLO	Village Level Organization
WLL	Wireless in Local Loop
WLPA	Wild Life Protection Act

Glossary

Adi	beginning or of earliest times
Anganwadi	kindergarten
Avapattikar Churna	ayurvedic herbal powder
Balchaturbhadra Churna	ayurvedic herbal powder
Chhindani	lopping tree branches and burning
Chiranjivi Yojana	a development scheme
Desh	country
Dhanvantari	ayurvedic god
Dhariya	bill-hook
Dilsukh Churna	ayurvedic herbal powder
Dodi	mahuda fruits
Faliyas	lanes
Gaucher	grazing/pasture land
Ghats	mountain pass
Girijan	people of the hills
Gram Panchayats/Sabhas	village institutions
Gram-mitra	village official
Gundas	unsocial elements
Hulchul Tel	ayurvedic herbal oil
Indira Awas Yojana	housing scheme
Indrajav Churna	ayurvedic herbal powder
Jagir	land or village obtained from the king as gift or reward
Jagirdar'	owner of the *'Jagirs'*
Jangli jati	people of the jungle
Jungle Satyagraha	non-violent struggle with reference to forests
Jungliness	wild, uncouth
Jyoti Gram	a development scheme
Kalajhad	blackwood
Kaliparaj	black people'
Kanchankaya Churna	ayurvedic herbal powder

Khandani	lopping tree branches and burning
Khandi	slash and burn cultivation
Kisan Credit Card	farmer credit card
Kodra	a type of grain
Kotars	ravines
Lathi	stick
Mahanarayan Tel	ayurvedic herbal oil
Nagli (Eleusine coracana)	a type of grain
Nakas	entry/exist gates
Nalas	culvert
Padtar	wasteland
Panchayati Raj	village statutory body
Peta mahal	a sub unit of administration
Prant	district or region
Raniparaj	people of the jungle
Sahukars	money-lenders
Sakhi Mandal	women's association
Sanads	title deeds
Sanjivani	a development scheme
Sardar Awas Yojana	housing scheme
Sarvashanti Churna'	herbal powder
Shigru Churna	ayurvedic herbal powder
Sudarshan Churna	ayurvedic herbal powder
Tendu patta	beedi leaves
Timru patta	beedi leaves
Van Bandhu Kalyan Yojana	a development scheme
Van Mandali	forest related organisation
Vanil Udyog	forest related industry
Vanyajati	people of the jungle
Vasi	resident of
Wadi Project	a development scheme

1
Introduction

This book is about the changing character of forests and its impact on the tribals of Gujarat since independence as related in the larger context of India. It attempts to analyse the changing character of forests in mainland Gujarat, the result of the changes in the forests on the tribal livelihood, interventions by the State and Central Government and the conflicts among the stakeholders of the forests. Long-term policy implications of this study will focus on the national scenario, taking Gujarat as a case study. However, the significance of this study needs to be seen in the light of how mankind as a whole has entered a new phase in the history with reference to the environment. In order to understand the world-wide phenomenon, we need to go back to the history of land use, forests, man-land ratio, state, individual and community, use of other natural resources and so on as human life has been closely dependent on the natural resource base for its survival. Exploitation of natural resources has been an age-old phenomenon. However, the quality and magnitude of this exploitation is a derivative of factors such as the level of contemporary technology, population, demand pattern, and socio-cultural attitudes of the society towards nature at different periods. Indian society has not been an exception to this.

I

Man-Land/Forest Relationship in India and Gujarat

Forestry traditions and management have existed even before the known sources of Indic traditions were written. And, these have continued to exist in the Vedic period, the later Vedic period and the Puranic literature. If we consider the Vedic reference, closer to a theory than the later Vedic and Puranic texts, they are definitely the practice manuals! Following these manuals common masses attempted to replicate the prescriptions on the ground for the benefit of humanity. Many references are available on the role that forests and trees played and how they were managed in *Vedas, Upanishads, Ramayana, Mahabharata, Arthasastra,* and *Brihatsamhita* etc. This has been illustrated with assessments of the different types of indigenous forests, trees and landscape management in various parts of India. This has much importance for the history of forest management and the future of sustainable forest management in India.

Ancient texts make explicit references as to how forests and other natural resources were managed. Sustainability in different forms has been an issue of development of thought since ancient times. For example, robust principles were created in order to comprehend whether or not the intricate web of nature is sustaining itself. These principles roughly correspond with modern understanding of conservation, utilization, and regeneration.

Utilization and regeneration principles mentioned in one of the hymns from *Atharva Veda* (12.1.35) reads: "Whatever I dig out from you, O Earth! May that have quick regeneration again; may we not damage thy vital habitat and heart". Implicit here are the following principles:

- Human beings can use the resources from the earth for their sustenance,
- Pattern of resource use must also help in resource regeneration,
- In the process of harvest no damage should be done to the earth,
- Humans are forewarned, not against the use of nature for survival, but against its overuse and abuse.

Although not in modern terminology, the three segment of sustainability—ecology, economy and society seem to get addressed simultaneously. There is considerable overlap in the formal and scientific forestry policy and practice, which provides hope that traditional knowledge systems can contribute to the management of natural resources. Gadgil and Guha (1992: 274) in this context note:

> Indeed one could argue that scientific prescriptions in industrial societies show little evidence of progress over the simple rule-of-thumb prescriptions for sustainable resource use and the conservation of diversity which characterized gatherer and peasant societies. Equally, the legal and codified procedures which are supposed to ensure the enforcement of scientific prescriptions work little better than earlier procedures based on religion or social convention.

On the question of arid and wet zones historian Trautmann (2011: 14-15) writes:

> It is in the areas of denser population that Indian Civilisation sprung up in the first place (the Indus Valley and the Indo-Gangetic Plain generally) and took root (the coastal region and the river deltas of the Peninsula). It is here that the agriculture yields a surplus large enough to sustain a complex social structure including kings and priests, and to finance the building of palaces, temples, and monasteries. By contrast, the drier areas or areas of rainfall agriculture are typically inhabited by peoples with a tribal organisation, far less complex and far more egalitarian, very often practicing a "slash-and- burn" form of agriculture, which sustains far lower densities of people....therefore, constitutes a kind of inferior frontier for Indian civilisation, a place of exile for princes in disgrace, a wilderness conducive to the meditations of a religious hermit, the home of forest peoples and wild.

To get a clear picture of the history of forests, we need to know the phases through which these forests underwent changes under different political regimes. Like most states of the Indian sub-continent, Gujarat State was also invaded and ruled by the Mohammedans, the Marathas, and the British until India got her Independence. In the pre-British India, the ownership of forests resided with the rulers of the different kingdoms across India. With few exceptions, access to forests was largely unrestricted throughout the pre-British period. The institutional framework was complemented by religious and symbolic functions of trees and forests, and caste system played a crucial role in forest management. For example, the protection of wild animals in India became serious business by the time of the Mauryan dynasty; being the first empire to provide a unified political entity in India, the attitude of the Mauryan towards forests, its denizens and fauna in general is of interest (http://en.wikipedia.org/wiki/Maurya_Empire). The Mauryan Empire (324 BC to 180 BC) used a forest classification system, based on the requirements of different social strata: reserved forests for the king of the state; forests donated to eminent Brahmins (priests under the caste system); and forests for the public. During the dynasty, at the village level, the use of all natural resources were managed by a local community institution known as '*Panchayat*', composed of five village elders, who managed all village affairs. A significant part of their duties revolved around settling disputes over land, access to water and mediating conflicts among villagers over the issues of forest and forest produce.

In Mughal India, the empire did not tax forest holdings and the state had no direct claims over lands other than hunting, but the local community was permitted to gather forest produce. The Mughal rulers relied on claiming a share of the actual crop which sometimes exceeded half of the produce. Habib (1984: 35). They needed more revenue. It could come mostly from agriculture. Almost all the Muslim rulers encouraged extension of cultivable land. Man was free to cut forests and bring them under cultivation. The idea of ownership of forests had not developed. The situation changed with the arrival of Islamic people and their state. They treated the forests differently. An important consideration was revenue from land and forest. Outside Mughal India, in many areas the control and management of local resources were vested in the local communities who designed a variety of practices for effective resource conservation through local knowledge and religious idioms.

The significance of forests in medieval Muslim Gujarat lay in its demand for wood for constructing boats, ships for merchants as well as navy in the rivers and the seas. For instance, in the rivers Mahi and Narmada boats were used for internal navigation as well as fishing. Wood was very important for the architecture of Gujarat, especially for houses and Haveli constructions. Then of course wood was used for sculpture in mainland and peninsular Gujarat and this wood had to be secured from the forests as it was not locally available. There were a large number of princely states in Gujarat, and their palaces were mainly made of wood. The large number of capitals which were small towns needed charcoal which came from forests. Precious stones too came from mines located in the forest areas.

During the British period, the sole purpose of forest management was to redistribute economic gains in favour of the colonial empire. The whole enfolding of policy was built on economic concepts favouring greater efficiency, increased control over the people and the resources and centralization of power. This was achieved by commercialization of timber, restriction on the rights of local people, and large scale deforestation. The exclusion of local people from forest resources led to conflict between them and the colonial empire. The unwritten oral local knowledge was lost in the colonial and post-colonial era, when priority was given to "scientific" forestry approaches originating from Europe. The local people searched for a solution through various non-violent movements, although some eventually turned to violent means. Thus the British period created large-scale conflicts among forest managers and forest dwelling people and marked the beginning of the breakdown of a symbiotic relationship between many communities and the forests in which they were located (Shah, 1996: 14ff).

Many forests were under the rule of princely states in India during the British colonial regime. The Princely states too more or less followed the same approach to forests as the British. Before the British rule, the present State of Gujarat was divided into several Princely states such as Cambay (Khambhat), Idar, Rajpipla, Chhota Udaipur, Devgadh Baria, Lunavada, Balasinor, Sunth, Sankheda, Bansda, Dharampur, Sachin, Dang and Baroda. British Gujarat (Ahmedabad, Kheda, Bharuch, Surat and Panchmahal Districts), and Princely states, both of which had forests, but the character of these forests and also of the forest-dwellers was different.

Although very little is known about the management of forests in Gujarat before the advent of the Britishers, yet the travelogues of the early 19th century and the Gazetteers give us the picture of a well-forested country whose pasture and forest resources were controlled and fairly managed by the local village communities. The forests were a communal property with no individual staking any claim to them, though all the individuals had accessed the forests for their needs. For the tribal communities in particular, the forests remained their life-blood. This symbiotic relationship between the tribals and the forests constituted the foundation of the independence of the tribals from the outside world. Forest regulations in the Princely states were only customary regulations of people's rights over forest-lands and forest-products; it did not pose any problem as there were vast tracts of forests and a relatively small group of tribal communities. These communities were bonded in mutual trust and common interests as far as the forests were concerned.

A review of the history of forests in the princely states and the British districts in the State of Gujarat needs to be undertaken. But one cannot deal with the forests of each of these states. The Gazetteers of these states and district Gazetteers contain a descriptive history of forests and how they were managed. As a case study, we have analyzed Idar, a princely state, and Dang, a mix of the princely and British State.

Idar—A Princely State

Some idea of the forest administration in Idar State is available from the Report on the Administration of the Bombay Presidency for the year 1885-87:7

> The Idar State alone attempts any forest conservancy. It has one or two teak reserves. The introduction of effective conservancy on a large scale would be most difficult in consequence of the immemorial rights of the Bhils to forest produce. The Bhils would certainly resent and resist any interference.

About the administrative set-up, the Administrative Report for the year 1886-87 makes the following observations: "The Idar State had some six forest reserves, in which teak was grown. These forests will in time become valuable. In the attached taluka of

Mohanpur, a start was made with forest conservancy. None of the other States had any regularly conserved forests, and indeed the immemorial rights of the Bhils to forest produce would materially interfere with anything like scientific conservancy" (*ibid*: 7).

The State of Idar was divided into three divisions and placed under a *Mamlatdar* (revenue officer of a region). The duties of the Darbar Karbhari (a Minister of a State), a First Class Magistrate, and the Assistant Political Agent were more supervisory in nature than executive. In 1901 (Annual Administration Report 1900-1901), the Forest Department in the Idar Sate was supervised by a graduate of the College of Agriculture of Madras. The area under protection was over 35 miles extending over 12 villages in the Ahmednagar (Himatnagar taluka), 17 in the Bayad taluka and 5 in the Vadali taluka. Between 1901 and 1905, there were no major changes in the Forest policy of the State. However, in the year 1905-06, the contract to manufacture from the produce of the Khair trees in the Rajgadh forests was given to a Bohra merchant of Surat. However, the forest produce of the State did not find adequate sales as there was little demand owing to the distance of the forests from the railway. Although the Reserved Forests had not been actually surveyed, it must be pointed out that in, 1912-13, their area was approximately 30,000 acres. The local forest produces usually consisted of ordinary teak, *sadad, khair, timru, rayan, dhav* and *bamboos*. In this year, the revenue from all the sources under the forests amounted to Rs. 1,107 (Annual Administration Report, 1912-13).

In 1931, the Forest Department was under the charge of the Assistant Revenue Commissioner. The post of a Forest Ranger was sanctioned but was not filled for want of a competent hand. In the same year, only 10 miles of the forest line and 8 miles of coupe line were demarcated, and many new changes were attempted by the State. Attempts were made for clearing useless trees by leasing coupes, but this effort was not successful as there were no good bidders. Plantation work was also undertaken in the Raigadh area; mahogany and *Kaju* seedlings from the State nursery were planted here, and the seeds of the *babul* tree were also scattered. Although, some of the trees perished, the general result was satisfactory; in the course of the year as many as 17 sandal, 53 mahogany, 27 *kaju* and 200 *babul* trees survived (Annual Administration Report, 1931-32: 47-48).

In 1935, the forests were taken under the charge of the Survey Superintendent. However, it was only in 1937 that the Forest Department was constituted as a separate Department under a regular Forest Officer. Later in 1937, the forests were classed as 'Reserved', 'Protected' and 'Village Forests' in the forest records. These terms, however, did not carry the usual definition of these classes as described in the Indian Forest Act of 1927. The Reserved Forests were set aside for the purpose of improvement, and the Protected Forests were subjected to *exploitation*. In the same year (1937), the coupe system under 30 years rotation was initiated for the purpose of exploitation of these forests. However, because of the poor quality of forest growth, a majority of the coupes remained unsold. This system was finally given up, and the coppice system with 18 years' rotation was initiated. However, major exploitation of the forests continued under the permit system, and the *ryots* could remove forests material from anywhere in the forests whenever they liked, on payment of the scheduled rate.

The forests of Idar were dense and luxuriant before integration of the State into the Indian Union. The enforcement of the Land Reforms Laws, particularly, the *Jagirs* Abolition Act, had also led to wanton destruction of the forest wealth of the district (Sabarkantha District Gazetteer, 1974: iv). Despite some of the native states were under the general control of the Mahikantha Political Agency, no attempts were made either to classify these forest areas (except areas which were parts of Baroda State) or to prepare schemes or plans for its working and development. In most of the areas, even surveys were not undertaken, and therefore, no maps existed. Owing to the lack of control and absence of sound implementation management policies, the forests were left in a degraded state. Even though the Forest Department was established as a separate administrative unit in some of the States; however, it was usually the *Diwan* under the king who had the final authority in all matters of administration in the Princely states.

The general public was allowed a free hand and enjoyed liberal privileges of cutting the trees and exploiting the forests after the payment of duty, fixed from time to time by the Diwan. This led to the fall in forest growth. This practice received further impetus during Second World War. The wanton cutting of trees, heavy grazing and regular fires left no scope for the natural regeneration of forests. The disastrous consequences of ill-conceived forest policies developed by the former States ruined the forests so much so that in many areas such forests were difficult to retrieve (Jadhav, 1959). The prices of forest produce soared, and the practice of indiscriminate cutting of forests spread unchecked resulting in utter ruin of forest wealth (Gazetteer of Sabarkantha, 1974: 22-23).

The Dang—Bhil Rajas and the British

The word 'Dang' suggests a hilly village as opposed to '*desh*', which means a village situated in the plains. The Dang district was heavily forested area both during the time of the princely rulers and under British rule. It was one district and had the smallest area, with the least population and the most backward in terms of social and economic growth, but the richest in forest reserves. It is predominantly populated by tribals, who are by and large illiterate. The Dangis as a people have special customs and traditions and peculiar agricultural practices as stated in the Gazetteer (Dangs Gazetteer, 1971: i). The history of the tract is traceable as far back as 1818 when the British Government first came in contact with the Bhil Rajas, who ruled over petty tracts comprising the Dang. Forest land was freely cultivated prior to 1812 without any restrictions whatsoever by the four kings (*Nayaks*), their *Bhaubands* (lineage) and other tribals.

Under Notification No. 26 F, dated 1st March, 1879 issued by the Chief Secretary to the Government of Bombay the entire district of Dang was notified as Reserved Forests. The exercise of privileges in certain areas later on, including cultivation, was thought to be needed and set aside which were termed as Protected Forests. But it seems that no notification was issued for deleting these areas from the reserved forests and declaring them as protected forests. The First Forest Settlement made by Mr. A. Lucas was approved by the Government in 1892 under Resolution No. 5977, dated 22nd July, 1892, of the Revenue Department. Under the Resolution, 561.38 sq. km. (217.12 sq. miles) were set aside as reserved forests. But, for years, this reservation was only nominal, as there were neither law nor authority and no establishment to support it. The Bhil chiefs (Rajas) and their people conceived the Resolution as an attempt to deprive them of their rights; this made them rebel, and they vigorously started cutting, burning and cultivating in these reserves. In this process, large tracts of almost virgin forests were practically wiped out. Consequently, a Special Divisional Forest Officer was appointed in 1903 duly empowered with first class magisterial powers to make the chiefs abide by the terms of their agreement and to apply the spirit of the Indian Forest Act for infringement. Thereafter, the recommendations of the Divisional Forest Officer of the Dangs, and the Revenue Department (under Resolution No. 4265, dated 2nd May, 1911) sanctioned additional 294.26 sq. km. of forest area to the reserves, thus raising the total area of these reserved forests to 855.64 sq. km.

The question regarding village settlement of the Dang came up for consideration before the Government of India in the year 1957. It was opined by the Legal Department in 1959 as under:

> It is true that the present classification of the forests in the Dangs as Reserved and Protected cannot be held to have sanctioned in law merely because it has existed for many years and on the strength of past usage and convention. It is also possible to make a regulation for the Dang district under Para 5 (2) of the Fifth Schedule of the Constitution for this purpose. It is, however, competent for Government to issue now the necessary notifications under the Indian Forest Act, 1927, notifying the classification so far followed by any acts committed in pursuance of the same are challenged or are likely to be challenged; it does not appear necessary to make any such regulations.

Thus, the classification of the Dang Forests into Protected and Reserved was regularized. Formerly, an immense amount of shifting cultivation was carried out, and the forest was cut and burnt entirely or in parts. The Bhil and the Konkani tribes move their villages with the huge frequency, choosing fresh patches of forest, burning and clearing them for cultivation. For ages, they had been allowed to make roofs of the most temporary huts with fine teak saplings and poles, and they looked on all timber except picked logs as valueless (Working Plan of Dangs, 1912-13: 4).

Various methods of exploitation and extraction of forest produces were practiced which amounted to heavy selection felling of the best available timber. The timber was cut, sawed and dragged up the *ghats* (mountain pass) into Nasik and Khandesh districts. The disadvantage for such heavy felling of timber was the limited market demand and the lack of resources for export. There was a good deal of timber theft in the Baroda territory using the permit system as a cover. With the opening of the Tapti Valley Railway, now known as the Bhusaval-Surat (in 1897) section of the Western Railway, there was a boom in the irregular extraction of timber, amounting to the virtual depletion of teak from all available portions; almost 60,000 teak trees down to 90 girths were girdled and felled for railway sleepers in the northern Dang alone. The result of this and the previous working was that the protected forests and the new reserves in the West Purna valley were nearly all cleared of sound timber.

We may conclude the pre-independence history of Gujarat forests in pre-independence or premerger period the following manner:

- The Rajas were more interested in game and revenues and invited non-tribals to settle down in their princely states. They gave fertile lands in river-banks and valleys to these peasant castes who were better farmers than tribals. The different states were under the general control of the Rewa Kantha Political Agency. Under persuasion of the Agency, many states received schemes or Working Plans prepared by trained forest officers. Considerations of sustained yield, regeneration of forests, regulation and control of grazing and relevant forestry practices were ignored.
- The ex-princely States of Devgadh Baria, Lunawada, Santrampur and Sanjeli maintained their forests by suitably devising administrative and scientific measures as it was felt that forests contributed substantially to their revenue.
- Most of these states had a distinct set-up in their administrative machinery for managing forests. The forest areas were not demarcated in any of the states except in the Jambughoda State; the ruler had also obtained four inch toposheets of the maps showing forests.
- Working Plans were prepared for the Devgadh Baria in 1942, for the Santrampur (or Sunth State) by J.A. Wallinger and for the Lunawada State by E.K. Kotwal (date not known and the scheme is untraceable). But these Working Plans were never worked in practice. Forests were ruthlessly exploited much against the advice of the forest

officers, especially during the war years when timber fetched heavy prices and particularly before the merger of the states when many rulers wanted to extract as much as possible from these forests.

- The Ratanmahal forests of Baria State remained totally unexploited only because they were not easily accessible and also because they were annexed by the Devgadh Baria State upon the death of the Chief of the Ratanmahal State. These forests formed the *shikar* preserve of the ruler. To this day these have been extremely well preserved and provide a source for ecological studies of the forests of this region.
- The timber wood was costlier in British districts as there was a demand for railway sleepers. There was also smuggling of timber from the princely state to British districts where prices were higher.

After the abolition of the princely states and feudal estates, all uncultivated lands under their control became vested in the Indian State. The larger tracts were handed over to the Forest Department generally as protected forests, and the rest were vested in the Village Panchayats which are under the overall supervision of the Revenue Department. Another process of extending government control over forests was through acquisition of private forests. The necessary laws were passed by the various state governments in the two decades following Independence. "Massive felling of trees took place from these forests because of the fear that they would be nationalized, as indeed they were in the 1950's and 1960's. For many years after this take-over, an impression has continued in the villages that if trees are planted on private lands, not only would the trees belong to the Government but the land on which such plantation takes place would also revert to the Government" (Saxena, 2008).

After independence, from 1947 to 1987, the Government of India tried to redefine social-utility and social welfare functions, but the emphasis of forest management regimes continued to be on commercial exploitation and exclusion of forest dwellers. Forest management regimes did not take the cognizance of community-based natural resources management. This alienated the communities from being a responsible part of the eco-system and resulted into unsustainable and destructive harvesting of products and loss of bio-diversity. Furthermore, after independence, the 'Panchayat' was transformed from a system of local governance to one of a state regulated 'representative democracy' (Sarin, 1993). The former legitimacy of the local leadership and the tradition of collective decision-making was abolished; in their place, a new institution, which continued to be referred to as the 'Panchayat', took over.

The globalisation phase has seen population growth and increasing demand for goods and services, leading to exploitation of natural resources, including forests. Forests are complex multifunctional ecosystems contributing to sustainable economic development in the following manner: their role as carbon sinks and stores; their favourable impacts on local climates; their conservation of genetic diversity; their supply of hydrologic services of value regionally; and their role in reducing rates of soil erosion (Tisdell, 2012:4). Then of course forests provide safety nets for forest dwellers apart from providing employment, livelihood and satisfaction of their needs.

Conservation of nature is undoubtedly a good thing, but there are problems which one needs to consider. It is the forest dwellers who have paid a high price in terms of loss of their livelihood. We have conservationists who want to protect and conserve the forests with little regard for the livelihood of forest dwellers. They would even like to cordon off more and more forests land under the reserved and protected category of forests with sanctuaries for wild animals. This necessarily implies shifting forest dwellers or restricting their freedom and access to fuel, fodder and food. Some conservationists are caught between the preferences to the tiger to the man!

II

Gujarat and its Tribals

Gujarat state in western India has varied ecological systems: it has the longest coastal belt in India; it has desert system; plains irrigated system and dry hilly Eastern belt. Most of the forests are concentrated in eastern Gujarat. The rivers such as Banas, Sabarmati, Mahi, Karjan, Narmada, Tapi, Damanganga and others pass through these hills and flow into the Arabian Sea. The forest dwellers are mostly tribal who live especially in the hills but along the rich valleys where these rivers flow non-tribals live.

The depletion of forests in the State of Gujarat and the country as a whole is a major concern, but today the need for minerals what lies underground especially in forested areas has become a bone of contention. Hence, losses of trees with extractive industries are affecting the forest dwellers. One must note that the forests and mineral resources often co-existed, all forests were not located on the hills and the entire community in hilly and forest areas were not "tribals", and all "tribals" did not live in forests.

Forests are a treasure trove of a large variety of food. It is estimated that 60-70 per cent of the food consumed by the tribals comes from the forests. Food items comprising edible leaves bark of trees, fruits and vegetables, are procured from the forest. A number of the village industries are forest based. Commenting on the Khasis, Shangpilang (2010: xiv) writes that, for the Khasis, the forest is a well loved home, a game sanctuary and also as the abode of worship all rolled into one, around which his social, cultural and religious activities revolve. Forest is a sacred entity. This 'sacred' character of the forest finds expression in the customary practice.

The term "tribal" was introduced by the British, and it has no fixed scientific meaning, and is actually an administrative term, if not political or lineage (Shah, 2010: 205ff). The social activists have strongly advocated that the 'tribals' of India be considered as "indigenous" people of India. But, who is 'indigenous' in India has been a matter of contention! If the tribals are indigenous then who are the Dravidians? Who are the Indus Valley Civilisation people? The Aryan theory has also become highly controversial and critiqued from different sections. Hence, it may be appropriate to use the term forest-dweller, although most of the forest-dwellers are tribals.

Evolution from one stage of the economy to another with reference to forest-dwellers needs serious attention. Many forest dwellers on their own volition evolved into agriculturists. They would cut trees and clear a plot of land. Virgin land yielded good crops without much work on them for a few years. The assumption of static, conservative for dweller is unreal. Forest dwellers too had their own ambitions. Agricultural development also had stages: cultivation by broadcast of seeds; hoe cultivation; plough with the wooden share; plough with an iron share.

In languages such as Gujarati, Hindi or Bengali the word *jati* is used for both caste and tribe. In some older Gujarati texts, the term *jangli jati* is used to distinguish the *jati* of the mountains and forests from those of the plains (Desai, 1898: 379). In South Gujarat, the term *kaliparaj*—denoted 'black people'. But this was applied only to a related group of *jatis* and did not extend to the tribals of central and northern Gujarat, who were known as Bhils. Terms such as *jangli jati* or *kaliparaj* were, from the point of view of the tribals, hardly flattering, and in the twentieth century Gandhian social workers coined polite equivalents such as *raniparaj, vanyajati* and *girijan*. These were intended to convey the idea of the wild yet noble denizen of the forests. They were, in fact, patronising terms, being used in a way that continued to imply *jungliness* and barbarity as well as simplicity and childishness, and they never became popular amongst the people so described. Another reason for the inappropriateness of these terms was that by the mid-twentieth century the majority of these people no longer actually lived in what little was left of the dwindling forest tracts of India.

Profile of Gujarat Tribals

The population of Gujarat in 2001 Census has been 50,671,017. Of these, 7,481,160 persons were the Scheduled Tribes (STs) constituting 14.8 per cent of the total population of the state. The state registered 21.4 per cent decadal growth of the Scheduled Tribe population in 1991-2001. There are twenty-nine notified Scheduled Tribes in the state. The Bhil with 3.4 lakh people represents the majority of the total ST population of the state (46%). Dubla (8%), Dhodia (7.9%), Rathawa (7.2%) and Naikda (5.3%) are the other major STs each was having a sizable population. Along with Bhil they constitute about 74.3 per cent of the state's total ST population. Gamit, Kokna, Chaudhri, Varli, and Dhanka account for 3-4 per cent each of state's ST population. Table 1.1 shows the population of major STs in the State of Gujarat in 2001 Census.

The Scheduled Tribe (ST) population in Gujarat is predominantly rural with 91.8 per cent residing in rural and 8.2 per cent, in urban areas. Of the twelve major STs having more than one lakh people, Dubla has recorded the highest 15.7 per cent urban

Table 1.1: Population of Major STs in Gujarat—Census 2001

Name of Scheduled Tribe	*Total Population*	*Proportion to the Total ST Population*
Bhil	3,441,945	46.0
Dubla	596,865	08.0
Dhodiya	589,108	07.9
Rathwa	535,284	07.2
Naikda	393,024	05.3
Gamit	354,362	04.7
Konkana	329,496	04.4
Chaudhary	282,392	03.8
Varli	255,271	03.4
Dhanka	252,637	03.4
Pateliya	109,390	01.5
Koli	95,655	01.3
Other ST	245,731	03.1
Total ST	**7,481,160**	**100.0**

Source: Census 2001.

population. Significant urban population has also been recorded among Dhodiya (12.4%), Pateliya (12.4%), and Koli (10.2%). On the other hand, Varli has recorded the lowest at 0.6 per cent urban population.

District-wise, The Dang has recorded the highest 93.8 per cent of its population as Scheduled Tribe, although its share is 2.3 per cent of the total ST population in the state. Besides, the district of Dangs, the Narmada (78.1%), Dahod (72.3%) and Valsad (54.8%) have recorded more than half of the total population of the district as Scheduled Tribe.

As per 2001 census, sex ratio of the ST population is 974, which is close to the national average for all the STs (978). Individual ST-wise, the Varli and Gamit have recorded sex ratio above 1000. The sex ratio among Chaudhary (996), Konkana (990), Dhodiya (989), and Dubla (983) has been recorded above the state average for STs. Sex ratio is comparatively lower among Dhanka (937) and Pateliya (955). The state has recorded child sex ratio (0-6 age group) of 966, which is lower than the national average for STs (973). Among the individual STs, Pateliya has recorded low child sex ratio of 926.

The ST population of Gujarat has recorded 47.7 per cent literacy rate, which is at par with the national average for STs (47.1%). The male and female literacy at 59.2 per cent and 36 per cent respectively indicate that women are lagging behind male counterparts by 23.2 percentage points. Of the twelve major STs, Dhodiya with 75.9 per cent literacy is ahead of others. Their female literacy rate is 66.5 per cent and male (85.3%). Table 1.2 shows the literacy rate (seven years and above) for major Scheduled Tribes.

Table 1.2: Literacy Rate (Seven Years and Above) for Major STs in Gujarat

Name of Scheduled Tribe	*Literacy Rate*		
	Male	*Female*	*Total*
Bhil	56.9	31.3	44.3
Dubla	56.8	38.7	47.8
Dhodiya	85.3	66.5	75.9
Rathwa	50.2	22.8	36.8
Naikda	45.6	25.2	35.6
Gamit	61.7	44.2	52.9
Konkana	62.6	40.3	51.5
Chaudhary	71.3	53.4	62.4
Varli	42.1	22.2	32.1
Dhanka	66.7	38.1	52.9
Pateliya	78.5	45.9	62.5
Koli	38.4	26.3	12.8
Total ST	**59.2**	**36.0**	**47.7**

Source: Census 2001.

In the age-group 5-14 years, total of 56.9 per cent of the ST population is attending schools or other educational institutions. Of the twelve major STs, Dhodiya has recorded the highest 84.5 per cent. Other STs who have recorded above state average are Chaudhary (80.7%), Pateliya (74.9%), Konkana (66.5%), Dhanka (63.6%), and Dubla (60.9%). Naikda (44.1%) and Varli (44.9%) have recorded less than half of their population in the age-group 5-14 to be attending schools or any other institution.

Merely 2.5 per cent of total literates in the ST population have educational level graduation and above. The Chaudhary and Dhodiya are well ahead, among the twelve major STs, to register high of 5.3 per cent of their literates as graduate or above. On the contrary, Varli, Dubla, and Naikda are at the bottom, each having less than one per cent.

In 2001 census, 51.7 per cent of the ST population has been recorded as workers, which is much more than the aggregated national figure for STs. Of the total workers, 70.4 per cent have been recorded as main workers and 29.6 per cent as marginal workers. The Work Participation Rate (WPR) at 47.8 per cent among ST female workers is slightly lower than ST male workers (55.5%). Gender disparity, however, is different in the category of main workers; 87.2 per cent males and only 50.3 per cent females. Of the twelve major STs, Gamit has recorded the highest WPR at 58.3 per cent.

As regards category of workers, 41.9 per cent of the total main workers among the STs have been recorded as 'cultivators' and 36.1 per cent 'agricultural labourers'. Thus, a total of 78 per cent of the total Scheduled Tribe main workers are involved in the agricultural sector. Of the twelve major STs, Rathwa has recorded the highest 68.4 per cent of their total main workers as cultivators, closely followed by Pateliya (64.7%), and Konkana (60.9%). It is important to note that merely 1.8 per cent main workers among Dubla have been recorded as cultivators. 73.6 per cent of Dubla main workers have been recorded as agricultural labourers and many of them are bonded labourers.

There are five minor tribes recognized as primitive tribes because of their extremely poor economic existence and another eleven minor groups mainly in mainland and Saurashtra areas of Gujarat (Lal, 1998).

Tribal communities have suffered heavily due to deforestation and depletion of forests; they have to raise monoculture crops and suffered a reduction of food sources (plant and wildlife). Due to large scale development projects and extractive industries along with destructive environmental modifications for the benefit of the tribal societies, there has been an abrupt change in tribal population-forest relationship especially affecting population density, as well as hunting and gathering. Increased migration has caused cultural heterogeneity. Mines and industries in the tribal areas have exposed the people to changed physical, chemical and biotic environmental stresses; the sudden alteration of diet might have caused profound disturbance of water and electrolyte balance causing various diseases. Migration to another environment might have deleterious effects on social and cultural status leading to poor housing, sanitation, and water supply and exposure to infectious diseases.

It is seen that a satisfactory assessment of the environment of the tribal communities is yet to be made. For a proper assessment of tribal communities, one requires extensive research in the physiological characteristics of their capacity for physical work, about their pattern of migration, physical adaptation, method of food intake, nutritional status, and design of clothing, etc. Many people living in or in the vicinity of forests especially in recently deforested areas may have modified or radically altered their living conditions either by improving or worsening hygiene and exposure to different infections. Such data would be extremely important for the proper formulation of development programmes for socio-economic and socio-cultural upliftment of the tribal communities in the State.

III

Gujarat Forests and their Management after Independence

Gujarat was a part of the Bombay State from 1947 to May 1960. The forests were under the Ministry of Agriculture till 1976. In 1976 forests and wildlife were transferred from the State to the Concurrent list by the 42nd Amendment. This enabled both the Central Government and the States to make laws under clause (2) of Article 246 of the Constitution. In the event of inconsistency, the laws made by parliament prevailed. In 1985, the Government of India created the present Ministry of Environment, Forest, and Wildlife (MoEF) by moving Forests and Wildlife from the Ministry of Agriculture and merging them with the Department of Environment.

The Forest Department is responsible for the administration and management of forests in Gujarat. The eighteen districts of the study area fall under different circles created by the Forest Department for administrative convenience. Each of these circles has a number of offices headed by the Divisional Conservator of Forests. Table 1.3 reflects the administration of forests under the Forest Department.

As per State of Forest Report 2009, Gujarat had 2.46 per cent of the total recorded forest area of India in the year 2009 which was 2.52 per cent in the year 1991. Forest cover was 1.81 per cent in the year 1991 and had increased to 2.12 per cent of country's total forest cover in the year 2009. Tables 1.3 and 1.4 give the picture of the recorded forest area, and forest covers situation in the state of Gujarat and India.

Table 1.3: Forest Administration in Mainland Gujarat after Independence

Districts	*Circle Offices of Forest Department*	*Offices of DCF under Forest Department*
• Banaskantha • Sabarkantha • Mehsana • Patan • Gandhinagar • Ahmedabad	• Gandhinagar	• Sabarkantha – North • Sabarkantha – South • Palanpur • Gandhinagar
• Panchmahal • Dahod • Kheda • Anand • Vadodara	• Vadodara	• Godhra • Baria • Chhota Udepur
• Narmada • Bharuch • Surat	• Surat	• Rajpipla – East • Rajpipla – West
• Surat • Tapi • Navsari • Valsad	• Surat • Valsad	• Vyara • Valsad – North • Valsad – South
• Dang	• Valsad	• Dang – South • Dang – North

Table 1.4: Comparative Recorded Forest Areas for Gujarat and India

Recorded Forest Area	*Recorded Forest Area (in square km)*					
	Gujarat			*India*		
	1991	*2005*	*2009*	*1991*	*2005*	*2009*
Reserved Forest	13,763	14,067	14,122	414,916	419,028	430,582
Protected Forest	1,022	696	479	233,081	216,605	206,219
Unclassed Forest	4,603	4,199	4,326	122,081	133,993	132,711
Total	**19,388**	**18,962**	**18,927**	**770,078**	**769,626**	**769,512**

Source: State of Forest Reports—1991, 2005 and 2009, Forest Survey of India.

Table 1.4 shows that the reserved forest areas have been increased by 2.61 per cent for the period between 1991 and 2009 in the State of Gujarat. During the same time, the reserved forest areas have been increased by 3.78 per cent at all India level. If we look at the protected forest area, Gujarat's protected forest area has been decreased by 53.08 per cent while India's by 11.52 per cent during the same time. Unclassed forest area has also been decreased by 2.38 per cent against 8.71 per cent increase at all India level during the period between 1991 and 2009. Total recorded forest area has been decreased by 2.38 per cent between the year 1991 and 2009 for the state of Gujarat while the same has been decreased by 0.07 per cent at all India level.

Table 1.5 shows the comparative forest cover for the State of Gujarat and India. Gujarat had 1.81 per cent of total forest cover of the country in the year 1991 which has been increased to 2.12 per cent in the year 2009. If we look at the data of dense forest (which include very dense forest and moderately dense forest), situation of Gujarat is worse than all India situation. 9.62 per cent forest cover has been decreased between 1991 and 2009 in Gujarat, which is just 0.22 per cent at all India level for the same time. Open forest area has been increased by 70.17 per cent for the State of Gujarat during the same time which is just 14.96 per cent at all India level.

Table 1.5: Comparative Forest Cover for Gujarat and India

Forest Cover		*Forest Cover (in square km)*					
		Gujarat			*India*		
		1991	*2005*	*2009*	*1991*	*2005*	*2009*
Dense Forest	Very Dense		376	376		83,472	83,510
	Moderate		5,319	5,249		319,948	319,012
	Dense Forest	6,224	5,695	5,625	385,610	403,420	402,522
Open Forest		5,286	8,909	8,995	250,842	286,751	288,377
Total		11,510	14,604	14,620	636,452	690,171	690,899

Source: State of Forest Reports—1991, 2005 and 2009, Forest Survey of India.

Table 1.6 shows the details on scrubs, mangroves and tree cover for the period between 1991 and 2009. Areas of scrubs have been decreased by 37.13 per cent in the State of Gujarat while the same is 30.31 per cent at all India level for the period between 1991 and 2009. Mangroves areas have been increased by 163.48 per cent in Gujarat for the same time. The rate for all India level is just 9.31

Table 1.6: Comparative Areas of Scrubs, Mangroves and Tree Cover for Gujarat and India

Area (in square km)

Area	*Gujarat*			*India*		
	1991	*2005*	*2009*	*1991*	*2005*	*2009*
Scrubs	2,327	1,419	1,463	59,641	38,475	41,525
Mangroves	397	991	1,046	4,244	4,581	4,639
Tree Cover	NA	7,621	8,390	NA	91,663	92,769

Source: State of Forest Reports – 1991, 2005 and 2009, Forest Survey of India.
NA = Not available

per cent for the period between 1991 and 2009. In 1991, 9.35 per cent of India's total mangroves area had been in Gujarat, which has been increased to 22.55 per cent in the year 2009. If we look at the comparative tree cover area for Gujarat and India, the tree cover area has been increased by 10.09 per cent for the period between 2005 and 2009 which is just 1.21 per cent at all India level. Gujarat had 8.31 per cent of total tree cover area of India in the year 2005 which has been increased to 9.04 per cent in the year 2009.

IV

Methodology

The study area was broadly identified as mainland Gujarat with a focus on the Eastern hilly regions of the State where tribal communities and forests are located. The area under study has different geographical and topographical features which extended from the hilly tracts of North Gujarat to the Eastern hilly areas and the Dang district. Eighteen districts covered under this study, are divided into five zones: (i) Banaskantha, Sabarkantha, Mehsana, Patan, Gandhinagar, Ahmedabad in north Gujarat; (ii) Anand, Kheda, Panchmahal, Godhra, Vadodara in central Gujarat; (iii) Narmada, Bharuch, Surat; (iv) Tapi, Valsad, Navsari and (v) Dang in south Gujarat (see Map 1.1).

Secondary data on forests was collected from archival documents such as Gazetteers, Annual Administrative Reports, Gazettes and so on. Population and demographic informations have been collected from the Census of India and Anthropological

Survey of India. The struggles and conflicts reported between the forest department and the forest dwellers are presented indicating the location, specific changes in the forest issues/conflicts, struggles/movements and forest areas. Land use data from the following three sources was elicited:

1. Satellite imagery of four periods: 1972, 1990, 2000 and 2007 and change detection maps based on satellite imagery (post-monsoon) were produced at district, taluka and village levels.
2. District Census Handbook of 18 districts of mainland Gujarat.
3. Working Plans of the Forest Department.

The whole of Eastern Gujarat (18 districts) was subdivided into five zones and from each region a cluster of villages from the distinct talukas were taken for primary data collection. The selection of the sample was based on the criteria of forest, community, people and gender. The village sample was taken from three settings: (1) where forests were degraded, (2) where forests were regenerated, and (3) where forests remained unchanged. The sample also took care to include different tribes in different districts.

Primary data was collected from 184 villages of 18 districts through a semi-structured questionnaire on the following topics: household data, conflict data, change in forests, Joint Forest Management (JFM), relationship between the forest department and the tribals, socio-cultural changes, alternative sources of livelihood, implementation of the Forest Rights Act 2006 and so on. In this study, 184 villages of 14 talukas in 11 districts of the State of Gujarat in India were selected (see Annexure 1). The following parameters were worked out before choosing the study villages in different zones:

- Decrease or increase in forest areas
- Conflicts between forest officials and the local tribals
- Forests before Independence
- Forests during the administration of the Princely States
- Dependence on forests for livelihood by tribals
- Migration of tribals for livelihood

Table 1.7: Zone-wise Forest Areas with Types of Forests

Zones	*Forest Types*	*Forest Area (in Ha)*
I.	• Dry Deciduous Scrub Forests • Dry Mixed Deciduous and Tropical Forests • Desert thorn Scrub Forests • Dry Teak Forests • Dry Deciduous Forests • Tropical Dry Deciduous Forests	2,57,824.01
II.	• Dry Teak Forests • Very Dry Teak Forests • Dry Deciduous Scrub Forests • Dry Mixed Deciduous and Tropical Forests • Tropical Dry Deciduous Forests	2,78,926.07
III.	• Slightly Moist Teak Forests • Dry Teak Forests	1,40,001.68
IV.	• Slightly Moist Teak Forests • Moist Deciduous Forests	1,90,384.41
V.	• Moist Deciduous Forests	91,484.66

Source: District Census Hand Book—Gujarat, Census of India 2001, Gujarat Forest Statistics—May 2006.

- The ground realities of the various welfare schemes of either the Government of India or the Government of Gujarat

The forests of mainland Gujarat comprise of different types of forests such as tropical dry deciduous, tropical moist deciduous, dry deciduous or teak and dry deciduous thorny types. Total forest area covered in our study area is 9,58,621 hectares (Table 1.7). Out of the forest areas covered in the study area, zone I to zone V covers 26.90 per cent, 29.10 per cent, 14.60 per cent, 19.86 per cent and 9.54 per cent respectively (see Table 1.8).

Field work was done in the month of March-April 2009 in 184 villages (see Table 1.8). Ethnographic case studies were conducted in four villages, in several sub-zones. The criteria kept in mind while choosing those villages were: areas having forests in and around the village, inhabited by the tribals totally or partially dependent on the forests, villages bordering the neighbouring States. Other criteria for selection were the size of the village—not less than 150 households, and one village being a Forest Village. Forest villages were created by the Forest Department for labouring families in the forest itself. Their status is different from revenue villages. Unlike, revenue villages, the forest villages do not have developmental benefits of the state. They are clamouring for revenue status which is under consideration of the state.

Table 1.8: Zone-wise Number of Study Villages

Zone	Forest Area (in percent)*	Total Number of Districts	Total Number of Talukas	Number of Districts for Study	Number of Talukas for Study	Number of Villages for Study	Study Villages (in percent)**
I.	26.90	06	55	01	02	28	15.21
II.	29.10	05	48	03	05	52	28.26
III.	14.60	03	22	03	03	49	26.63
IV.	19.86	03	15	03	03	33	17.93
V.	09.54	01	01	01	01	22	11.97
Total	100.00	18	141	11	14	184	100.00

Note: * Percentage of forest area (of total forest area of study area).
** Percentage of cluster villages (of total cluster villages selected).

There are many different groups of tribal communities in the study villages covering total study area. Table 1.9 gives the details about the scheduled tribes in the study area.

Dungari Bhil and Garasiya Bhil have different surnames. In Zone I they have a surname like Ninama, Modiya, Bhagora, Gamar, Damor, Dhrungi and many more. In Zone II, they have a surname like Damor, Katara, Pasaya, Ninama, Bhuriya and many more. In Zone III, they have the Vasava surname, while, in Zone V, they have many surnames. The same is true in the tribe of Dhanka, Kunkana, Kolcha, Varli, Dhodiya and Gamit.

Among Dungari Bhils in Gujarat, Vasava is more in number and have settled in Bharuch, Narmada, Vadodara, Surat and Panchmahal. Dhanka has three sections: Tadavi, Valvi and Tetariya. They have sub-sections with surnames such as Parmar and Chauhan. They live in Vadodara, Narmada, Bharuch and Tapi district of Gujarat. Dhodiya lives in Valsad, Surat, Tapi, Navsari and Bharuch. Kunkana and Varli mainly live in Valsad and the Dang. Rathwa lives mainly in Vadodara and Panchmahal districts. They have different surnames like Bamaniya, Bariya, Mahaniya, Kathari and many more.

In analysing the study area, we have also focused on Scheduled Tribal areas (43 Talukas) within the 18 districts of mainland Gujarat. Focused group discussions were held in the sample villages and

Table 1.9: Zone- and District-wise Scheduled Tribes in Study Area

	Zones with Districts	*ST Population (Census 2001)*	*ST Population (Census 2011*)*	*Names of Scheduled Tribes*
I.	Banaskantha	4,12,003	NA	• Dungari Bhil • Garasiya Bhil • Kathodi • Kotwaliya • Parghi
	Sabarkantha	1,89,871	NA	
	Mehsana	13,861	NA	
	Patan	(with Mehsana)	NA	
	Ahmedabad	54,104	NA	
	Gandhinagar	7,119	NA	
II.	Panchmahal	17,72,885	NA	• Rathwa • Bariya • Nayakada • Nayaka • Pateliya • Dhanka (Tadavi) • Dungari Bhil (Damor) • Koli
	Dahod	(with Panchmahal)	NA	
	Kheda	52,134	NA	
	Anand	(with Kheda)	NA	
	Vadodara	10,44,245	NA	
III.	Narmada	(With Bharuch)	NA	• Dungari Bhil (Vasava) • Chaudhary • Gamit • Dhodiya
	Bharuch	894,615	NA	
	Surat	15,56,884	NA	
IV.	Tapi	(With Surat)	NA	• Chaudhary • Gamit • Kotwaliya • Dhodiya • Konkana • Kolcha • Dhanka (Tadavi) • Varli
	Navsari	(With Valsad)	NA	
	Valsad	15,01,375	NA	
V.	The Dang	1,72,054	NA	• Konkana • Varli • Gamit • Dungari Bhil

Source: Census 2001 and Census 2011*.

* District-wise ST Population Tables are not declared under Census 2011.

personal interviews of local tribal families had also been taken to get the wider perspective of the study. Interviews were held with the forest bureaucrats (see organogram in Annexure 2) and the Non-Governmental Organisations (NGOs) working with tribals and forest related issues.

The remaining chapters in this volume contain legal, political and developmental programmes of the State; changing behaviour of forests; migration and tribal people, conflicts between tribals and the Forest Department; profiles of 184 study villages, its respondents and households; changing patterns of tribal livelihood; changes in forest and tribals covering state interventions and NGOs interventions; summary of the findings; and finally using Gujarat as a case study of the policy outline that will take care of issues and concerns on environment, forests and tribals.

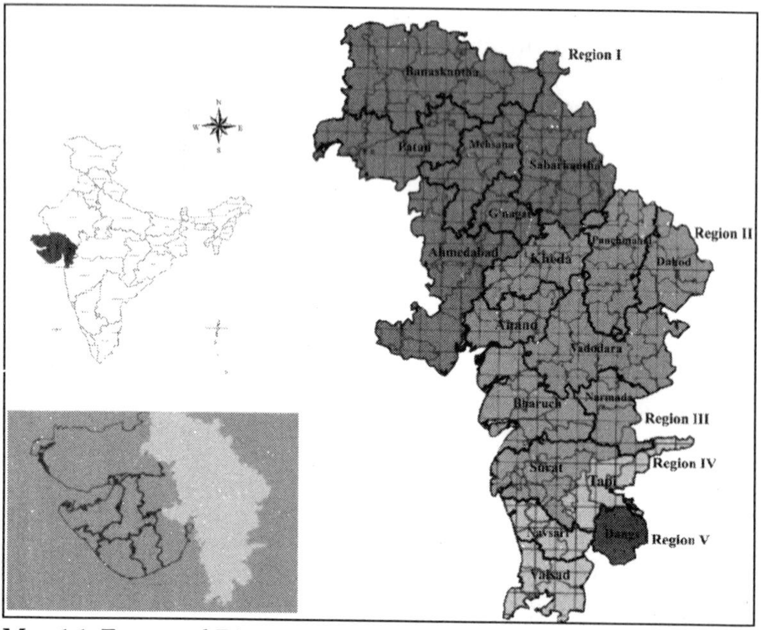

Map 1.1: Zones and Districts in Study Area of Mainland Gujarat

2
Legal, Political and Developmental Interventions in Forests

It is necessary to review the forest laws and the various Forest Acts adopted by the British as well as by the Government of India regarding forests and the tribals. This symbiotic relationship was acknowledged and crystallized as customary rights over forest produce. But these rights were not recognized and recorded by the government while consolidating state forests during the colonial period as well as in Independent India. How this aspect was neglected by the policy formulators, is the subject matter of this chapter. First section of this chapter explores legal history of forests, viz., how the colonial state intervened in the abode of the forest-dwellers through laws and acts, and converted it into a resource thereby eventually denying the forest-dwellers their life support system. The colonial state enacted laws to corner the forest resources and commodities in the market thereby excluding and alienating the tribals. Second section explores the political interferences in the forests after independence, and the third section describes to what extent people have been affected when forest lands have been diverted and transferred for development projects in Gujarat.

I

Legal Intervention in Forests

A number of foreign invasions and the consequent integration of migrant groups from other civilizations into Indian society influenced and altered its approach towards the exploitation of its natural resource base. The significance of forests for the British changed over time. In order to understand how British attitudes evolved, it is essential to examine briefly how pre-colonial regimes viewed uncultivated lands. British intrusion in terms of trade and control of land went beyond that of the previous rulers (Habib 1963: 9). The sub-continent was being drawn into a transcontinental empire, and the new rulers brought with them a particular legacy in terms of how they viewed forests.

Pre-colonial Views on Forests

There is little to suggest that there was an ecological equilibrium in pre-British India. The question is not merely whether or not forests were cut and cleared. After all, India includes some of the oldest agrarian civilizations in the world. It is necessary to ask how far pressure for revenue and agrarian extension actually influenced the process of denudation. There were indeed some customary restraints on the use of trees, as in the sacred groves protected by villagers. Many of these areas survived into the late nineteenth century were described by British Official (Brandis, 1897: 12). Such groves were still in existence, in areas as diverse as Wynad in the Southern parts of the peninsula and Gorakhpur in North (NAI, PWD 1871: 3). However, it would be misleading to ignore the extent of fluidity of the border between forests and cultivation. Every epoch in Indian history had its own 'forest line', besides its political and military boundaries (Habib, 1999: 1).

States such as the Delhi Sultanate under Muhammad Bin Tughluq (1325-51) tried to encourage agrarian extension by remitting revenues and providing credit to those peasants who cleared fresh land for agriculture. Conversely, excessive taxation could contribute to the contractions of cultivation. This was especially so in medieval India, where labour was a scarce resource and peasants could merely move away rather than pay high taxes (Habib and Raychaudhari, 1982: 2).

Not only was the 'forest line' a shifting boundary, it also demarcated areas where rebels, robbers and peasants fleeing taxation could find refuge. The clearance of woods, therefore, caused more revenues and also enabled increased political control by governments. For example, in the fourteenth century, the middle Doab was still covered with thick forests where cultivators could avoid tax collectors. By the end of the sixteenth century, cultivators had developed these lands for agriculture (*Ibid*: 48). However, the low population density in many parts of the Mughal Empire meant that cultivators could still convert forested land into arable (Habib, 1963: 117). Even densely populated and intensively cultivated areas had patches of land covered with trees and undergrowth. For example, the Mughal Emperor Jahangir (1605-28) was aware "the villagers and cultivators of the other side of the Jamuna river persistently engaged in burglary and robbing travellers and shelter behind dense forests and fastness difficult of access" (Habib, 1984: 11). There was a close connection between deforestation and military campaigns. In addition to long-term measures for the extension of agriculture, forests became a target of attack in order to extend the military and political power of conquerors and landed elements. Woodcutters and cultivators accompanied the Mughal army from the time of Shah Jahan (1628-56), and 'there was a general order that whosoever cleared a forest and brought land under cultivation, such land should be *zamindari*' (Alam, 1991:66).

Fayrer describes how armies in the Maratha areas 'hide themselves in the woods, which they also set on fire, to leave their opponents destitute of recesses' (Fayrer, 1921: 310). During his Coorg campaign, Tipu Sultan (died in 1799) had his *amirs* and *khans* cut away and burn the trees and bushes for three miles along the roadside (Miles, 1884: 79). Other Indian rulers, such as Sikhs, also denuded the countryside during conquest and counter-insurgency operations (Bayly, 1988: 138). Battles in woodlands often became battles against forests.

The relationship of Indian princely states with forest areas was not entirely a negative one. However, there was a hierarchy of user-rights rather than an absolute notion of property. In Mughal period, logs of wood were floated down several rivers for use in ship-building and construction (Habib, 1983: 25). Moreland found 'no hints' of Mughal efforts to conserve or exploit forests on a systematic basis. He argues that restrictions were mostly limited to the exaction of dues by local or imperial authorities (Moreland, 1920: 144). Some forest products were important for trade, and rulers tried to stake a claim to the wealth by asserting their rights.

Successor states followed similar policies of claiming property rights over certain varieties of trees. For example, Tipu Sultan asserted rights over sandalwood, a valuable tree. Some of the successor states of the Mughal had additional intrusive policies for managing forest utilization. These included measures by rulers and by landed groups either to provide hunting grounds or for the strategic defense of forts.

Thus, the pre-colonial period was not an idyllic one, and there were many ways in which the policies of states led to change in forested tracts. There were some significant initiatives by successor regimes after the fragmentation of the Mughal Empire, but, in general, they were concerned with pushing back the forests, not with controlling access or extraction of forest produce. It is against such background of limited but significant state intrusion that the British entered the picture.

There are significant differences among the scholars over the question of how the pre-colonial situation was distinct from the colonial one. Guha and Gadgil argue that "in the earlier situation village communities had control over management and disposal of forests and uncultivated lands. Demands by dominant landholders and rulers were limited, and never approached the scale they did in the subsequent period of colonial rule" (Guha and Gadgil, 1994: 141). At the other extreme, Groove contends "deforestation had assumed significant proportions before the advent of colonialism. He also argues that initiatives for state control of forests in Sindh anticipated colonial conservation" (Groove, 1995: 167). But, in general, the point is that there is no evidence of environmental collapse with adverse consequences for village communities in the pre-colonial period. Nor is there significant evidence of sharp conflicts over control of forest resources. There was no functional harmony, but fresh arable land was abundant, and state intrusion was limited. In general, Indian rulers and landholders were content to take a share of the surplus. They did not attempt to outlaw or suppress any particular form of land use. So stock keepers and animal trappers, shifting cultivators and nomadic communities were never subject to the kind of control that was to be attempted by the British.

With the Industrial Revolution in their homeland, the main task of British administrators in India was to expropriate India's natural resources for their own imperial demands that were dictated by their military and commercial interests. India being one of the richest colonies of the British in terms of its natural resources was an obvious target for the fulfilment of their rapacious greed. The legitimacy needed to appropriate the resources in the colonies was secured by passing various laws. The constitution of Forest Department and the enactment of several Forests Acts were part of such attempts in colonial India.

The British systematically and legitimately exploited India's forests. In the process, they deprived India's rural population of the environmental base on which it was dependent for its livelihood since time immemorial. The process of commercialization introduced by the British did not leave any fraction of Indian society untouched. The transformation from sustainable style of living to commercialization was not very smooth for the rural community. The process of adjustment took a heavy toll causing resistance among the different sections of the society.

The need to stop mindless destruction of forests began to be felt by British administrators only when the demand for the steady supply of timber for shipbuilding and sleepers for railway arose. Formerly the Royal Navy and Railway Department depended on oak for their requirements. But the oak plantations in Britain were almost exhausted by the end of the nineteenth century. For them, the teak from India was the next best alternative (Albion, 1936: 367). Hence, the solution was sought for improving methods of exploitation—both by the British administrators of India and the contractors. However, even when protection was accorded, for many years it was given only to certain species of trees and not to the forests as a whole.

Early British Forest Policies in India

The first concrete action taken by the administrator of British India towards forest protection and conservation was an order issued by the Bengal-Bombay Joint Commission appointed in 1800, to inquire into the internal circumstances of different forests in India and to make regulations prohibiting the felling of teak below 21 inches girth (Robbentrop, 1900: 67). In 1805, a dispatch was received from the Court of Directors of the East India Company inquiring about the extent to which the might of the King's Navy, in view of growing deficiency of oak in Britain, depended on a permanent supply of teak timber from the forests of India, particularly from the forests of Malabar and the Dangs. Consequently, a Forest Committee was appointed to enquire into both the capacity of forests themselves and the status of proprietary rights over them. It was necessary for Britain to get over the problem of shortage of timber for ship building and railways and to maintain its supremacy on the sea against the French. The Court of Directors was aware that Indian timber had long been prized and that, in fact, Arabs imported teak from Bombay for building their fleet (Stebbing, 1926: 63).

The reports submitted by the Forest Committee appointed by the Court of Directors indicated that the added accessible teak forests of peninsular India had been almost exhausted. Tapping the distant forests would require construction of costly roads. Nevertheless, the Committee pointed out that if protection was afforded, these forests could gradually regenerate. This highlighted the necessity to protect the forests along with the improved methods of utilization. The immediate result of the Committee's report was that, in 1806; an officer was appointed as Conservator in 1807, a general proclamation was issued, that the royalty rights in teak trees proclaimed by the former government in the Indian continent was vested in the Company, and all further unauthorised felling of the teak were prohibited (Baillie, 1951: 178). In the new set-up, the Conservator, assumed much larger powers than were entrusted to him earlier. On 10 November 1806, Captain Watson of the Police Department was appointed as the first Conservator of Forests in India. But, on the recommendations of the Governor of Madras, Sir Thomas Munroe, and with the consent of the Supreme Government, the conservatorship was abolished in 1823 following a lot of discontents among the peasantry, who were deprived of the privilege of cutting wood for fuel and other ordinary purposes—a privilege they had enjoyed from time immemorial.

According to E.P. Stebbing, "This showed a complete ignorance of the point of view of the private proprietors of forests, timber merchants and their methods of working. It sounded the death knell of hundreds of thousand of acres of fine teak forests (1926: 84-85)." After the abolition of the Conservator's office and the previous restrictions, the forest holders, or the persons who obtained from them or the state permission to fell timber, bothered only about their interests. Probably, as a reaction to the prohibition, they began to clear the land completely, indiscriminately cut all trees without leaving any young plants for regeneration. As a result, some of the more accessible forests were destroyed or were materially injured.

In 1837, the government's attention was drawn to the indiscriminate exploitation of forests. The first step adopted by the Bombay Government was to issue orders in 1839, prohibiting the felling of teak without permission. In the next year Gibson, the Superintendent of the Botanical Gardens, was directed to inspect and report on the forests of the Bombay Presidency. His report, in fact, confirmed the destruction of teak forests that was taking place (*Ibid*: 78). The common elements of early British forestry in India were already evident by this time in different provinces. The local inhabitants were either totally excluded, or else incorporated into a regime of control. The forests of Dang were the best example of this British policy on forestry.

The Bhil Rajas of the Dang were at par with all the surrounding territories and were quite independent. In order to prevent raids, the British maintained a military cordon around the Dang. But the Dang Chiefs always resisted tooth and nail interference from outsiders. This obscure term to some extent ended when the British got forest leases from the Dang Chiefs in 1842. After the lease of forests in 1842, the Dang district was placed under the administrative jurisdiction of the Collector and Political Agent, Khandesh. Here, the British administration had included the Bhil Rajas and Chiefs into the regime of control by way of giving judicial powers to them. However, the right of exploitation of forests lay with the British administration (Government of Gujarat, 1971: 3-4). So, British policy on forests either way served the wider British interests in timber and revenue. Technical strategies for manipulating forest use had far more in common with the techniques of forestry in France, Prussia and Bavaria than with plantation forestry which was in vogue in Britain (Stebbing, 1926: 463).

The broad features of developments in the early phase of British policies on forestry in India can be summed up as follows:

- Groups on the fringes of arable society were considered responsible for deforestation, in addition to being lawless and unproductive.

- The changing relations on the agrarian frontier framed the context in which the desiccation theory left a mark on British attitudes.
- Officials in many provinces were concerned with the supply of timber for strategic and commercial ends.

Evolution of Forest Policy, and Laws during 1850-1900

The British administration had a basic mistrust for anything that was Indian, the Indian traditions or their administrative patterns. They lacked confidence in the capacity of Indians to lookafter themselves. The Forest Department was founded in 1864 on the assumption that the Indian lacked the sense of Conservation (Grove, 1995: 35). This was the opinion held by a majority of the British administrators, though there were a few exceptions. The culmination of this feeling gave birth to the Indian Forest Act of 1865. The appointment of Brandis in December 1862 was the landmark stone for the starting of laws on forests in British India. As an Officer on Special Duty, he examined and advised on systems of forest management in various provinces. He thus became the first official with such extensive powers on the issue. The crisis in the supply of timber for the railways led to the consolidation of existing initiatives for conservation. The Forest Act of 1865 was the first step towards a rule of property for the forests of British India.

The Indian Forest Act of 1865 empowered several local governments to declare certain areas as State Forests without in any way interfering with the rights of the people. As per the Act, state forests meant land covered with trees and brushwood or jungle. A revenue official and not a forest official determined the merits of a particular block of forest chosen for reservation (Robbentrop, 1900:15). The 1865 Act empowered the local governments to draft local rules for their respective provinces for the better management and preservation of forests, and prescribe punishments for infringement of rules. These rules, when confirmed and published were to have the force of law. Penalties could be imposed after vexatious seizures and arrests. The rules under this Act further dealt with the details of forest conservancy such as staff to be employed for administration of the forests, the procedure to be followed while creating "Reserve Forests" and "Unreserved Forests", their demarcation etc.

However, from the point of view of the administrators, the 1865 Act was imperfect and unsound in principal (Baden-Powell, 1893: 35-36). Despite significant differences, there was a broad unity among the officials for the need of a new legislation. The first General Conference on Forestry in India was held in 1874 at Allahabad and the second at Simla in 1875 generated three main streams of thoughts or opinions. Madhav Gadgil and Ramchandra Guha called them as 'annexationist', 'pragmatic' and 'populist' (Gadgil and Guha, 1992: 126-128). The 'annexationists' were for complete control of the State over the forests; the 'populists' believed that tribals who were traditionally enjoying rights over forest lands should continue to exercise these sovereign rights, while the 'pragmatic' aimed for a balance between the two, preferring selective control over forests.

Finally, after long deliberations among the scholars and officials of the British administration and based on a memorandum prepared by Brandis in 1875 and the paper prepared by Baden-Powell the Indian Forest Act 1878 was passed and the prolonged debate finally ended in favour of 'annexationists'.

The Indian Forest Act 1878 provided for the following:

1. The power to declare government lands as reserved State forests.
2. The power to demarcate these reserved forests and to enquire into the record and settle rights over them once and for all, as it was thought that the forests were often burdened with rights adverse to the public interest and therefore; they had to be dealt with in a special way.
3. The power to commute such rights whenever they prevented the conservation of the area as forests.
4. The power to prevent the springing up of new rights except by government grant.
5. Provisions for the protection and management of reserved State forests protected forests and unclassified forests.
6. Provisions for providing suitable punishment for breaking of the forest law. This was because forests contained a great variety of produce and acts of petty theft, trespass, mischief, which constituted forest offences, were varied. Therefore, it was thought that they had to be treated by a special law.

7. The power to protect forest products in transit to check its theft.
8. A forest was considered to be particularly liable to accidents—some due to natural causes and others due to the carelessness of malice of men, for example fire. Hence, provisions were made to prevent such accidents.

With this Act, provision was made for the Constitution of reserved forests and protected forests. The reserved forests were the only forests par excellence because they alone were properly and fully secure. The reserved forests secured a permanent settlement whereas in protected forests; existing rights were recorded but not settled.

In the 1878 Act, Chapter III made provisions for the constitution of Village Forests. The idea behind forming village forests was that village communities, and private persons had a right to expect that the government should provide security to their forest property, protection against trespass and damage and also against the accrual of new rights. The village forests were to be under the management of the government officer. The surplus revenue from the village forests was to go to the village community.

Settlement of rights was the most crucial aspect incorporated in the 1878 Act. Under the provisions of the Act, the rights of the user were subjected to certain limitations. These limitations were held necessary in order to secure the enjoyment of rights, without imperiling the maintenance of the forests which supported them. Legally the forest owner had the freedom to:

1. Indulge in all Acts that did not touch the easement in any way.
2. Acts that affected the easement to some extent, but were still necessary for the due maintenance of the estate.

The second provision was clearly a loophole in the hands of the Forest Department, which later became a source of discontentment among the people. In the Act, the provisions are also made for curtailment of rights. If this curtailment amounted to the serious infraction of the rights, people could get rid of entirely by compensation. These rights were classified in the following manner:

(a) Grazing or pasture
(b) Grass cutting
(c) Lopping boughs and gathering leaves
(d) Wood rights
(e) Right to fallen leaves for litter or manure
(f) Right to other forest produce
(g) Hunting and fishing
(h) Temporary and shifting cultivation

With great care, the 1878 Act specified which were to be considered offences and how they were to be dealt with strictly. Forest Offences were divided into:

1. Offences against the forest itself covering Reserved Forests and Protected Forests
2. Special offences
3. Cattle trespass
4. Offences relating to the forest produce in transit and to drift timber

The Act of 1878 applied the Indian Penal Code for forest offences like theft, receiving stolen property, mischief, criminal trespass, attempt to commit an offence, abetment of an offence and unlawful assembly.

Hence, stringent restrictions were imposed on the people regarding the use of the forests. People were denied their rights which had existed from time immemorial. This naturally became the cause of discontentment among the people. Doubts were expressed by the revenue officers whether they could in their position risk a high amount of general discontent for the sake of the forests, and whether it was better to let the forest estates go altogether than have people discontented on account of them (Standing Orders of Bombay Presidency, corrected up to 1910, Bombay, 1912: 296). However, this discontentment went largely unacknowledged by the government for almost a decade until it reached its peak in the mid-eighties leading to the appointment of the Bombay Forest Commission in 1885. The recommendations of the Bombay Forest Commission were as follows: (Bombay Forest Commission Report, vol. I, 1887: 28-55). Residents of forest villages were allowed to graze their cattle and cut grass at no cost in the unclosed portion of the forest block.

- The grazing rights of each village depended on its cultivated area.
- No consideration was taken about how much former free grazing land was contributed by each village while determining the grazing rights.
- All residents of the village would have these rights regardless of whether the land taken from the village was grazing land or not.
- Anyone cultivating land in the village, regardless of whether they were a resident or not, were given grazing privileges.
- Professional graziers resident or not would be excluded from this privilege.
- Moderate fees for grazing of the cattle belonging to non-forest villages which were attached to the forest of other village.

The general conclusion drawn by the Commission (Stebbing, 1926: 43-47) was that the tribals would have no interests in the preservation of the forests if the regulations made it impossible for them to earn a sufficient livelihood there from. The Commission concluded that as long as these tribes were practically dependent on the forests for their living, they were to be considered as first claimants on the forests. The Commission proposed not to grant any privileges to the wild tribes which would not be shared by all the poorer inhabitants of forest villages. These privileges, it thought, were necessary to enable the classes who were dependent on forests to earn a sufficient living and to prevent their becoming a source of anxiety in the future. The Commission proposed the rules regarding privileges to be simple and consistent enough for the villagers to comprehend and also simple enough to administer so that friction between the officials and villagers could be minimized.

As the government largely ignored the recommendations of the Commission, the discontentment among the people continued to rise. Forest offences were increased by nearly 200 per cent within three years from 1889 to 1892 at all India level. Petty thefts continued to take place. Forest fires were another matter of major concern for the forest officials. It was observed that a large number of forest fires were due to the irritation felt by the people, at the strict enforcement of forest regulations (Revenue Department Files, 1894: 24 and 1888: 65). The passing of the resolution by the state in 1889 to discontinue the privilege of collecting dead wood in the forests led to high discontentment among the people causing immense unrest throughout the villages in and around the forest areas.

By the end of the nineteenth century, though amid great discontentment among the people, the fact that forests belonged to the State was found all over India, and the forests were demarcated, surveyed and mapped before being entrusted to the care of the Forest Department. After settling the forests, thus a need was felt to lay down certain general principles on which they were to be managed. At this stage, the Government of India invited Dr. J.A. Voelcker to head the Royal Commission on Agriculture to examine the state of agriculture and suggest how it could be improved.

Dr. Voelcker submitted his "Report on the Improvement of Indian Agriculture" in 1893. In Chapter VIII of this monumental report, he discussed at length the conditions of the forests and stressed the need for formulating a forest policy. On the basis of his recommendations, the Government of India issued Resolution No. 22 F dated 19th October 1894, declaring its first forest policy. This was a landmark in the history of forest management of India (Forest Policy Report of the Royal Commission on Agriculture in India 1928). Following were the main features of the Forest Policy of 1894.

The sole objective of management of forests was to be directed at promoting the overall well-being of the country—

- The maintenance of adequate forests was aimed primarily for the preservation of the climatic and physical conditions of the country and secondly to fulfil the needs of the people

These were subject to the following conditions:

- Permanent cultivation was to come before forestry, and
- The satisfaction of needs of the local community at non-competitive rates, if not free, was to override all considerations of revenue.

The state owned forests were classified with reference to their primary functions as follows:

(i) Forests, the preservation of which was essential on climatic or physical grounds,
(ii) Forests that afforded a supply of valuable timber for commercial purposes,
(iii) Minor forests, and
(iv) Pasture lands.

The above classification was not intended to be rigid, and particular forest could fulfil more than one function. Although, this policy was partially a response to the serious discontent among the agricultural classes caused by strict forest administration, it was based on the Principle of State Monopoly of Forests. While this policy seemed to have cleared the bias towards serving agricultural interests more directly, it cautioned that the needs of the agricultural community were to be met only "to the utmost point that was consistent with Imperial interests" (Gadgil and Guha, 1992: 135). The Forest Policy clearly stated that the claims of cultivation were stronger than the claims of forest preservation. Accordingly, whenever an effective demand for cultivable land exists and could only be supplied from forest areas, the land should ordinarily be relinquished without hesitation.

However, Forest Policy of 1894 remained valid throughout the British Rule in India, though it was under many discussion and not always followed. Considerable progress had been made in the drawing up of forest working plans during this stage. Brandis (1865-1883), Schlich (1883-1885) and Ribbentrop (1885-1900) were the three Inspector Generals of Forests who shaped the forest administration in India during the time of Forest Policy of 1894.

Evolution of Forest Policy and Laws during 1900-1950

The attitude of the British government towards the villages and their understanding of the subsistence agricultural practices did not change all through their administration in India. The Imperial Gazetteer of Bombay in 1909 is an example where it was said that, in spite of the great care taken by the Forest Department to control forest operations in the interests of the people, these operations did not become popular. During the British government era, another important change brought about in the Forest Department during the period 1900-1950, was that, in 1927, the Forest Act XVI was passed. Till then the Indian Forest Act of 1878 was the model for corresponding Forest Acts of the major princely states of India. This Act was updated in 1927 as Indian Forest Act 1927. The changes made by the Indian Forest Act, 1927 were small.

However, no action was taken until 1939 when a new bill was drafted. Its enactment was delayed by the war, but subsequently many of the provinces and princely states passed their own Acts or updated their own forest related laws and rules. Princely States like Baroda, Rajpipla, Bansada and Palanpur had passed laws on forests to curb the menace of forest destruction for the sake of fodder and manure for agricultural crops. The Forest Act of Baroda State passed in 1823 and updated in 1933, the Forest Act of Rajpipla State passed in 1896-96 and revised in 1931, and the Forest Rules declared by the Kings of Bansada in South Gujarat and Chhota Udepur in Central Gujarat had clearly prohibited the *chhindani* or *khandani* of trees for manure. Lopping of trees was also clearly banned, and heavy penalty and punishment was imposed under the Forest Act. Bombay Presidency passed a more comprehensive Bill in 1942 (Act XXVIII). Their underlying principle was to manage the forests according to the approved working plan with the alternative of forests taken over by the State.

This Indian Forest Act of 1927 "gave more power to the state in the reserved forests, increased the number of listed offenses and enhanced the punishment for some of these offenses" (Nadkarni, 1989: 60). It extended also to private lands by allowing that "State governments may regulate timber cutting, cultivation, grazing and burning or clearing of vegetation on private forest land". According to Singh (1986: X), the Indian Forest Act of 1927 does not conform to the principles embodied in the Constitution. As a legal rationalist Singh, therefore, holds that the Act should be held unconstitutional, and another basic Act legislated instead. Singh criticizes the 1927 Act on many counts, chief among which is the question of expropriation of land (Singh, 1986: XII).

This Act was succeeded by the 1878 Forest Act. Finally, 81 of the 84 sections of the 1878 Act were incorporated into the 1927 Act. This legal complex enabled the colonial state to take over

Common Property Resources (CPR), thereby extinguishing the property rights of the forest-dwellers and closing off the resources which had hitherto been at their disposal. Singh's argument hinges on two further points: that the "theft" of the forests was a new policy and not a continuation of the policy and practice of earlier rulers and that the British motive was the exploitation of resources rather than their sustainable use. Both these questions, which are essentially historical rather than legal, have been extensively debated, and much moral prestige is attached to them.

Provisions of the Indian Forest Act 1927 were found insufficient in preventing the rapid decline of the forests into wastelands with its consequent dangers by some or other reasons. The Act, therefore, affected the work of the Forest Department considerably. However, another important point which was of general interest during this time was the maintenance and development of fuel and small timber supplies for local consumption and also the fodder for the survival of cattle in the villages. With the struggle for Independence assuming a more serious form it had become necessary for the British Government, by this time, to give consideration to people's needs and complaints to avoid conflicts.

In 1928, the Royal Commission on Agriculture in India made inquiries into the uses of forest lands which were under the management of the Forest Department for agricultural purposes such as providing fodder for livestock, fuel and timber for the rural community and protection of soils which were in danger of erosion.

In spite of many recommendations made by the Royal Commission, the issues related to fuel and timber supply, forest grazing and fire protection continued to bother the forest officials and conflict between the villagers and the forest officials became routine. Forest Officials became critical of the tendency of the Congress Ministry to grant many concessions to the villagers on these issues during 1935-1938.

The Indian Forest Act of 1927 is still in operation even after the Independence of India. Ministries after the independence had never thought of the review of these draconian forest laws even after nine decades.

Forest Policies and Laws after 1950

The failure of the Forest Department to protect the forests from degradation as seen in the loss of tree cover was taken as evidence of a general environmental crisis. Apprehensions about an exponential environmental crisis are widely shared both at elite and general level. While the decline in political institutions is often dated to the mid-1960s, the late 19th century, the Second World War, the time after Independence when private forests were nationalized, and the last four decades have all been quoted as the onset of the environmental crisis. The Stockholm Summit on the environment in 1972 and the Chipko movement both sensitize decision-makers and others to the situation, and when the satellite photos became available, the reality of the crisis was confirmed.

The first major step towards reform occurred with the recommendations of National Commission of Agriculture (NCA) established in 1976. The NCA appraised the whole agricultural sector devoting volume IX of its report to forestry (National Commission on Agriculture, 1976).

Gadgil and Guha suggest that the stress on commercial forestry was adopted "retrospectively" by the NCA under the influence of the FAO, which had advocated commercial forestry from the early 1960s (1992: 187). It is probably true that the report was influenced by the FAO, and the report itself notes that the World Bank was promoting man-made forests. However, the NCA does not appear to be a doctored document. Instead, the report systematically opened up for a range of new developments stressing profitability and underlining the need for economically viable projects. The report noted that there was a wide gap between the production of industrial wood from state forests and the increasing demand. This gap was made up by felling trees on private lands and pilferage from the state forests. On this basis, the report" (National Commission of Agriculture, Report of the Forestry, 1976: 4) argued the intensification of forestry:

> If the forests are bled both by the rural sector and industrial sector, there will be no incentive or initiative left to change over from existing low-cost low-yield forestry to a commercial high investment economic forestry development.

An important result of the report was the priority accorded

to social forestry. The concept of social forestry was coined by Jack C. Westoby of the FAO but brought into prominence in India by the NCA. It means farm and community forestry to meet the needs of communities for fodder, fuel, small timber etc. in order to "lighten the burden on production forestry" (Arnold, 1992: 5). Social forestry schemes are made on farm lands, community, pasture and wastelands, tank foreshores as well as on road margins and along railway lines and canal banks (Reddy, 1993: 26-32).

While social forestry brought forestry and agriculture closer, administratively the two have diverged. In 1976 forests and wildlife were transferred from the State to the Concurrent list by the 42nd Amendment. This enabled both the Central Government and the States to make laws under clause (2) of Article 246 of the Constitution. In the event of inconsistency the laws made by parliament prevail. In 1985, the Government of India created the present Ministry of Environment, Forest, and Wildlife and (MoEF) by moving Forests and Wildlife from the Ministry of Agriculture and merging them with the Department of Environment. The MoEF has administrative jurisdiction over national forest policy, forestry development and the Indian forest service.

The first major Central Act relating to forest was the Forest Conservation Act (FCA) of 1980. This Act was not based on a detailed study or scientific recommendations. Instead, the FCA was an exercise in fast policy-making by an ordinance which was later converted into an Act. The FCA was spurred by the need to bring into line states such as Uttar Pradesh and Kerala, which had hesitated to implement Government of India directives. The FCA was further grounded in the 42nd Amendment which made the protection of the environment, the forests and wildlife constitutionally binding through Article 48A. The FCA furthered centralization by providing for the following:

> The Forest (Conservation) Act of 1980 prohibits state governments from declaring any reserved forest, or any part thereof, as non-reserved without the prior approval of the central government. It also prohibits the state governments from allotting any forest land, or any part thereof, for any non-forest purpose.

This provision in FCA created a conflict between the central government and many state governments. Every state government has to take permission from the central ministry for converting any of the forest land for non-forest purposes. The FCA has been severely criticized on two issues:

1. For allowing deforestation when not needed, and
2. For not allowing afforestation when needed

But, as intended, FCA has had an impact on the regularization of encroachment. It was possible to convert large amounts of forest lands to non-forest purposes despite the FCA, but the case shows that it requires very considerable political clout to do so. Initially, the FCA had no penal clauses and the Act did not specify who should deal with infringements of the Act. A penal clause was inserted only eight years later, in 1988.

The 1988 Amendment made it very difficult for many local non-governmental bodies to follow the intentions of the National Forest Policy of 1988 to improve the management of degraded lands such as village forests as this would often require central clearance. "In May 1992, Forest Conservators were authorized to clear cases of de-reservation of up to 5 hectares of land. It was discussed in 1993 whether industries should be allowed to invest in forestry on government-owned degraded forest land" (*Times of India*, 1993).

The FCA has been a very efficient Act which over a period has brought down the annual loss of forests as measured in terms of formal de-classification. However, it has been counter-productive in so far as it has prohibited afforestation. It has also been an inordinately centralizing Act. Therefore, it has rightly been criticized by proponents of commercialization, development and livelihood rights who uniformly consider it impossibly restrictive.

In the year 1982, Government of India had drafted the Forest Bill to replace the Indian Forest Act of 1927. A careful reading of the government's draft Forest Bill showed that its real aims were: (i) to restrict people's rights in reserved forests, and (ii) to limit the area of village forests in which local communities could exercise more effective and independent control (Guha and Gadgil, 1994). The proposed Act would be known as "The Conservation of Forests and Natural Ecosystems Act". As the very title indicates, there would be a strong, perhaps even dominant emphasis on conservation and environmental protection. The detailed provisions of the Draft Act also made it clear that its intention was to create or maintain reserved forests under strict state control, for preserving the ecological balance. By prohibiting the Constitution of Village Forests from the reserved forest land, new draft Forest Bill overturns a provision in the existing Indian Forests Act of 1927, wherein village forests can in theory be constituted from reserved forests. According to the social activists, this was the most dangerous feature of the Draft Bill. On the whole, the proposed Forest Bill was based on the NFP of 1988. There was a definite change from the colonial and regulatory tone of the Indian Forest Act of 1927. The provisions relating to village forests and regulation of saw mills introduced desirable changes. However, certain provisions of the Draft Forest Bill went against the interests of the people and particularly the tribals, which needed to be modified or deleted. Due to the mass movement and countrywide agitation, the Government of India had not moved ahead in the draft Forest Bill of 1982, and the draconian Indian Forest Act of 1927 is still in force for the whole of the country.

National Forest Policy (NFP) 1988

During the last years of British Rule, Sir Herbert Howard outlined a new forest policy. He agreed with the policy in effect from 1894 that forests primarily should safeguard the environment. He prioritized the needs of the agriculturists over the needs of commercial forestry arguing "the satisfaction of the wants of local community free or at noncompetitive rates comes before revenue." Howard's draft policy was never implemented, but according to Taylor it was used by the Congress government after Independence when it formulated the First Forest Policy of Independent India in 1952 (Taylor, George, 1981: 45-52).

The National Forest Policy (NFP) of 1988 succeeded the 1952 policy. The Central Board of Forestry (CBF), which advises the Central Government, had worked on this policy since the seventies. As late as December 1986, the CBF attempted to steer the process in a conservative direction stressing departmental control over all forests including private forests. A similarly restrictive position was taken by the National Committee on Development of

Backward Areas, which recommended the curtailment of rights of tribal communities.

However, a Committee formed by the Ministry of Home Affairs opposed such views advocating instead "an ecosystem management approach" based on an understanding of the "symbiotic relationship between forests and forests dwellers". Additional input was received from a high-powered technical committee established in February 1972 shortly before the Environmental Summit in Stockholm. The National Committee on Environmental Planning and Coordination consisted of representatives of the Government of India, experts and voluntary agencies, and was serviced by the Department of Science and Technology. It drafted a national environmental policy statement which strongly influenced the debate on the environment. One member of this committee was the ecologist Madhav Gadgil. In 1983, Gadgil produced a proposal for a new forest policy (Gadgil, Madhav, Narendra Prasad and Adi Rauf, 1983: 2ff). The proposal was revised by the Government of India and published as "Recommendations regarding the revision of the National Forest Policy".

The National Forest Policy (NFP) 1988 which eventually emerged, sought to protect the livelihood rights of the forest dwellers without relinquishing departmental control:

> The holders of customary rights and concessions in forest areas should be motivated to identify themselves with the protection and development of forests from which they derive benefits. [...] The life of tribals and other poor living within and near forests revolve around forests. The rights and concessions enjoyed by them should be fully protected. Their domestic requirements of fuelwood, fodder, minor forest produce and construction timber should be the first charge on forest produce. These and substitute materials should be made available through conveniently located depots at reasonable prices [...] (See Section 4.3.4.2 to 4.3.4.4. of the NFP, 1988).

The policy tried to be simultaneously pro-people and pro-environment. As the policy was thought to be in tune with national and international developments, it was widely considered a progressive policy statement.

One of the few, who has criticized it, is Shyam S. Sunder, a retired IPS officer from Karnataka. In an unpublished study Sunder has stressed that the Forest Department should maintain a tight control over the reserved forest to secure "national needs". He regards this as entirely feasible. Sunder, therefore, argues against the growth of the forest villages on par with revenue villages as visualized in the policy (Shyam, S., n.d.: 10ff). According to Sunder, forest based industries use less than 5 per cent of the output from the forests, and the industrial needs are, therefore, not the cause of degradation. If, as the NFP prescribes, the forests are considered gene pools and if exotic species are also subjected to long-term trials before being introduced, the production of the reserved forests risks stagnating. According to Sunder, the real need is not to open the reserved forests to people and people's management, but to restock the wastelands, 89 per cent of which is outside the reserved forests. Around 80-87 per cent of the biomass produced in India's forests is used as fuel wood. The country needs 150 million tonnes of firewood a year of which only 7.5 million tonnes is departmentally harvested. The rest is obtained legally or illegally by local communities. To restock, the wastelands, Sunder argues that Land Ceiling Laws should be raised above the present ceiling of about 20 ha. The use of the wastelands should be regulated by formulating a land use policy including both agriculture and cattle-grazing.

Despite Sunder's criticism, NFP 1988 is an important document and not an irrelevant exercise. One of the major ways in which some of the ideas contained in the NFP 1988 have been sought to be fleshed out is through participatory forest management known as Joint Forest Management (JFM).

After the Participatory Forest Management, the long drawn struggles of tribals and the support given to them by the NGOs have put pressure on the government to enact the Scheduled Tribes and other Traditional Forest Dwellers (Recognition of Forest Rights) Act, 2006 (soon known as Forest Rights Act). But it has remained controversial and uneven in its implementation.

II

Political Intervention in Forests

Pre-independence Era

The implementation of the Indian Forest Act of 1878 resulted in several problems. The discontentment among the people rose higher in the last two decades of the nineteenth century and first two decades of the twentieth century. It was conveniently believed by Forest Officers like Baden-Powell (Imperial Forest Officer and architect of the land revenue system in India) that people did not like "restrictions". Hence, discontentment was natural, though it was not to be a cause for worry. But as the freedom movement got momentum, the Indian National Congress leaders utilized this discontent as a tool against British Rule in India. As recorded in the Imperial Gazetteer of Bombay:

> In spite of the great care taken by the Forest Department to control forest operations in the interest of the people, these operations did not become popular. The reason behind this was perceived as the inability of the people to comprehend the necessity of foresight in forest utilization. They did not hesitate to burn the valuable forest for the sake of temporary supply of green fodder or to lop and fell trees to provide manure for their crops without thought, as to whether the supply of forest produce will continue to meet the needs of his successors. People's these actions had been supported by the freedom movement leaders of Indian National Congress to give momentum to their movement in the interior villages (*Imperial Gazetteer of India*, Bombay, 1909: 64-65).

Curiously enough, the British officers who always complained that the Indian forests were badly destroyed by the Indians due to their destructive ways of exploitation not only justified but praised the ruthless exploitation by the British State during the two World Wars. Private contractors had been engaged by the forest officials to cut the forests. All this was done at the cost of interests of the people as poor tribals were exploited by private contractors. The

Map 2.1 shows the Surat Collectorate areas with forest areas. The issue of this massive destruction of Indian forests and exploitation of tribal communities all over India had been raised tactfully and successfully by the freedom movement leaders under the Indian National Congress.

The forest officials' eagerness to meet the timber requirements and the revenue targets of the British Government made them overlook the subsistence needs of the tribals. The lack of understanding indigenous customs and traditions made matters even worse. Many a times the resistance was in the form of individual offences. But, revolts of tribals were not an uncommon phenomena during the freedom struggle controlled by the leaders of Indian National Congress. Birsa Munda is an example of one of the tribal leaders of the tribal revolts during the freedom struggle. The leaders of the Indian National Congress had mobilized the tribal communities by way of "*Jungle Satyagraha*".

Post-Independence Era

The process of alienation of tribals from the forests did not come to a halt even after independence. Political leadership after Independence had started the process of urbanization, building of big dams, industries and many other developmental activities, which altered the lives of the entire rural and tribal people of the country. Most of them had either taken to marginal farming or had become unskilled labour in the nearby towns.

One can identify and discuss the result of political interference in four phases in Gujarat:

(i) First Phase 1947–1960,
(ii) Second Phase 1961–1977,
(iii) Third Phase 1978–1990, and
(iv) Fourth Phase 1991–2007.

First Phase: 1947–1960

The evil of illicit cutting on a commercial scale had originated during the early years of free and independent India. Coupe was given for cutting to the private contractors during the pre-independence period, continued even after independence.

Looking at the exploitation of the tribals, some of the leaders in South Gujarat had started an awareness movement by entering into the deep forest area. In 1948, Sarvodaya and Gandhian leaders assembled in Surat. After Many discussion and many deliberations, they found the first Forest Co-operative called the "Sadhhvav Vibhag Jungle Kamdar Sahakari Mandali" in the Mandvi Taluka of Surat district under the direct leadership of Gandhian leaders. During this phase, 175 Co-operative Forest Workers' Mandalis had been established (Joshi, Satyakam, 1992). These Mandalis took the contract from the Forest Department for the cutting of forests. They gave more wages to the tribals who cut the forests as members of these Mandalis. Having taken an in-depth look into the politics reigning in the *Jungle Kamdar Sahakari Mandalis* in South Gujarat, Joshi (*Ibid*) concluded that Gandhian leaders tried to change the life of the tribals by using these Mandalis as a livelihood tool; he also claimed that they were successful to some degree as no serious political influence or politicization process had started during this period.

The important thing to be noted here is that the destruction of forests continued even after Independence. Maps 2.2 and 2.3 of the Bharuch Collectorate of the pre-Independence period and for the year 1972 clearly shows the level of destruction. Lots of forest areas had been destroyed under the coupe felling system either cut by the private contractors or the *Jungle Kamdar Mandalis*. Another major reason for the destruction of forests during the later years of this phase was the nationalization of private forests. Princely state rulers had cut forests indiscriminately calculating only financial wealth and not taking into account the maintenance of ecological balance.

Second Phase: 1961–1977

The rulers of the Princely State had indiscriminately cut forests during the initial years of this phase. As they did not get proper compensation from the handing over of their own natural resources and wealth, most of them cut the forests before handing these over to the Government. In fact, political leadership had no vision for ecology and environment at that time. Lack of strong political will was responsible for the major destruction of forests at the time of the handing over of the private forests to the Government.

Besides this, the socio-political environment started changing at high speed in the forest areas during the second phase. Due to the presence of Gandhian leaders and their social workers in the whole tribal belt of the State of Gujarat, which separated from the Bombay State in the year 1960, the social upliftment activities like awareness campaign for education, eradication of habits like drinking alcohol, domestic violence, etc. had been started on a massive scale among the different tribal communities. Many voluntary organizations had also started primary schools to educate the tribals.

The Jungle Kamdar Sahakari Mandalis established in the forests areas, in the State of Gujarat, had struck roots, and they contributed to some extent in creating a lobby against the Forest Department (Joshi, 1992). These Mandalis built up confidence among the tribals and assured them that they could confront the forest officials and the Forest Department in an organized way. The tribals were repeatedly told that the forest officials were not their masters but their servants. Some of the timber traders had also joined hands with them, but it is a known fact that some of the "so called" Gandhian leaders at that time had encouraged local tribals to fell trees and supply timber; most of these traders knew how to take advantage of the loop-holes in the Forest Administration, and they knew the weaknesses of the Gandhian leaders.

Leaders of the Jungle Kamdar Sahakari Mandalis had groomed one whole generation. During the early seventies, a new generation of tribals had started taking part in party politics and was elected to the State Legislative Assembly, the District Panchayat and the Taluka Panchayat. They were different from the old generation of Gandhian and Sarvodaya leaders. Some of the leading tribal leaders from South Gujarat and Central Gujarat started illicit cutting in the forest areas and made quick money. Some of them misused the funds of the Jungle Kamdar Sahakari Mandalis for their personal interest and advancement of their political career. This new tribal leadership which entered the vote bank politics was extra aggressive in nature and was able to provide leadership to the other tribals.

During this phase, the political situation had undergone a tremendous change. The value of the vote and the vote bank of tribals were given greater importance in the state level political arena. The tribal leaders were pampered by all the political parties for their power game as all the political parties started wooing the tribals towards them. In this overcharged environment, more and more tribal people joined the group opposing forest administration. The illicit timber *"mafias"* had supported the leading tribal leaders financially and in return the illicit cutting of forest areas went on unabated during this time (Nayak, D.M., 1989). In our interview with the retired Chief Conservator of Forests for the Government of Gujarat, D.M. Nayak in the month of September 2009 at his home in Vadodara stated that the timber *mafias* had started carrying lethal weapons and *"gundas"* for protection while transporting timber and that they had also threatened and sometimes attacked forest officials who dared to intercept their vehicles carrying illegal timber, making forest bureaucracy totally ineffective. All this had the blessings of the leading prominent tribal leaders belonging to different political parties. The staff of the Forest Department succumbed to political pressures and did not discharge their duties with a full sense of integrity and commitment. The Map 2.4 of Dang district for the pre-independence period and Map 2.5 for the year 1972 clearly shows the deforestation in the area during this time.

Because of the vote bank politics, poor tribals living in the vicinity of towns had also learned to cut small sized timber and carry them as head loads to the towns and sell them or to use to build their homes. They grew in big numbers giving support to each other evidently with the blessings of their political leadership. Voluntary organizations, social workers and politicians always treated these poor tribal people on humanitarian grounds for their power games at the State or the District level. However, the real culprits who indulged in the illicit cutting were never or rarely booked because of the political patronage and financial strength that they enjoyed.

Third Phase: 1978-1990

By the end of the seventies and in the initial years of the eighties, the situation in the tribal belt had gone from bad to worse. The tribal people turned out in greater numbers for illicit cutting of the forests areas. Indirectly the policies of Janata Morcha Government at the State level had turned the cards in favour of the tribal leaders of Congress party. Between the year 1975 and 1980, during the Janata Morcha regime, the Forest Department had stopped giving couples to Jungle Kamdar Sahakari Mandalis. This decision created a revolt like situation in the tribal belt. The tribal leadership of the Congress Party had propagated that the Janata Morcha Government at the State level was anti-tribal. During this time, with the instigation from the tribal leaders of the Congress Party, more and more tribals turned out in large numbers for illicit cutting and felling of trees in the forests areas. They started attacking forest officials at different places. They also ransacked the premises of the forest officials and threatened them with dire consequences. Groupism in the ruling political party in the early eighties had also damaged the environment in the whole tribal belt of the State of Gujarat. Ultimately, due to all these circumstances, the rule of terror was found in the forest areas.

Anti-reservation stir in the State of Gujarat also played a major role in creating chaos and brute force ruling in the forest and tribal areas. The State was burning during the decade between the years 1981 and 1990 due to some reason or the other. The tribal leadership and timber *mafias* had played their game, and illicit cutting became rampant as the State was busy trying to maintain law and order in most of the major cities and towns in the State. In this entire gambit, the forest officials were relegated to a position of being mere spectators as only the leaders who were holding powers at the State level were involved. Forest officials lost their hold on illicit cutting completely. The anti-social elements had emerged strong and forceful with the blessings of the highest level of political authority that were ruling the State. During this period, forest officials started concentrating on the counting of illicit cutting and felling of trees in the forests areas and assessing the value of forest wealth lost.

Vyara taluka of Tapi district, Mandvi taluka of Surat district and Sagbara taluka of Narmada district are the examples of the illicit cutting during this phase. The land use patterns in Map 2.6 for these talukas for the years 1972 and 1990 are self-evident:

Fourth Phase: 1991-2007

During this phase, the Joint Forest Management (JFM) had been introduced and implemented successfully at several places. Development related work had been started in the tribal areas. The regeneration of forests was also started during this phase, and this regeneration of forests was considered a very vital phase. Another important reason for the regeneration of forests is the halting of coupe cutting in the forest areas. Coupe cutting had been completely banned from year 1988. Satellite imageries for different taluka in all the five zones show the regeneration of forests.

Chaos and terror in the tribal belt has been controlled with the help of various NGOs in the whole State. NGOs like AKRSP, N.M. Sadguru, VIKSAT and many more started their work in the tribal areas, in the State of Gujarat. In the year 2008-09, Government of Gujarat spent Rs. 2,513.00 crores towards the development of Tribal Area Sub-Plan (TASP or TSP) and Rs. 321 crores towards New Gujarat Pattern under Chief Minister's Ten Point Programme for the tribal development (http://guj-tribaldevelopment.gov.in/cms.aspx?content_id=7). Government of Gujarat generated revenue of Rs. 27.99 crores in the year 2008-09 from forest produces collected from the forests of the state (http://www.gsfdcltd.co.in/collection.html). The tribals have begun getting alternative sources of livelihood for the survival of their families. All these factors have somewhat calmed down tribal communities.

Political interference has continued but now the political leadership of all the parties concentrates on the development of the tribal areas instead of illicit cutting of forest trees. Rise in education, in the tribal community is also playing a major role in the changing tribal behaviour. Instead of getting easy money by illicit cutting of the forests, the influential political leaders in the tribal areas have now started making easy money by misusing the different developmental projects for the tribals.

After the introduction of the Forest Rights Act in the year 2006, a few social activists have encouraged illicit cutting of forests to regain the control of the forest lands. Lots of forests have been cut to start cultivation. The need of the hour for the State Government and the implementing agencies is to take care of the environment and the forest dwellers in such a way so as to ensure that both benefit from the new Act.

III

Developmental Interventions in Forests

It is well-known that natural resources are finite and cannot be produced keeping in mind market demands. By treating these resources as commodities, we face the danger of exhausting them, thus depriving future generations and also risking the loss of a rich bio-diversity. Since Independence, the State of Gujarat has been undertaking developmental projects such as water resources (large, medium and small dams), transport and communications, industries, mines, non-hydel, defence and security, environment protection, human resources, farms and fisheries, urban development, refugee resettlement, social welfare, tourism, government offices and so on. Land acquired for these projects by the State during the last sixty years have been of three types: revenue (private), forest and Government (Common Property Resources). While revenue land is acquired by the State with some compensation, the forest and Government lands are transferred to project. Therefore, people dependent on forests and Government lands are likely to suffer the most. The tribals of Gujarat have singularly been victims of water resource development projects.

New Economic Policies and Land Acquisition

In the 1990s, there was no going back on the policy of economic liberalization set in motion in the previous decade. After 1991, when under international pressure, the Government adopted the stabilization and structural reform measures known as the New Economic Policy (NEP).

The introduction of market friendly economy set India on the fast track of industrialization and development. A growth rate of 6 to 8 per cent, way behind that of market-socialist China but hitherto deemed unattainable in India, was achieved soon, but its benefits were reaped only by monopoly houses and multinationals. In real terms, it further accentuated the misery of the ordinary people because of the rising costs of living and the higher rate of unemployment (Chowdhury and Chowdhury, 1997: 74).

Many newly set-up ventures tolled the death knell of the country's environment. For example, in the 1990s, the global trend, partly to compensate for the damage to forests due to mindless industrial expansion and consumerism, has been on conserving whatever forests have survived. This trend has also taken the form of the creation of National Parks and Sanctuaries, ousting the mostly tribal inhabitants of the forests. Besides, vast stretches of India's coastline have been besieged, while the bio-rich tropical forests and wetlands across the country are about to be decimated. The views of the local residents, whose lives depend on these environments, have never been sought. They have not been properly compensated for the destruction of their habitats or the loss of their livelihoods.

The study by Lobo and Kumar (2009) provides hard data on the number of families displaced and deprived by various developmental projects in Gujarat. It is also an attempt to study the impact of displacement and deprivation on different strata of society. The data covers a span of nearly sixty years from 1947 to 2004. They examined land acquisition documents, and visited project offices in the different parts of the State to get information about monetary compensation under different projects. Moreover, the study has carried out a sample survey of the households affected by different categories of projects, to understand the conditions of the displaced people in the new locations. This study shows that almost 2.5 million households have lost their land and/or habitat, and fall in the category of displaced in post-independent Gujarat. Eighty per cent of the displaced are powerless and belong to the lower strata of society. Water resources and transport are the main development projects, which caused a large number of displacements.

Ghanshyam Shah in his foreward to the above mentioned book observes, "Gujarat's model of development is a shadow of the model prevalent in India and the world at large. This is a model that relies heavily on the use of non-renewable energies, increases urbanization at the cost of rural life, and causes environmental damage and destruction. This model helps a few to gain at the cost of the pain and misery of many. A large number of people face the risk of losing their knowledge just as they lost their lands, resources, languages and lives" (*ibid*, xix).

Sxity-one per cent of the total lands acquired for water resources are mostly in tribal areas in the eastern forested regions of Gujarat. Twenty-three per cent of the total lands acquired are for the cause of transport and communication, 07 per cent for industries and 09 per cent for other causes. Subsequently, 59 per cent of the total families displaced or affected are tribals. The location of water resources, viz., large, medium and small dams, are mostly in forested tribal areas. The authors analyzed that Central Gujarat accounts for 39 per cent of the land acquired for water resources and 40 per cent of the families affected and subsequently; South Gujarat for 28 per cent of the land acquired and 35 per cent families affected and finally North Gujarat for 22 per cent land acquired and 19 per cent of the total families affected or displaced. Central and South Gujarat account for 67 per cent of the land acquired and 75 per cent of the families affected or displaced. As noted earlier, most of them are tribals.

It has been observed in the study (*ibid*, 52) that, in mainland, large dams like Sardar Sarovar, Ukai, Madhuban (Damanganga) and Dharoi were constructed. The Ukai Dam, submerged 170 villages (about 19 villages submerged in Gujarat for the SSP) and relocated in four resettlement sites. The Madhuban Dam oustees, mostly tribals, were relocated in 15-20 villages, without sufficient rehabilitation plans. These projects were mainly responsible for displacement and alienation of people in the Eastern hilly tracts of the State. South Gujarat gave its land for power, mines and transportation projects. Major schemes like Ukai and Karjan submerged more than 82 per cent of the land belonging to individuals and about 10 per cent Government land and rest forest land. Whereas, the Sardar Sarovar Project had submerged about 30 per cent of the private lands and 34-35 per cent of lands belonging to both Forest and Government. Except for some minor schemes which had 20-25 per cent of the land under submergence, most of the major and medium dams have submerged 30-100 per cent of the private lands.

As a result of such a large scale land acquisition for different purposes, millions of people were displaced in the name of development. *Narmada Bachao Andolan* (NBA) and many other organizations had spearheaded the movement against the dams. NBA has continued its fight for the rights of the displaced peoples by the dams on the Narmada River. Their mode of campaign includes hunger strikes and garnering support from noted personalities. Medha Patkar, the leader of NBA had organized a 36-day long, solidarity march among the neighbouring states of the Narmada valley from Madhya Pradesh to the Sardar Sarovar dam site. She said that the march was "a path symbolizing the long path of struggle (both immediate and long-term) that [they] really had" (Fisher, 1995).

All India scenarios are not different. This resulted in much greater displacement and many more struggles after independence than before it. Studies of displacement and deprivation have been conducted in Orissa (Fernandes and Asif, 1997), Jharkhand (Ekka and Asif, 2000), Andhra Pradesh (Fernandes *et al.* 2001), Kerala (Murickan *et al.* 2003), in Goa (Fernandes *et al.* 1999), West Bengal and Assam (1947-2000) (Fernandes Walter *et al.* 2006). Some studies are in progress, in three other states. These studies show that the displacement is high. In India, the 60 million displaced persons and project affected people (DPs/PAPs) of development projects are four times that number; there are more in Pakistan and Bangladesh. Unfortunately, in India, awareness about the subject is weak, leading to the perception of an attitude that seems indifferent. A possible reason for the lack of concern is that most DP/PAPs are voiceless: for instance, tribals constitute 8.08 per cent of India's population; studies show that they constitute over 30 per cent of the DP/PAPs (Fernandes, 2007b), 22 per cent of the DP/PAPs are Dalits (Mahapatra, 1994), and an unknown but the significant proportion of the rest are other rural poor (Muricken *et al.* 2003), particularly the 'backward' till recently. Recent studies show that the backward classes may account for as much as 22 per cent of the DP/PAPs (Muricken *et al.*, 2003). Thus, 80 per cent of the DP/PAPs are powerless, can be displaced without their consent, and are ignored. Table 2.1 gives the magnitude of the social background of the displaced and affected people in states where studies have been carried out.

Many of the displaced experience a marginalization that goes beyond impoverishment—it is a deterioration of their social and cultural status. The loss of land alienates the DP/PAPs from the traditional identity attached to it; it dispossesses them of their cultural heritage, spiritual beliefs, history, legends and myths, and disrupts and dislocates their traditional lifestyles, social networks and cultural practices, and affects their psyche. They find it difficult to adjust to a more powerful society and economy into which displacement has thrust them. Outsiders who come to the project township consider themselves superior to the locals and impose a new culture on them. The DP/PAPs internalise this, develop a low self-image and come to consider their community inferior and incapable of improving itself (Fernandes and Bharali, 2006).

An example of their loss of hope in their future is their transition from a tradition of sustainable use of forests to destructive dependence on them because of the shortage of resources. For sheer survival, they exploit the forests, cutting down trees for sale as firewood. With their impoverishment, they lose their social and

Table 2.1: Social Backgrounds of the Displaced and Affected People

State/Type	Tribals	Dalits	Others	Total	NA	Total
Andhra Pradesh	9,70,654	6,28,824	14,67,286	30,66,764	1,48,856	32,15,620
Assam	4,16,321	NA	6,09,015	10,25,336	8,93,538	19,18,874
Goa	NA	NA	NA	0	60,913	60,913
Gujarat	18,21,283	4,62,626	17,91,142	40,75,051	0	40,75,051
Jharkhand	NA	NA	NA	0	15,48,017	15,48,017
Kerala	NA	NA	NA	0	5,52,233	5,52,233
Orissa	6,16,116	1,78,442	6,71,351	14,65,909	0	14,65,909
W. Bengal	13,30,663	16,89,607	25,66,223	55,86,493	13,57,999	69,44,492
Total	51,55,037	29,59,499	71,05,017	1,52,19,553	45,61,556	1,97,81,109
Percentage	26.06	14.96	35.92	76.94	23.06	100

Source: Fernandes, 2007; Lobo and Kumar, 2007.

psychological infrastructure and internalize an ideology of being incapable of developing themselves (Fernandes and Raj, 1992).

The Deprivation of Forest Resources

As seen earlier in this chapter, in Gujarat, forest resources were taken away from the people during the early 19th century, after the British decided to utilize timber for the construction of railway sleepers. The commercial exploitation of timber resources led to the suppression of the tribals and forest dwellers. Forest dwellers were relocated at the periphery of the forests in order to allow the Forest Department to carry out a hassle-free commercial exploitation of timber. On the eve of Independence, the forest dwellers were mostly settled by Forest Settlement Officers (who demarcated zones for plantations and human settlement). The state's 'eminent domain' principle imposed the monopolistic rights of the State over forests by regulating the activities within them.

Forest dwellers who survived on forest produce, hunting and fishing, were forced to practice settled agriculture. Prabhu (2002: 253) points out "Settled agriculture with alien practices and implements resulted in starvation. Denied food sources in the forests, the tribals, were pushed into the open hands of the money lender for their needs of food, implements, animals and seeds. Indebtedness among them was strikingly endemic, accepted as a fact of life, as natural as to have a wife and children".

Forest in Gujarat are 9.66 per cent of its geographic area (State of Forest Report, Forest Survey of India, 2009). The state lost significant forest cover to the development projects particularly dams and water related projects till 1970. The degradation of forests, as well as their ownership pattern, has deprived the tribals of their livelihood.

Diversion of Forests for Development Projects

Apart from the land acquired for Forestry Programmes, the State also transferred 97,972.75 hectares for various purposes between 1961 and 2006 (State of Forest Report, The Forest Survey of India, 2009). Table 2.2 reflects the diversion of forest area for the period between 1961 and 2006 in the State of Gujarat for different developmental purposes.

Out of the 97,972.75 hectares of forest lands diverted, 41,976.89 hectors (42.8%) of forest lands had been diverted for developmental projects, 19,414.46 hectares (19.8%) for rehabilitation and 36,581.40 hectors (37.4) for agricultural purpose. Forest Department data reveals that though giant steps were taken towards environmental protection; it was not able to stop large-scale land transfer for several projects. The Gujarat Forest Statistics (May, 1983) revealed that 56,214 hectors occupancy rights were given and as per estimates and the Forest Department released 24,790 hectors for authorized cultivation to the people of the Dangs.

Decadal changes in forest land transfer reveal an increase in the rate of transfer after the 1990s in the name of liberalization. This is the result of the numerous incentives that the State Government

Table 2.2: Diversion of Forest Area (1961-2006)

(In Hectares)

Decadal Years	*Submergence*	*Rehabilitation*	*Agriculture*	*Construction of Roads etc.*	*Establishment of Industries Township*	*Misc.*	*Total*
1961-1970	15,210.04	9,347.39	1,082.36	249.68	1,259.58	3,682.36	30,831.41
1971-1980	8,539.83	7,726.34	3,435.30	109.18	422.43	6,038.21	26,271.29
1981-1990	2,081.46	2,340.73	80.94	26.87	1.69	347.59	4,879.28
1991-2000	0.00	0.00	12,417.87	19.08	0.00	1,947.59	14,384.54
2001-2006	1,048.76	0.00	19,564.93	732.32	0.00	260.22	21,606.23
Total	26,880.09	19,414.46	36,581.40	1,137.13	1,683.70	12,275.97	97,972.75

Source: Based on Gujarat Forest Statistics (As on 31/03/2006) May 2006.

offered to the industries and the infrastructural projects. The transfer of forestlands for development projects is regulated by the Central Government's Environmental Laws (Forest Conservation Act, 1980). This has deterred industries from procuring forest lands for their profit. One is compelled to note how easy it was to lose forestlands to development projects particularly for industries in Gujarat before the Forest Conservation Act of 1980.

Although the tribals are having varying amounts of land, it is not fertile for good yielding of crops for their livelihood. The tribals of the forests of Rajpipla and the Dangs who were dependent on the forestlands for cultivation, hunting, gathering, grazing and fishing have been forced over time to vacate their lands and resettled at the periphery of the forests or new sites altogether. The State suppressed their protests and demands, treating them as encroachers or criminals who were hindering the State's development plans.

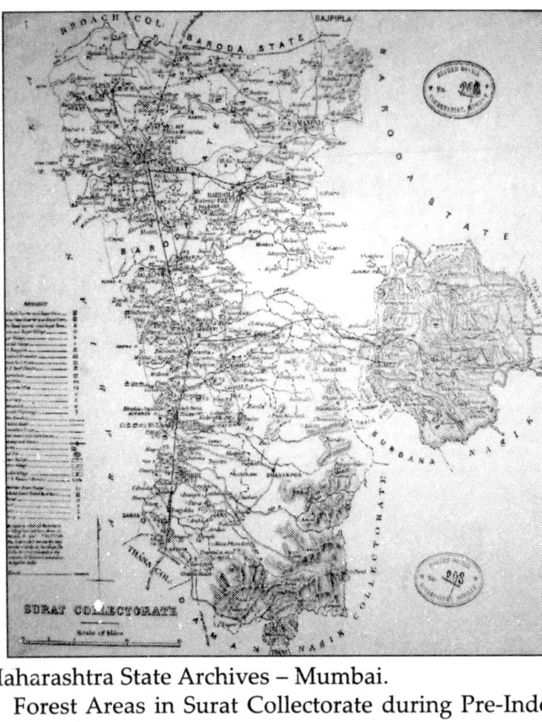

Source: Maharashtra State Archives – Mumbai.

Map 2.1: Forest Areas in Surat Collectorate during Pre-Independence Period

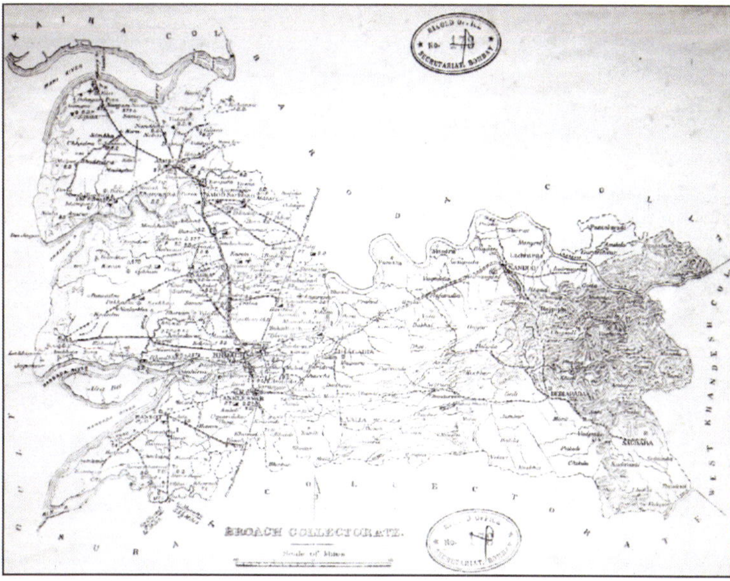

Source: Maharashtra State Archives – Mumbai.

Map 2.2: Forest Areas in Bharuch Collectorate during Pre-Independence Period

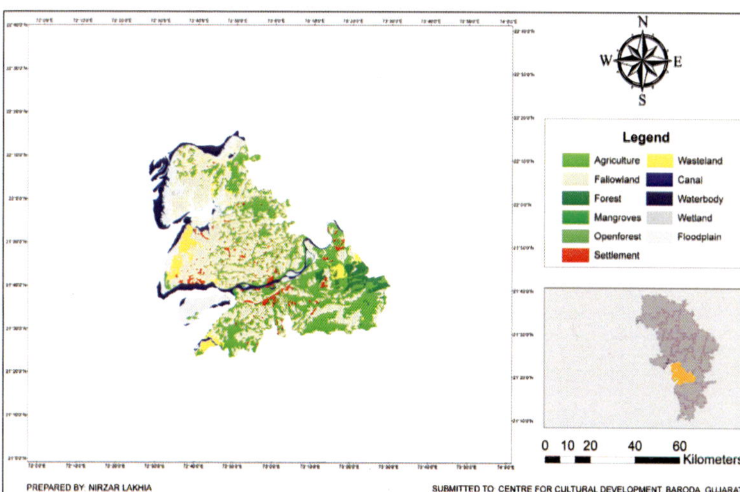

Map 2.3: Forest Areas in Bharuch District in the Year 1972

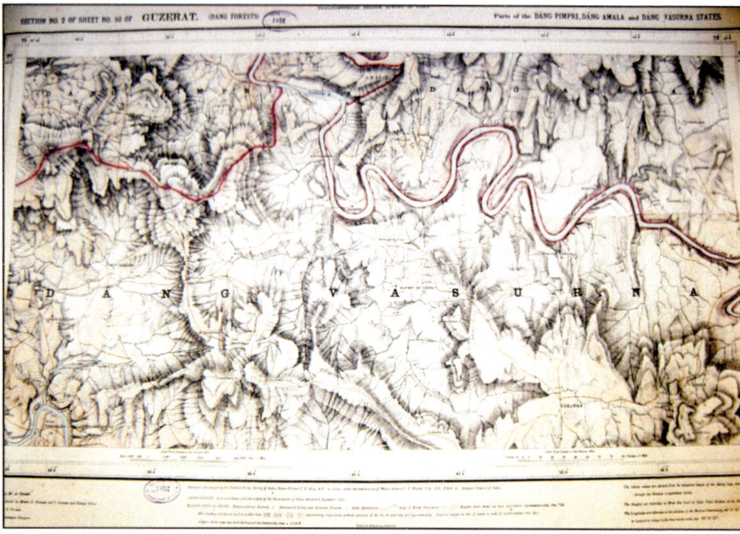

Source: Maharashtra State Archives—Mumbai.

Map 2.4: Forest Areas in Dang (Pimpari-Amala-Vasurna States) during Pre-Independence Period

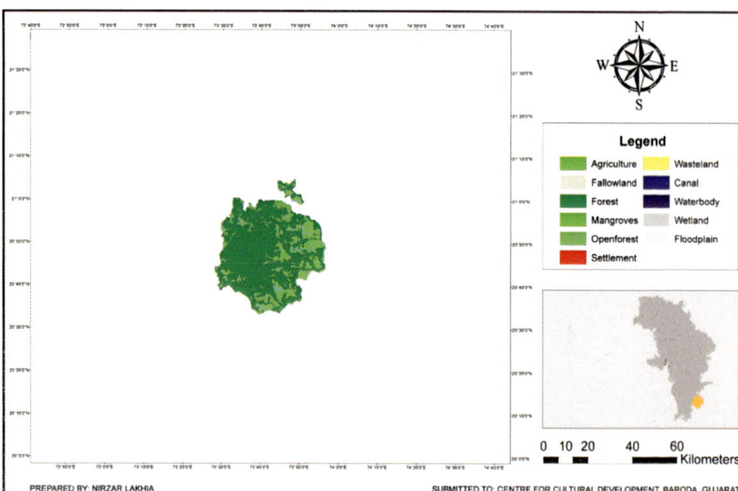

Map 2.5: Forest Areas in Dangs District in the Year 1972

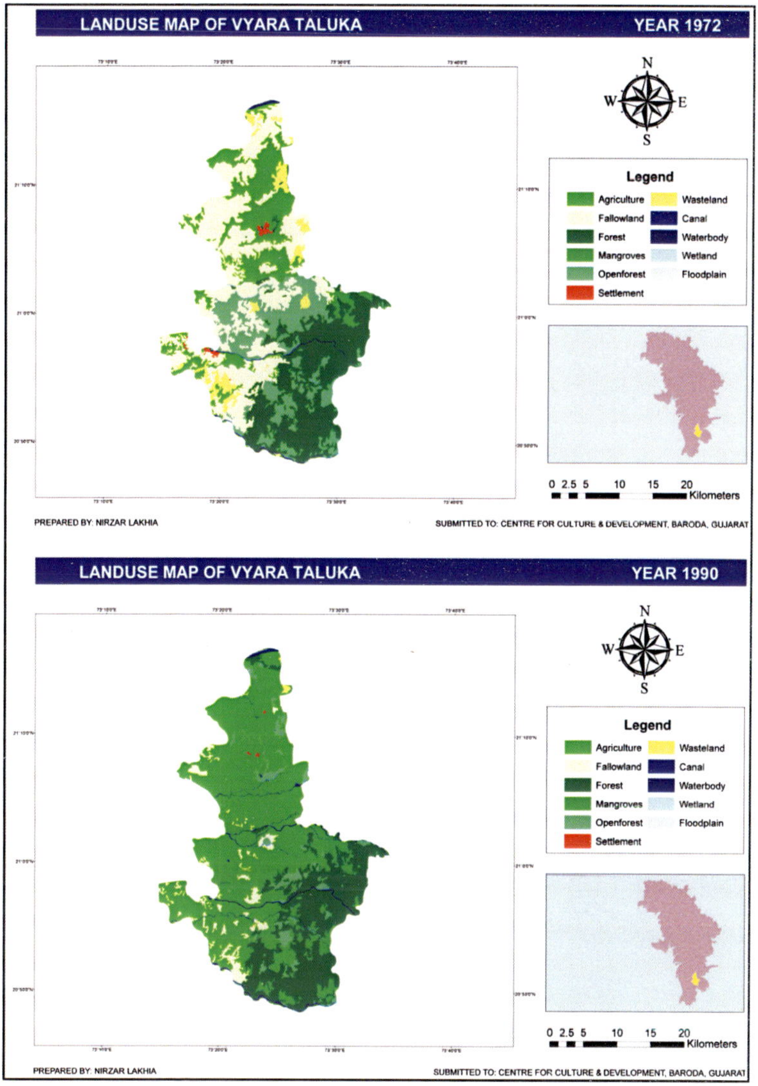

Map 2.6: Landuse for Vyara and Mandvi Talukas in the Year 1972-1990 (*Contd.* next page)

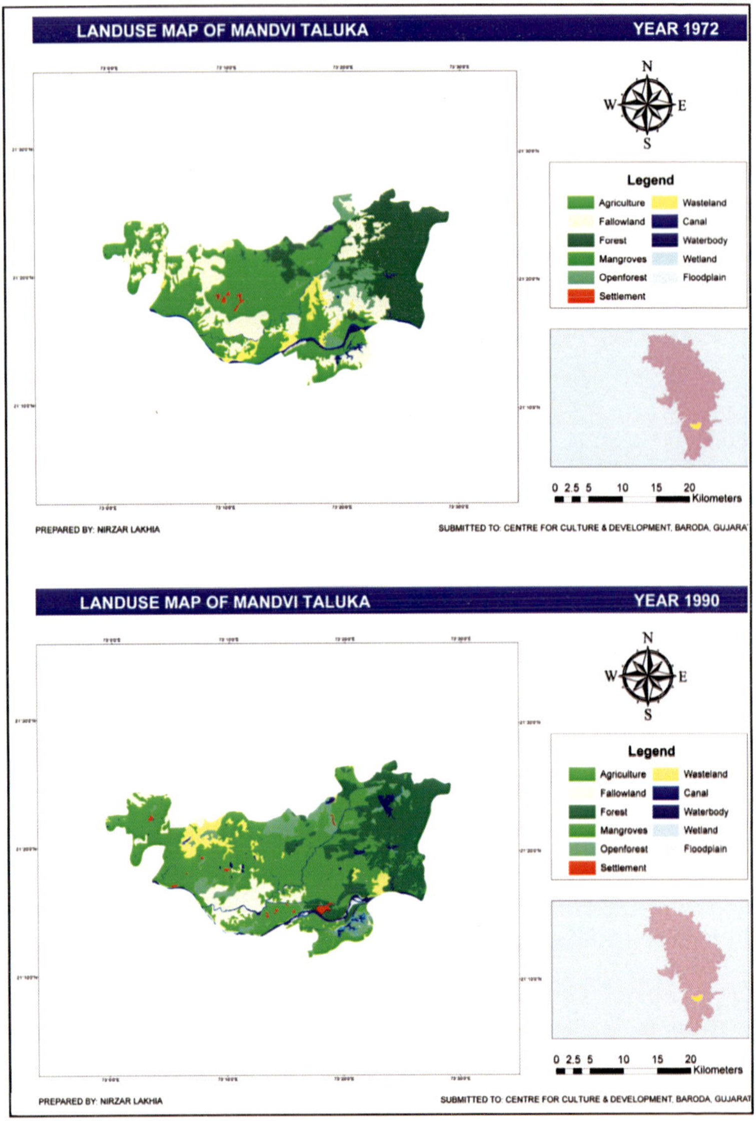

Map 2.6: Landuse for Vyara and Mandvi Talukas in the Year 1972-1990

3

Changing Behaviour of Forests in Gujarat

This chapter reviews the changing behaviour of forests based on satellite imageries for the year 1972, 1990, 2000 and 2007. Based on Census data it also enquires into migration of tribal people. Furthermore, it also analyses the association between migration of people and the changing behaviour of forests. Land use data has been compared from satellite imageries, Forest Working Plans, Forest Survey of India and District Census Handbooks in the five study zones as well as in the non-scheduled and scheduled talukas of mainland Gujarat. This chapter also examines the changing behaviour of forests in mainland Gujarat: the increase in forest cover, decrease in forest cover, and no change in the forest cover at different points of time and in different five zones of the study area.

Section one defines terms like 'forest', 'land use' and 'land cover' and these definitions will be used throughout. There are 13,043 villages in 146 talukas of the 18 districts in the study area. Banaskantha is the biggest district in the State occupying almost 12.68 per cent land; Ahmedabad takes second place with 9.26 per cent and Sabarkantha is the third largest district occupying 9.08 per cent of the total land. Dang is the smallest district with only 2.12 per cent of the total land.

I

Definition of Forest

Forests are generally conceived as areas having tree cover. The Forest

Survey of India has accordingly recognised very dense, moderately dense, open and scrub forests based on the percentage of canopy cover. The Indian Forest Act, 1927 does not define the forests, and the legal extent of these forests depends upon the process of Notifications. In the current study, the term 'forest' means the combination of 'very dense forest' and 'moderately dense forest' while the term 'open forest' means the combination of 'open forest' and 'scrubs' as defined by the Forest Survey of India in their State of Forest Report, 2009:82 for preparing maps using satellite imageries. The meaning of the word 'mangroves' in this study denotes the same meaning as defined by the Forest Survey of India in their State of Forest Report, 2009 for preparing maps using satellite imageries. In all other places where we used the term 'forest' or 'forest cover' in this study means the combination of 'very dense forest', 'moderately dense forest', 'open forest', 'scrubs' and 'mangroves'. This study has used the following terms as defined by the Forest Survey of India in its State of Forest Report 2009 (82ff):

- *Forest Area*: The area recorded as forest in the Government records. It is also referred to as "recorded forest area"
- *Forest Cover*: All lands, more than one hectare in area, with a tree canopy (cover of branches and foliage formed by the crowns of trees) density of more than 10 per cent irrespective of ownership and legal status. Such lands may not necessarily be a recorded forest area. It also includes orchards, bamboo and palm.
- *Protected Forest:* An area notified under the provisions of the Indian Forest Act or other State Forest Act, having limited level of protection. In protected forest, all activities are allowed unless prohibited.
- *Reserved Forest:* An area so constituted under the provisions of the Indian Forest Act or other State Forest Acts, having full level of protection. In reserved forests, all activities are prohibited unless allowed.
- *Unclassed Forest:* All area recorded as forest but not included in reserved or protected forest category.
- *Very Dense Forest*: All lands with forest cover having a canopy density of 70 per cent and above.
- *Moderately Dense Forest*: All lands with forest cover having a canopy density between 40 to 70 per cent.

- *Open Forest*: Lands with forest cover having a canopy density between 10 to 40 per cent.
- *Scrub:* Degraded forest lands having a canopy density of less than 10 per cent
- *Mangroves:* Salt tolerant evergreen forest ecosystem found mainly in tropical and sub-tropical coastal and/or inter-tidal regions.

II

Changing Character of Land Use in Study Area

Agricultural Land

In 1972, agriculture contributed to 35 per cent of the land in the study area. Banaskantha being the biggest district in terms of the total land contributes highly to the total agricultural land (5.50%) Deesa, Tharad and Vav Talukas are other major contributors. 3.95 per cent of the land in Mehsana district was used for agricultural activities; other districts like Sabarkantha (3.96%) have almost 50 per cent of the land under agriculture. The Dangs shows no major agricultural activity during these years as a large part of it is covered with only forest and open forests with little water bodies occupying 0.03 per cent of the total area.

In 1990, the increase in agricultural land was seen through the last two decade as agricultural areas have increased from 35 per cent to nearly 50 per cent. No major increase in agriculture is seen in Banaskantha (5.60%) except Vav taluka whose agricultural land has increased from 1.30 per cent to 1.60 per cent since 1972. Vadodara district (5.00%) through its Jetpur Pavi, Sankheda and Savli Talukas have also seen some major increase in the agricultural land. Except Dahod city and Garbada, all other talukas have contributed in the increase in agricultural land, among them most being in Devgadh Baria taluka in Dohad district that has increased agricultural land from 0.08 per cent to 1.60 per cent since 1972. Jambughoda is the only taluka which has contributed least to increase in agricultural land in Panchmahal district where agricultural land increased from 1.75 per cent in 1972 to 3.60 per cent in 1990. Surat, Sabarkantha and Mehsana had 4.7 per cent, 4.46 per cent and 4.42 per cent of total agricultural area. Only

Daskroi taluka showed some distinctive increase in Ahmedabad district.

In 2000, Ahmedabad, Banaskantha, Sabarkantha and Vadodara showed the highest increase in agriculture lands. The majority of the agricultural land are seen in talukas like Daskroi and Sanand of Ahmedabad district; Deesa, Dhanera and Palanpur of Banaskantha, Dehgam and Gandhinagar of Gandhinagar, Chikhli of Navsari and Karjan of Vadodara district. Among the districts that have shown some reduction in agriculture land from the year 1972 are Bharuch and Narmada along with few talukas of Patan, Surat and Vadodara. The overall comparison shows a 4.00 per cent reduction in agricultural lands from the year 1990.

In 2007, Banaskantha, Mehsana, Patan, Sabarkantha and Vadodara were among the highest contributors of agriculture land, while Patan and Vadodara are the only two districts showing some major growth from 2000. Their overall land holdings have increased by 1.27 per cent in the last decade.

To summarise, the State has witnessed a steady growth in agricultural land and indeed, this trend may continue. For this growth to be realistic it is proposed that a deliberate attempt should be made by the State Government to achieve greater growth in agricultural land which will lead to food security and more importantly, it will be a source of revenue to the State. Waste lands seem to have reduced between 1990 and 2000, and this signifies a desirable change if they are made cultivable.

Forest Land

The forests of mainland Gujarat comprise of various types of forests such as tropical dry deciduous, tropical moist deciduous, dry deciduous or teak and dry deciduous thorny types. Table 3.1 gives a clear picture about different types of forests in the study area.

Annexure 3 shows the list of trees, shrubs, grasses, and creepers that these forests contain with their local, botanical and scientific names.

In 1972, the total forested cover was 10.42 per cent of the total land area in use. Surat is the second largest district in the study area after Banaskantha. Surat has the most forest lands (1.62%) compared to the Dang (1.46%). The Dang is a densely forested cover with almost all of its land under forest cover. There is no sign of any kind

Table 3.1: Types of Forests in the Study Area (District-wise)

Forest Types	*Districts of Study Area*
Moist Deciduous Forests	Dangs and Valsad
Slightly Moist Teak Forests	Surat, Bharuch and Narmada
Dry Teak Forests	Vadodara, Panchmahal, Dahod, Drier parts of Bharuch, North and East part of Sabarkantha
Very Dry Teak Forests	Panchmahal, Dahod
Dry Deciduous Scrub Forests	Vadodara, Panchmahal, Dahod, Banaskantha, Sabarkantha, Mehsana and Patan
Tropical Dry Deciduous Forests	Gandhinagar, Kheda and Mehsana
Dry Deciduous Forests	Western and Southern part of Sabarkantha
Dry Mixed Deciduous and Tropical Forests	Vadodara, Panchmahal, Dahod and Southern parts of Banaskantha
Desert Thorn Scrub Forests	East, North and West part of Banaskantha

Source: Gujarat Forest Statistics—May 2006.

of settlement or other agricultural activities here. Dediapada taluka of Narmada district, Songadh taluka of Surat and Kaprada taluka of Valsad are among the other highly forested areas.

In 1990, it was found that the urban area was increasing, and so were the agricultural activities, the total forest covers seemed to reduce by 1 per cent. Surat (1.49%) still had the largest forest covers, but it clearly seemed to be affected by developmental activities. The Narmada (1.31%) and the Valsad (1.26%) areas have increased their forest cover through these years. The Dang (1.23%) is another major forest covered area but 0.23 per cent of its forested area has been reduced because of increased agricultural activities. Sabarkantha (10.82%) and Banaskantha (9.48%) also show an increase in its forests especially during the 1990's. However, an important reduction in the forested areas is seen in the Panchmahal district; its forests reduced to half from 1.34 per cent in 1972 to 0.61 per cent in 1990.

In 2000, Surat (1.45%), Sabarkantha (1.40%), Valsad (1.21%) and Dang (1.21%) possessed the maximum amount of area under forest cover. The Narmada area has seen some significant reduction during this decade with its forest land reducing to nearly 0.4 per cent. Banaskantha and Bharuch has also reduced its forest cover by 0.12 per cent and 0.08 per cent respectively. The Panchmahal and Sabarkantha districts have shown an increase in its forest cover by almost 0.30 per cent. At the sub-district level, talukas like Amirgadh (0.30%) and Bhabhar (0.4%) are found to be the forest covered area of Banaskantha. Dediapada (0.55%) and Nandod

(0.30%) of Narmada have most of the forest cover in the district. Bhiloda (0.43%) and Vijaynagar (0.42%) of Sabarkantha are high forest covered area. While Songadh (0.59%), Uchchhal (0.20%) and Vyara (0.23%) are known as the largest forest covers of Surat district. Dharampur (0.40%) and Kaprada (0.72%) of Valsad are the main forest covers of Valsad.

In 2007, most affected areas were Dohad, Sabarkantha, Panchmahal and Valsad, which have reduced its forests by almost 0.25 per cent due to the urban sprawl. Contrastingly Surat, Navsari and Bharuch have shown some reduction in its agriculture areas but have also shown some increase in its forest cover by 0.20 per cent.

To summarize, indeed, between the time of 1990 and 2007, there has been a steady increase in the spatial expansion of settlements in Eastern Gujarat compared to the time between 1972 and 1990. There is a possibility of continued increase over the coming years. This may, therefore, suggest that the urbanization has increased in producing functions that attracted large scale migration into this area. There is a continual reduction of the forested areas, and it is, therefore, proposed that the Gujarat Government should encourage the local tribals to regenerate forests.

Settlements

In 1972, only the major towns seemed to be visible during these early years of development. Ahmedabad and Surat are among the few towns that have developed. Vadodara and Surat are in the early phase of development. Human settlements occupy 0.54 per cent of total land-use. It is prominently in the city of Ahmedabad and Surat. Development at the sub-district levels is mainly observed in talukas like Deesa and Tharad of Banaskantha districts, Vagra and Ankleshwar of Bharuch, Bardoli of Surat district and Nandod of Narmada district. Compared to the growth in population, agricultural activities are less in the Banaskantha and the Mehsana districts. The Dang and Valsad show no visible signs of urban development during this year whereas Dahod shows negligible signs of development.

In 1990, in nearly two decades, settlements have increased by 0.10 per cent. Major developments in terms of settlements or urban sprawl are seen in cities like Ahmedabad, Surat and Vadodara along with a few talukas like Ghandhinagar and Choryasi. Talukas like Anand, Ankleshwar, Godhara, Kalol, Mehsana, Vagra and Valsad have also shown some development. (The amount of water and wasteland have also increased with a significant amount of reduction of open forests. A large number of water bodies are seen in talukas like Bhiloda, Jambusar, Khambhat, Nizar, Songadh, Uchchhal and Vagra).

In 2000, settlements increased by two folds. But there has been no marked reduction of the forests. There has also been some reduction in the wastelands which might have been used for agricultural purposes or other developmental purposes. Looking at the overall development where human habitation is concerned, Ahmedabad, Bharuch, Surat, Vadodara and Banaskantha are the only districts whose urban sprawl can be easily noticed in the satellite images. The majority of urban sprawls is seen around the city areas and in the talukas like Daskroi of Ahmedabad, Ankleshwar of Bharuch, Choryasi and Olpad of Surat and Karjan of Vadodara.

In 2007, little reduction was seen in the area covered by forests while no significant change was noticed in the overall agricultural area in recent years. Settlements have increased from 1.66 per cent in 2000 to 1.90 per cent in 2007. There has also been an increase in water bodies from 1972 to 2007. Banaskantha and Mehsana are among the areas most used for agriculture while their overall settlement areas have increased to almost three fold from 1972. Among others Kheda, Narmada, Surat and Valsad districts show some increase in settlements.

To summarise, the land consumption rate which is the measure of compactness indicates a progressive spatial expansion of the city; this growth was constant in 1972 and 1990, high in 1990 and 2007 and this increase is expected to be consistent in the future. Therefore, this suggests that the rate at which new lands are acquired for development is high. It seems to be expanding towards the outskirts rather than concentrate development at the city center.

III

Changes in Forest Covers between the Year 1972 and 2007

Changes in the forest are seen over a period of time through change detection maps. An important aspect of change detection is to determine what is actually changing to what, i.e., which land use category is changing to the other. Some general observations have been given here for the zonal scale. Change detection represented here has been divided into five different categories based on the 30 per cent changes in the spectral radiance in the images, and land use map digitized from the satellite image. The criteria adopted in this project for change detection is shown in Table 3.2.

Table 3.2: Description of Categories used in Change Detection

Categories	*Description of Categories*
Unchanged	Open forest in 1972 and open forest in 2007
Slightly decreased	Forest in 1972 and open forest in 2007
Slightly increased	Forest in 2007 and open forest in 1972
Highly decreased	Forest in 1972 and open area in 2007
Highly increased	Forest in 2007 and open area in 1972
Slightly decreased	Open forest in 1972 and open area in 2007
Slightly increased	Open forest in 2007 and open area in 1972

Zone I

Gandhinagar, Mehsana and Sabarkantha are the three main districts showing a positive development in their forest cover (see Table 3.3). While all the talukas of these districts show a positive trend we have seen that talukas like Khedbrahma, Vadali and Meghraj show a negative trend in the increase of forest cover; Meghraj being the most affected with 1.31 per cent of decreased forest cover. All the talukas of Sabarkantha except Vijaynagar show a good development in the increase of forest cover. While Deesa, Kankrej and Palanpur

Table 3.3: Five Categories Showing the Percentage of Change in Forest Cover of Zone I

Categories		*Percentage of Change*	*Colors used in the Map*
Decreased	Highly decreased	06.57	Red
	Slightly decreased	25.43	Orange
	Total decreased	32.00	
Unchanged		33.88	Yellow
Increased	Slightly increased	19.85	Light green
	Highly increased	14.27	Dark green
	Total increased	34.12	

have reduced their forest cover, Amirgadh, on the other hand, has shown an increase in its forest covers and the Banaskantha district villages like Kapasia, Dabhila, Juni, Rohgadhada, Nichlo Bandh and Uplo Bandh have shown a positive increase.

Ahmedabad, Banaskantha and Patan districts have been affected by the development of the human habilitation and for these reasons have shown reduced forest cover. The urban sprawl of Ahmedabad city has grown three folds since 1972 while the forest cover of Daskroi taluka has been affected because of the human habilitation.

Zone II

Dahod and Panchmahal are the two main districts which have a high negative impact of forest change with the ratio of the percentage of negative/positive being 1.47/0.13 and 3.22/0.68 respectively to 14.29 and 11.96 per cent of their total land mass. Some villages like Vav Kulli, Navagam, Jambuvania, Goya Sundal and Bhojpura show negative trends in Ghoghamba taluka. However, some other villages of Ghoghamba, Halol and Jambughoda talukas of Panchmahal district have a positive trend of forest development, while Kadana, Lunawada and Santrampur are the most affected talukas. All the villages of Dahod have shown a negative trend (see Table 3.4).

Table 3.4: Five Categories Showing the Percentage of Change in Forest Cover of Zone II

Categories		*Percentage of Change*	*Colors used in the Map*
Decreased	Highly decreased	18.51	Red
	Slightly decreased	49.51	Orange
	Total decreased	68.02	
Unchanged		17.58	Yellow
Increased	Slightly increased	09.24	Light green
	Highly increased	05.16	Dark green
	Total increased	14.40	

Vadodara and Kheda are the other districts with major forest reduction with the negative/positive ratio being 0.94/0.54 and 0.74/

0.43 respectively. Anand also showed some reduction in the forest covers with the negative/positive ratio of 0.37/0.11 from these statistics it can be concluded that all the five districts of these zones have been greatly affected by deforestation, and this is a major concern.

Zone III

While there are no significant changes in the forest cover of Surat district, Bharuch has increased its forest cover whereas, Narmada has reduced its forest cover by 0.56 per cent. Mangrol, Songadh, Uchchhal and Vyara are some districts whose forest cover have almost reduced to half while Bardoli, Choryasi, Kamrej and Mahuva are the talukas contributing to greater forest cover in the Surat distric (see Table 3.5).

Table 3.5: Five Categories Showing the Percentage of Change in Forest Cover of Zone III

Categories		*Percentage of Change*	*Colors used in the Map*
Decreased	Highly decreased	05.94	Red
	Slightly decreased	12.50	Orange
	Total decreased	18.44	
Unchanged		46.77	Yellow
Increased	Slightly increased	22.10	Light green
	Highly increased	12.70	Dark green
	Total increased	34.80	

All the talukas of Bharuch have shown an increase in their forest covers, Dediapada is the only major taluka showing decrease in the forests, in the Narmada district.

Zone IV

We have included three districts of this zone in our study, two of which show contrasting developments. While Navsari shows a fair amount of development in their forest cover, Valsad shows a good amount of growth in its human development but a negative trend in forest conservation (*see* Table 3.6).

Table 3.6: Five Categories Showing the Percentage of Change in Forest Cover of Zone IV

Categories		*Percentage of Change*	*Colors used in the Map*
Decreased	Highly decreased	06.63	Red
	Slightly decreased	20.07	Orange
	Total decreased	26.70	
Unchanged		56.62	Yellow
Increased	Slightly increased	11.70	Light green
	Highly increased	04.98	Dark green
	Total Increased	16.68	

Vyara, Kaparda and Pardi have shown some decrease in its forest cover as compared to the other parts of the zone.

Zone V

As the Dang was one of the only districts with almost 100 per cent of forest cover, there was no chance of further increase in the forest cover. While more than 70 per cent of the areas of the Dang have still remained as forests, this area has also shown some major changes in its remaining zones as compared to 1972. There is a significant amount of reduction in forest cover of the villages like Kudcas, Pimpri, Nadagadi, Chikatiya, Gaurya, Sati, Wangan, Wawanda, Isdar, Mahal, Dewantembron, etc. while a trend in the reduction of the forest cover is clearly seen in other parts as well (see Table 3.7).

Table 3.7: Five Categories Showing the Percentage of Change in Forest Cover of Zone V

Categories		*Percentage of Change*	*Colors used in the Map*
Decreased	Highly decreased	04.19	Red
	Slightly decreased	18.46	Orange
	Total decreased	22.65	
Unchanged		70.56	Yellow
Increased	Slightly increased	06.12	Light green
	Highly increased	00.67	Dark green
	Total increased	06.79	

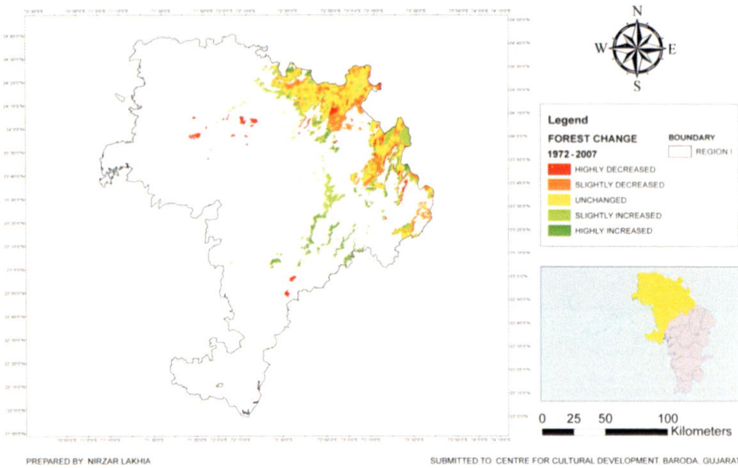

Map 3.1: Change Detection Map of Forest Cover in Zone I

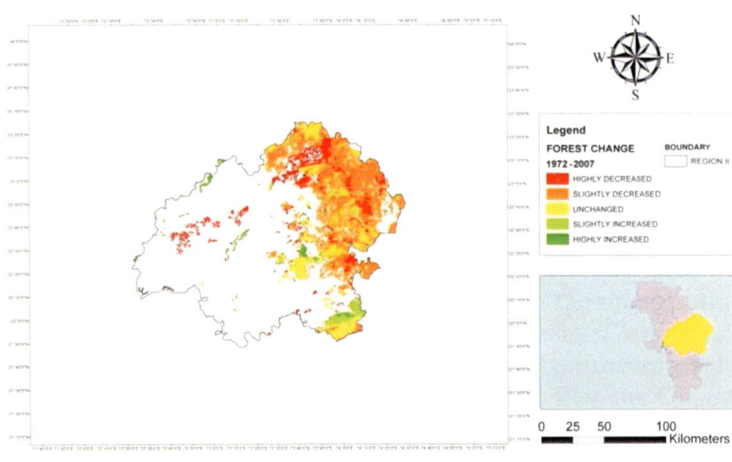

Map 3.2: Change Detection Map of Forest Cover in Zone II

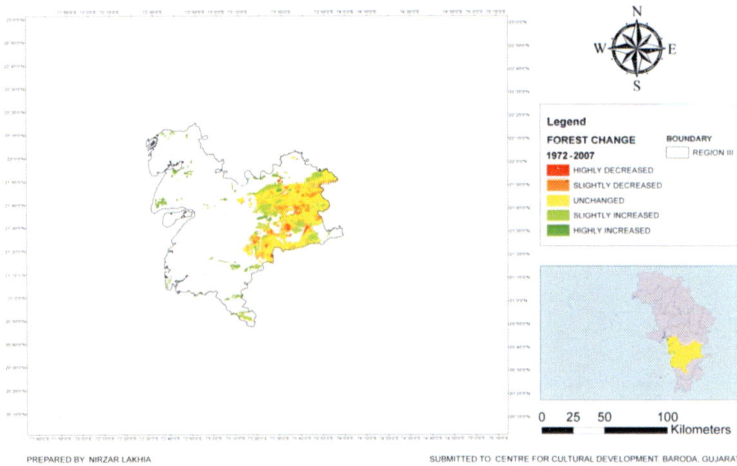

Map 3.3: Change Detection Map of Forest Cover in Zone

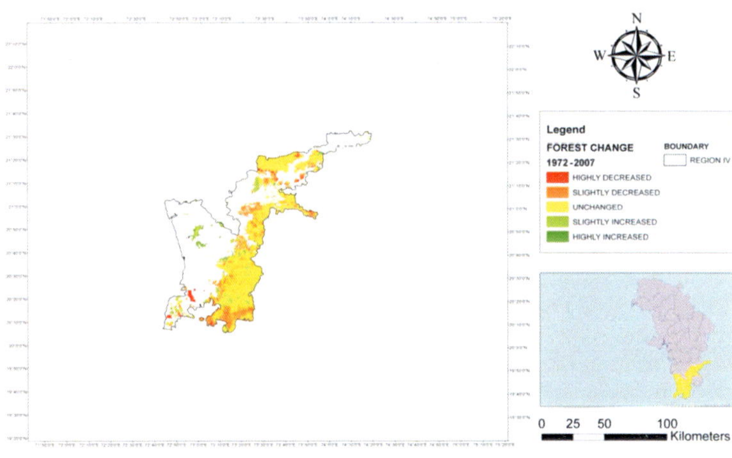

Map 3.4: Change Detection Map of Forest Cover in Zone IV

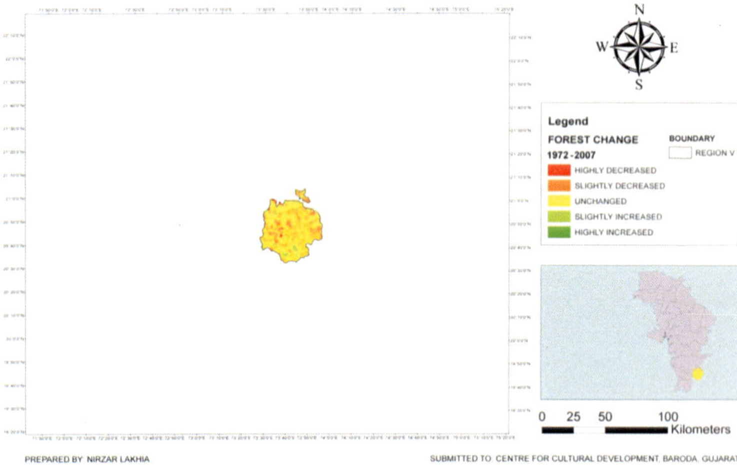

Map 3.5: Change Detection Map of Forest Cover in Zone V

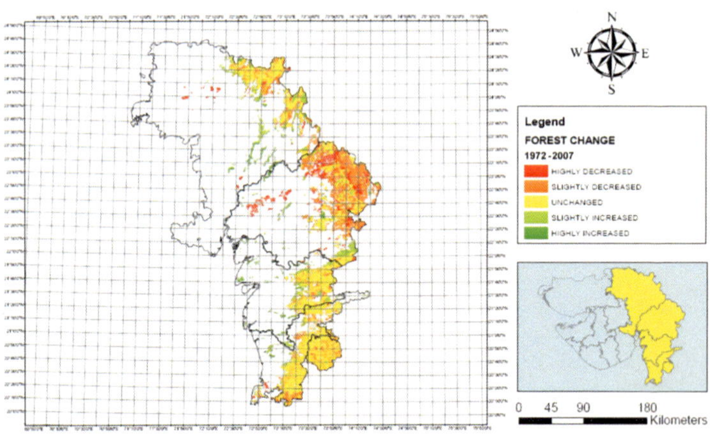

Map 3.6: Change Detection Map of Forest Cover for the Study Area

4

Migration and Change among Tribals

By and large migration is driven by a search for a better and more secure livelihood. The literature on tribal communities and agricultural development often ignores or underplays the role of migration. Rather than seeing migration as a livelihood strategy (adopted in combination with other activities) the literature also often represents migration as a response to failing tribal livelihoods. Policies and development programmes often aim to reduce out-migration pressures on urban areas. However, such attempts fail to understand how migration can be a critical element in the livelihood of tribal households and communities. Migration between urban and rural areas has fundamentally changed interactions between rural and urban settlements and the way in which we perceive the countryside. Tribals migrate on both a temporary and permanent basis, from rural to urban areas, between rural areas, from one town or city to another. However, many rural-urban migrants retain strong links with their home villages to the benefit of household members in both locations, (for example, through remittances, food supplies, childcare, and work at harvest time).

In this chapter, we will examine the migration in the tribal community between the year 1971 and the year 2001 in section one. Section two will discuss the impact of change in forest cover on the migration of the tribal community. Impact of migration will be discussed in section three.

I

Migration of Tribal Population for the Period between the Year 1971 and 2001

The general perception is that, on account of the degradation of forests, there is a large scale migration of tribal populations to mainland Gujarat. To substantiate our claims, we had mapped the Census of 1971 and the Census of 2001 (http://censusindia.gov.in) data on village-wise tribal community of our study area. In this section, we will see the zone-wise migration in the tribal community over the thirty years.

Zone I

It is seen that the villages on the North-East border of the zone have gained from the migration in the population while the villages on the South-Western part show a reducing trend. Sabarkantha is a major contributor to the migration of tribal people in this zone. This migration is mainly observed in Khedbrahma, Bhiloda and Vijaynagar talukas. There are a few talukas like Dholka and Sanand of Ahmedabad and Vagdod of Patan, which have shown a negative trend by 0.01 per cent from 1971. While Danta of Banaskantha (1.75%) Bhiloda (1.64%), Vijaynagar (1.08%) and Khedbrahma (2.86%) of Sabarkantha are among the major contributors in this zone. The other main sites for tribals are Amirgadh, Dhanera and Palanpur talukas of Banaskantha (see Table 4.1).

Table 4.1: Migration of Tribal Population for the Period between 1971 and 2001 in Zone I

Districts	*Percentage Migration in Tribal Population*
Banaskantha	3.48
Sabarkantha	6.98
Mehsana	0.14
Patan	0.09
Gandhinagar	0.57
Ahmedabad	0.53

Zone II

As can be clearly seen from the images (Map 4.2), the Eastern part of the zone shows a growing trend while the Western part shows a reducing trend in the ST population migration (see Table 4.2). Dahod taluka contributes considerably to the migrating population of tribals in this zone with almost 50 per cent of the tribals moving to this part of the zone. One of the reasons for this is that it lies on the border of Madhya Pradesh. All the talukas contribute to the migrating population of Dahod, Zalod being the major contributor to this district with 5.38 per cent. Santrampur, Kadana and Ghoghamba contribute most in the population migration of tribals in Panchmahal district whereas in Vadodara, Jetpur Pavi, Chhota Udaipur, Kawant and Nasvadi provide the main resources. More research is needed to unravel the real reasons for so much migration from this zone.

Table 4.2: Migration of Tribal Population for the Period between 1971 and 2001 in Zone II

Districts	*Percentage Migration in Tribal Population*
Dahod	19.65
Panchmahal	09.47
Kheda	00.35
Anand	00.39
Vadodara	13.62

Zone III

The trend of the population migration is reducing in the North-Western zone while there is an overall increasing migration in the other parts of this zone. There are a few villages of the zone which have also shown a reducing trend like Borbhatha, Diva, Divi, Matied, Samor of Ankleshwar, Amleshwar, Kasva of Bharuch, Rundh of Jhagadia, Gandhar, Keshwan, Sachan of Vagra, Kanerva, Sabariya of Vagra talukas of Bharuch. While, in Narmada, the villages like Koliwada, Moti Daberi, Nani Bhamari, Navagam, Sada of Deduaoada taluka, Kevadia, Mokhdi, Rajpipla of Nandod taluka, Naldhara of Mahuva taluka, etc. Jhagadia and Valia contribute the most to the tribal population migration in the

Bharuch district. Talukas like Bardoli, Mahuva, Mandvi and Mangrol contribute more than 50 per cent of the migration in the Surat district. Dediapada and Nandod talukas are also the main contributors with 50 per cent of the migration in the Narmada district (see Table 4.3).

Table 4.3: Migration of Tribal Population for the Period between 1971 and 2001 in Zone III

Districts	*Percentage Migration in Tribal Population*
Narmada	05.21
Bharuch	04.33
Surat	08.55

Zone IV

Villages like Vadichonda of Bansada taluka, Bhil Bhavali, Raygadh, village of Nizar, Abhankuva of Uchchhal in Navsari district, Madhuban of Kaprada, Vapi in Valsad district are the villages with the reducing trend in this zone. Valsad is the second largest district after Dahod in terms of tribal population migration. Talukas contributing to this migration are Kaprada and Dharampur. Bansada and Chikhli are the major contributors to this migration in the Navsari district (see Table 4.4).

Table 4.4: Migration of Tribal Population for the Period between 1971 and 2001 in Zone IV

Districts	*Percentage Migration in Tribal Population*
Tapi	07.52
Navsari	06.85
Valsad	10.02

Zone V

The Dangs has 2.27 per cent of the total tribal population migration from the entire study area. Ambapada (Waghai), Borigaotha (Waghasia), Taklipada show a reducing trend in the Dang while few villages like Ahirdi, Ahirpada, Ahwa, Chikhalda and Gunjpeda have remained unchangea since 1971. Samgahan, Saputara, Pimpri and Gadhvi have contributed up to 0.03 per cent to the total tribal population migration (see Table 4.5).

Table 4.5: Migration of Tribal Population for the Period between 1971 and 2001 in Zone V

Districts	*Percentage Migration in Tribal Population*
Dang	02.27

Some Emerging Trends

Table 4.6 shows the percentage migration in the tribal community in five Zones. One can superimpose the maps of the change in forest covers and the migration in the tribal community to verify the relations of development and examine the same.

Table 4.6: Migration of Tribal Population for the Period between 1971 and 2001 in Study Area

Zones	*Percentage Migration in Tribal Population*
I	11.78
II	43.48
III	18.08
IV	24.39
V	02.27

Zone II has the maximum migration in tribal people (43.48%) over a period of thirty years while Zone V has a minimum migration in tribal population (02.27%). Zone I does not have a significant migration in tribal people (11.78%) compared to Zone II, Zone III and Zone IV. Zone IV shows significant migration in the tribal people (24.39%) over the last three decades. Increase in education among the tribal communities has a positive impact on the migratory pattern. Migration is high in the areas with low education, than those areas with more education. In Zone III, there is more education but the migration is low while, in Zone II, there is less education but more migration. Tribals with low level of education or illiterate tribals seemed to use traditional sources and were not quite comfortable with modern alternative sources for their livelihood. Tribals with more education are seen to have started taking advantage of welfare schemes for them and using modern techniques in agriculture and alternate sources of livelihood like dairy farming, buying jeep or rickshaw or truck or matador tempo.

This study shows that tribals migrate for additional sources of livelihood; seventy per cent of them either migrate for better employment opportunities or in search of better sources of livelihood (Refer Table 4.7). It is seen that 63 per cent of the total respondents in Zone II have migrated for a better employment compared to other causes of migration. Twenty-two per cent of the total respondents of Zone I and Zone III have migrated for livelihood requirements. An insignificant number, that is, hardly 01 per cent of the total respondents migrated for higher education.

Table 4.7: Zone-wise Distribution of Causes of Migration among the Respondents

Causes of Migration	*Zones*					*Study Area*
	I	*II*	*III*	*IV*	*V*	
To get better employment	176 (48)	467 (63)	273 (47)	282 (55)	207 (44)	1405 (53)
In search of livelihood	81 (22)	52 (07)	128 (22)	118 (23)	66 (14)	445 (17)
Educated – hence leave village	04 (01)	07 (01)	12 (02)	10 (02)	05 (01)	38 (01)
No facility of education	07 (02)	07 (01)	23 (04)	05 (01)	00 (00)	42 (02)

Note: Percentages are given in parenthesis.

Regarding the temporary or seasonal nature of migration, respondents from Zone V and Zone IV informed that they had migrated during the sugarcane cutting season. Sugar factory owners picked them up in vehicles from their villages and also paid them in advance. The men went in pairs to work in the fields and at times migrated with the whole family for three to six months. Respondents from Zone II said that they generally migrated for construction work anywhere in the State of Gujarat and sometimes even outside Gujarat. Some of them also worked in mines and dolomite factories crushing stones in Chhota Udepur, Kadi Pani and Kawant area. These mines and factories are mostly in the nearby areas of their villages. Respondents from Zone III migrated to nearby industrial areas like Ankleshwar and Jhagadia to work as unskilled workers on a temporary basis. Hence, it seems that one of the main causes for migration was to improve their economic standards. And this migration had definite effects on the employment patterns of tribal communities.

Migration needs to be further examined to determine whether it is dependent on the degradation of forests or the level of education or even on better infrastructure facilities or on heightened expectations among the tribals. Due to global warming, there is a change in temperature and rainfall patterns. The summers seem to have become warmer than before. The rainfall pattern has also changed. Two decades ago, the Saurashtra area received very scattered rainfall and South Gujarat region enjoyed high rainfall. However, it has been seen that the pattern has changed since the last five years. Rainfall in the Saurashtra region has increased, but the rainfall has decreased in the South Gujarat region (see Chapter 8 for more details). This changing pattern of rainfall pattern has had an impact on the agricultural products, and the forest produces. Hence, it is this changing pattern of weather that could have had an indirect effect on the migrating attitude of tribals and their livelihood. The following are the major factors responsible for the migration attitudes of tribal communities:

1. Many tribal areas have recently undergone administrative changes, including reorganization of certain districts such as, Surat, Valsad, Bharuch and the Panchmahal.
2. Ecology has seen changing patterns due to the effect of global warming that has affected the tribal economy. This has resulted in changing the pattern in agriculture and forest produces.
3. Development of infrastructure like roads, concrete houses, railways, schools, colleges, and health centres, mineral and non-mineral mines, setting up of industrial areas, welfare centres etc. have brought about socio-economic changes and changes in the cultural situation.
4. A high number of mines have come up in almost all parts of the tribal areas in the State of Gujarat. This brought in employment, improved communication systems and changed the pattern of living of the tribals living in the nearby areas.

5. Owing to the growth of the tribal community over the last four decades, there has been an increased demand for fuel wood, bamboo and timber, and this led to ecological depletion, which ultimately led to migration.
6. Awareness about schemes to regulate and replace migrating cultivation (for which land capability and soil survey studies have been undertaken) have brought in changes. Barren areas were also produced under various horticulture crops. All such activities have changed the lifestyle of the tribal people.
7. Various schemes and development programmes have been initiated by the Government of India and the Government of Gujarat to improve socio-economic conditions of the tribals and the outcome of this has been a rapid change in the livelihood structure of tribal society.

In fact, all these factors mentioned above are responsible for the rapid migration in socio-economic and cultural attitudes of the tribals.

II

Change in Forest Cover and the Migration of Tribal Population

Our study observed that the link between the changes in the forest and migration of the tribals is weak. Even when there was an increase in the forest cover, i.e., regeneration of forests, the tribals migrated.

The relation between the increase and decrease in the forest cover with the migratory pattern of the tribal people is shown in Table 4.8. 20.21 per cent migration has been recorded in the areas where there is a decrease in the forest cover. The percentage of migration is 16.43 per cent in the areas where there is an increase in the forest cover. The difference is not significant.

There are many additional factors responsible for the migration of tribals. Migratory pattern is now not only based on the dependency on forests among the tribal communities. Even where there is no change in the forest cover, migration has been more than double (37.69%) than in areas where the forest cover has increased (16.43%) or decreased in the forest cover (20.21%). This trend in recent times is due to tribals not merely because of depending on the forest or on the forest products. They have adopted alternative sources of livelihood such as dairy farming, horticulture, agriculture etc., besides using modern techniques in agriculture like drip irrigation and better seeds.

Increase in the population among the tribal communities (which is always more than the general population growth rate) also has an impact on the tribal demography. Increase in their community since the last four decades resulted in the cutting down of forests to some degree in order to get additional land for cultivation to get extra food for the survival of their families. As the population of tribals is growing, the land holding is divided among the new generations which leads to the fragmentation of land holding. Land holding plays an important role as one of the main causes for the migration of tribal. Migration of some of the family members with small land holdings is also seen across the study area.

When the study area is divided into two divisions (i) Scheduled Areas (43 talukas) and (ii) Non-scheduled areas (103 talukas), this study observes the differences in the migratory patterns of the tribal communities. Migration is found high in the scheduled areas (80.44%) (Refer Table 4.9) compared to the non-scheduled areas (19.56%) (Refer Table 4.10). Tribals from scheduled talukas of districts like Vadodara (10.24%), Surat (13.09%), Valsad (8.42%) and Panchmahal (5.79%) have more migration than those districts having non-scheduled talukas in districts like Vadodara (3.38%), Surat (2%), Valsad (1.60%) and Panchmahal (3.67%). A possible reason for these disparities between the scheduled areas and the non-scheduled areas may be opportunities for better employment and better alternative sources of livelihood for the tribals in the non-scheduled areas compared to the scheduled areas.

III

Changes among Tribals

Literacy and education are the basic tools for the development of consciousness and reconstitution of any society. Table 4.11 shows the rate of literacy in 1991 and 2001; the data has been processed from the *District Census Handbook* for these years. It clearly reflects

Table 4.8: Zone-wise Migration of Tribal Population between the Years 1971 and 2001 with Respect to Forest Change

Zones	*Districts*	*Forest Change 1972 to 2007 (%)*				
		Decreased	*Unchanged*	*Increased*	*Others*	*Grand Total*
I	Banaskantha	0.21	2.27	0.19	0.82	**3.49**
	Sabarkantha	1.24	3.77	0.87	1.09	**6.97**
	Mehsana	0.00	0.00	0.03	0.11	**0.14**
	Patan	0.04	0.00	0.00	0.05	**0.09**
	Gandhinagar	0.00	0.00	0.35	0.22	**0.57**
	Ahmedabad	0.00	0.00	0.07	0.46	**0.53**
Total Zone I						
II	Anand	0.08	0.02	0.02	0.27	**0.39**
	Kheda	0.03	0.08	0.04	0.20	**0.35**
	Panchmahal	3.01	4.29	1.21	0.96	**9.47**
	Dahod	10.60	6.48	1.73	0.84	**19.65**
	Vadodara	3.02	3.37	1.94	5.29	**13.62**
Total Zone II						
III	Narmada	0.11	2.80	1.27	1.03	**5.21**
	Bharuch	0.01	0.65	1.15	2.52	**4.33**
	Surat	0.75	4.77	3.57	6.98	**16.07**
Total Zone III						
IV	Navsari	0.07	1.47	3.19	2.12	**6.85**
	Valsad	1.04	5.46	0.80	2.72	**10.02**
Total Zone IV						
V	The Dang	0.00	2.26	0.00	0.00	**2.26**
Total Zone V						
TOTAL		20.21	37.69	16.43	25.67	**100.00**

the increase in the level of literacy among tribals in all the five zones. An overall 10 per cent increase in the literacy level has been seen in one decade; that is, from 1991 to 2001. Zone III and Zone V show the highest increase compared to other zones. Zones I and II show the least increase if we compare them with Zone's III, IV and V for the same time.

If we look at the level of education of the respondents in the study area (refer Table 4.12), the result shows the same trend as shown by the Census data. Respondents of Zone's III and V look more literate than the respondents from the Zone II. An increase

Table 4.9: Zone-wise Migration of Tribal Population between the Years 1971 and 2001 with Respect to Forest Change in Scheduled Areas

Zones	*Districts*	*Forest Change 1972 to 2007 (%)*				
		Decreased	*Unchanged*	*Increased*	*Others*	*Grand Total*
I	Banaskantha	0.21	2.16	0.05	0.01	**2.43**
	Sabarkantha	1.22	3.65	0.68	0.84	**6.39**
Total Zone I		1.43	5.81	0.73	0.85	**8.82**
II	Panchmahal	2.19	2.96	0.48	0.16	**5.79**
	Dahod	10.60	6.48	1.73	0.84	**19.65**
	Vadodara	2.73	3.33	1.75	2.43	**10.24**
Total Zone II		15.52	12.77	3.96	3.43	**35.68**
III	Narmada	0.11	2.80	1.27	1.03	**5.21**
	Bharuch	0.01	0.65	0.57	1.05	**2.28**
	Surat	0.75	4.77	3.04	4.53	**13.09**
Total Zone III		0.87	8.22	4.88	6.61	**20.58**
IV	Navsari	0.07	1.47	2.02	1.11	**4.67**
	Valsad	1.02	5.41	0.70	1.29	**8.42**
Total Zone IV		1.09	6.88	2.72	1.40	**13.09**
V	The Dang	0.00	2.27	0.00	0.00	**2.27**
Total Zone V		0.00	2.27	0.00	0.00	**2.27**
TOTAL		18.91	35.95	12.29	13.29	**80.44**

in the level of literacy and education has also noted the migration in the clothing and food habits of the tribal communities. Table 4.13 shows the trend in changing attitude towards habits in clothing.

The women of Zone's IV (28%) and V (28%) show more changes than the women in Zones I (18%) and II (09%). Level of literacy and education among the tribal women are low in Zone I and Zone II and this aspect might be reflected in the changing patterns of clothing habits. If one looks at the variable of *clothing habits* where men are concerned, all the Zones have shown more or less similar trend. Where, the issue of introduction of the latest fashion in clothing is concerned, 27 per cent of the total respondents from the whole area of study stated positively and agreed that the latest fashions have an impact on their clothing habits. Merely 09

Table 4.10: District-wise Migration of Tribal Population between the Years 1971 and 2001 with Respect to Forest Change in Non-scheduled Areas

Zones	Districts	Forest Change 1972 to 2007 (%)				
		Decreased	Unchanged	Increased	Others	Grand Total
I	Banaskantha	0.00	1.10	1.14	0.81	**3.05**
	Sabarkantha	0.02	0.12	0.19	0.25	**0.58**
	Mehsana	0.00	0.00	0.03	0.11	**0.14**
	Patan	0.04	0.00	0.00	0.05	**0.09**
	Gandhinagar	0.00	0.00	0.35	0.22	**0.57**
	Ahmedabad	0.00	0.00	0.06	0.46	**0.52**
Total Zone I		0.06	1.22	1.77	1.90	4.95
II	Anand	0.08	0.02	0.01	0.27	**0.38**
	Kheda	0.03	0.08	0.04	0.20	**0.35**
	Panchmahal	0.82	1.32	0.73	0.80	**3.67**
	Vadodara	0.29	0.04	0.19	2.86	**3.38**
Total Zone II		1.22	1.46	0.97	4.13	7.78
III	Narmada	0.00	0.00	0.00	0.00	**0.00**
	Bharuch	0.00	0.00	0.59	1.47	**2.06**
	Surat	0.00	0.00	0.53	1.47	**2.00**
Total Zone III		0.00	0.00	1.12	2.94	**4.06**
IV	Navsari	0.00	0.00	1.17	0.00	**1.17**
	Valsad	0.03	0.04	0.10	1.43	**1.60**
Total Zone IV		0.03	0.04	1.27	1.43	**2.77**
TOTAL		**1.31**	**2.72**	**5.13**	**10.40**	**19.56**

Table 4.11: Literacy Rate among Scheduled Tribes in Different Zones

Zones	Literacy Rate (%)		
	1991	2001	Change
Zone I	30.22	36.85	+ 06.63
Zone II	23.22	31.80	+ 08.58
Zone III	32.01	43.91	+ 11.90
Zone IV	38.34	48.77	+ 10.43
Zone V	34.72	46.54	+ 11.82
Study Area	**29.87**	**39.59**	**+ 09.72**

Source: District Census Handbooks, 1991 and 2001.

Table 4.12: Level of Education among Respondents in Study Area

(In Percentage)

Level of Education	*Zones*					*Study Area*
	I	*II*	*III*	*IV*	*V*	
Illiterate	188 (51)	517 (70)	220 (38)	283 (55)	188 (39)	1,396 (52)
Primary	63 (17)	106 (14)	181 (31)	118 (23)	167 (36)	635 (24)
Secondary	58 (16)	72 (10)	90 (16)	75 (15)	69 (15)	364 (14)
Higher Secondary	47 (13)	29 (04)	48 (08)	12 (02)	24 (05)	160 (06)
Graduate and more	11 (03)	18 (02)	41 (07)	24 (05)	23 (05)	117 (04)
Total	367 (100)	742 (100)	580 (100)	512 (100)	471 (100)	2,672 (100)

Note: Percentages are given in parenthesis.

Table 4.13: Zone-wise Distribution of Change in Clothing Habits among Respondents

Change in Clothing Habits	*Zones*					*Study Area*
	I	*II*	*III*	*IV*	*V*	
Among Tribal Women	66 (18)	67 (09)	122 (21)	144 (28)	132 (28)	531 (20)
Among Tribal Men	99 (27)	186 (25)	139 (24)	138 (27)	104 (22)	666 (25)
Introduction of Latest Fashion	103 (28)	237 (32)	168 (29)	108 (21)	104 (22)	720 (27)
Not much Change	51 (14)	52 (07)	12 (02)	15 (03)	00 (00)	130 (05)

Note: Percentages are given in parenthesis.

per cent of the total respondents from Zone II have agreed that there has been a change in clothing practices among tribal women. Tribal women from Zone II had not much changed their clothing habits much even after exposure to the latest fashion in clothing; this might be due to the low rate of literacy and the low level of education. Table 4.13 shows that the rate of literacy has increased by only 6.63 per cent in Zone I, which is almost half of Zone III

Table 4.14: Zone-wise Distribution of Change in Food Habits among Respondents

Change in Food Habits	*Zones*					*Study Area*
	I	*II*	*III*	*IV*	*V*	
New Food Items in Daily Diet	183 (50)	423 (57)	348 (60)	297 (58)	179 (38)	1430 (54)
New Food Items on Occasions	15 (04)	15 (02)	12 (02)	26 (05)	90 (19)	158 (06)
Change in Food Habit on Special to Occasion not in Daily Diet	85 (23)	171 (23)	128 (22)	77 (15)	42 (09)	503 (19)
Not much Change	37 (10)	45 (06)	23 (04)	05 (01)	00 (00)	110 (04)

Note: Percentages are given in parenthesis.

and Zone V. Respondents from Zone I (14%) said that there was not much change in the clothing habits, and this strengthens our argument that, higher the level of education and literacy, more are the changes in the clothing practices of these communities.

Similar to the clothing habits, the food habits have also seen changes across the zones. Fifty-four per cent of the total respondents of the study area said that the new food items *roti* from wheat flour, *dal* and rice have been presented in their daily diet instead of their traditional diet of maize, *bajra, jawar* or rice. Respondents from Zone V (38%) have shown fewer preferences for new food items of *roti* from wheat flour, *dal* and rice instead stick to their traditional *roti* from *nangli* in their daily diet. During their religious or social occasions, the introduction of new food items seems very restricted. Six per cent of the total respondents show that there is a tendency to acquire newer food habits.

Respondents from Zone I (23%), Zone II (23%) and Zone III (22%) have said that they have introduced new food items like sweets, *farsan*, vegetables cooked in Punjabi style and many more during special occasions like marriage ceremony but not in their daily diet which consist of either *bajra* and *jawar* (Zone I), maize and *bajra* (Zone II) or *juwar* and *maize* (Zone III), while only 09 per cent of the total respondents from Zone V agreed on this change. Respondents from Zone V revealed some interesting facts in their responses on the change in their food habits. On the one hand, only 38 per cent of them had responded that they have introduced

Table 4.15: Total Workforce of Scheduled Tribes in Study Area

(In Percentage)

Zones	*Total Workforce**		*Main Workers***		*Marginal Workers***		*Non-Workers**	
	1991	*2001*	*1991*	*2001*	*1991*	*2001*	*1991*	*2001*
Zone I	42.88	58.45	77.88	73.10	22.12	26.90	57.12	41.55
Zone II	50.73	70.96	71.59	72.92	28.41	27.08	49.27	29.04
Zone III	55.02	67.15	84.54	81.79	15.46	18.21	44.98	32.85
Zone IV	53.34	66.07	82.00	79.71	18.00	20.29	46.66	33.93
Zone V	51.46	63.97	92.49	78.87	07.51	21.13	48.54	36.03
Study Area	**51.94**	**67.45**	**78.99**	**77.05**	**21.01**	**22.95**	**48.06**	**32.55**

Note: * Total ST Workforce and Non-workers—per cent of Total ST Population.

** Main Workers and Marginal Workers—per cent of Total ST Workforce.

Source: *District Census Handbooks,* 1991 and 2001.

new food items like *roti* from wheat flour, *dal* and rice instead of *roti* from *nangli* in their daily diet but, on the other hand, only 09 per cent of them said that they had introduced new food items during special occasions but not in their daily diet. If we thus correlate the food items with the literacy rates and the level of education, we could conclude that when the rate of literacy is higher, the change in food habits is more.

Change in Tribal Employment Patterns

A comparison of 1991 and 2001 censuses shows that the total scheduled tribal workforce participation rate had increased from 51.94 per cent in 1991 to 67.45 per cent in 2001 (Refer Table 4.15).

The share of marginal workforce of scheduled tribes in the total scheduled tribe workforce has also increased from 21.01 per cent in 1991 to 22.95 per cent in 2001, with the result that the main scheduled tribal workers had declined marginally from 78.99 per cent in 1991 to 77.05 per cent in 2001. Non-workers among tribal communities had decreased drastically from 48.06 per cent in 1991 to 32.55 per cent in 2001—a decline of 15.51 per cent in just one decade. This data reveals that there is definite change in employment patterns among the tribal communities. If labels like 'hunters' and 'food-gatherers' are put aside, this study finds that more and more tribals are now changing towards additional sources of employment. Artisans, self-employment in other domains, employment in different Government and semi-government organizations and also in private companies are some of the examples showing their Change in employment patterns.

Table 4.16: Distribution of Main Workers by Broad Categories for Scheduled Tribes in Study Area

(In Percentage)

Zones	*Cultivators*		*Agricultural Labourers*		*Household Industries*		*Other Workers*	
	1991	*2001*	*1991*	*2001*	*1991*	*2001*	*1991*	*2001*
Zone I	55.91	41.90	27.14	35.35	0.30	0.63	16.65	22.12
Zone II	60.06	49.92	31.59	37.66	0.13	0.30	08.22	12.12
Zone III	31.95	24.08	51.54	55.43	1.20	1.15	15.31	19.33
Zone IV	43.20	34.90	36.98	41.03	0.51	1.04	19.31	23.02
Zone V	73.85	60.37	16.35	29.19	1.41	1.00	08.40	09.44
Study Area	46.42	38.20	39.23	43.73	0.64	0.76	13.71	17.30

Source: District Census Handbooks, 1991 and 2001.

As regards diversification of the scheduled tribe workforce, agricultural employment (cultivators + agricultural labourers) seems to have declined from 85.65 per cent in 1991 to 81.93 per cent in 2001. Agricultural scheduled tribal labourers in the agricultural employment sector have increased from 39.23 per cent in 1991 to 43.73 per cent in 2001. Tribals have learned to do take on artisan related employment oriented projects like masonry, carpentry, furniture making, carpet making, plumbing, black-smithy, diamond cutting and polishing and electrical repair works. Some of them have started working as teachers, clerks and officers in government and semi-government organizations. The shares of other employments (household industries + other workers) have increased from 14.35 per cent in 1991 to 18.06 per cent in 2001—an increase of 03.71 per cent in just one decade (see Table 4.16).

A particular change in the attitude of educated tribal youths has also been seen. It has been seen that tribals with Graduate or Post-graduate Degrees do not go in for traditional sources of income; however, their employability is also an area of concern as not many are being absorbed in the sphere where they have received their education. Finally, many of them prefer to be unemployed rather than return to their traditional sources of income generation.

Change in Tribal Women Empowerment

Tables 4.17 and 4.18 give sex-wise distribution and marital status of the respondents in the study area. These two tables show the proportion of tribal women respondents and their marital status. This is necessary to present in order to get a clear understanding about the changing trends in women empowerment in the tribal areas of the study area.

Table 4.17: Sex-wise Distribution of the Respondents

Sex	*Zones*					*Study Area*
	I	*II*	*III*	*IV*	*V*	
Male	315 (86)	642 (86)	483 (83)	409 (80)	364 (77)	2,213 (83)
Female	52 (14)	100 (14)	97 (17)	103 (20)	107 (23)	459 (17)
Total	367 (100)	742 (100)	580 (100)	512 (100)	471 (100)	2,672 (100)

Note: Percentages are given in parenthesis.

Earlier tribal women were exploited and victimized. The level of domestic violence was at its peak. But, it seems that, after the increase in the levels of education and the production of additional sources of income, the tribal women have been empowered to a certain degree. Table 4.19 shows various aspects of empowerment among the tribal women. Thirty-seven per cent of the total respondents responded that education helped tribal women, while 8 per cent from the same area said that education helped tribal women to become equal partners with men and also aided them to take up leadership roles at every level, be it—the village, taluka, district, state or national. Tribal women are now playing active role in SHGs (Self-Help Groups) and *Sakhi Mandals* to create awareness on the necessity of economizing and budgeting.

Forty-two per cent of the respondents said that women work as daily wage earners by working outside their homes while 24 per cent of the respondents said that tribal women go outside the village for work. However, there are some new trends that have emerged from the analysis of our primary data. Ten per cent of

Table 4.18: Marital Status of the Respondents

Marital Status	*Zones*					*Study Area*
	I	*II*	*III*	*IV*	*V*	
Unmarried	05 (01)	05 (01)	18 (03)	07 (01)	06 (01)	41 (02)
Married	350 (96)	693 (93)	537 (93)	480 (94)	450 (96)	2,510 (94)
Widow/ Widower	12 (03)	41 (06)	24 (04)	22 (05)	15 (03)	114 (04)
Divorcee	00 (00)	01 (00)	00 (00)	02 (00)	00 (00)	03 (00)
Abandoned	00 (00)	02 (00)	01 (00)	01 (00)	00 (00)	04 (00)
Total	367 (100)	742 (100)	580 (100)	512 (100)	471 (100)	2,672 (100)

Note: Percentages are given in parenthesis.

Table 4.19: Zone-wise Distribution of Women Empowerment among the Respondents

Women Empowerment	*Zones*					*Study Area*
	I	*II*	*III*	*IV*	*V*	
Women become smarter with increase in education	151 (41)	282 (38)	232 (40)	215 (42)	104 (22)	984 (37)
Women become equal to men and take leadership	15 (04)	45 (06)	64 (11)	51 (10)	47 (10)	222 (08)
Getting equal wages as men	136 (37)	163 (22)	168 (29)	215 (42)	132 (28)	814 (31)
Women work as daily wage earners outside home	250 (68)	200 (27)	250 (43)	236 (46)	179 (38)	1115 (42)
Women go outside village for work	33 (09)	67 (09)	116 (20)	220 (43)	207 (44)	643 (24)
Women used to go outside village for work previously but not now	66 (18)	82 (11)	64 (11)	10 (02)	33 (07)	255 (10)
Decrease in domestic violence	165 (45)	334 (45)	249 (43)	190 (37)	165 (35)	1103 (41)
No sexual exploitation of women	147 (40)	260 (35)	267 (46)	241 (47)	184 (39)	1099 (41)
Tap and hand pump at home or near the home for drinking water	184 (50)	319 (43)	307 (53)	200 (39)	212 (45)	1222 (46)

Note: Percentages are given in parenthesis.

the respondents said that tribal women who used to go outside their villages for work previously, now no longer went to work. This is due to the improved economic situation either by dairy farming or growing agricultural productions as a result of better irrigation facilities; use of modern seeds, etc. Good private or government job of the male member of the family also made women are not going to work. This seems to be a new and changing situation for the tribal women.

On the subject of drinking water facilities, here too one can see a change. Forty-six per cent of the total respondents agreed that they had either a tap or a hand pump at home or near their home for drinking water facilities. Only 10 per cent of the total respondents said that the women have to travel far to get drinking water. If no facilities existed at home or near the home, they got water from bores or bore-wells near their homes.

Decrease in domestic violence and reduction, in sexual exploitation of women in the tribal areas, was particularly noted during the field work. Our study shows that there is a significant reduction in domestic violence. Forty-one per cent of the respondents responded that there is a decrease in domestic violence. During our field work interviews, the respondents gave credit to education when we enquired about these changes in their behaviour; education they said gave women dignity and self-respect. Increase in education among the tribal women and economic improvement have decreased domestic violence, sexual exploitation and victimization.

Though the tribal women of the area are found to be empowered on different aspects of their life, the basic necessities of managing the household are still their responsibility. In the past, the forests were dense, and women did not have to go far in search of fuel and fodder. The present state of degradation of forests has led to many difficulties among the tribals especially for the womenfolk who have to go deep inside the forest in search of fuel wood and fodder besides looking after their families. They have to go farther into the woods to collect fuel-wood, sometimes go across one hill to another causing them to leave their homes for longer periods of time, especially leave their young children. This led to more time spent on collection of fuel wood, caused physical fatigue, and worry about their small children, alone at home, caused dehydration due to trekking long distances, most times caused stress and fear etc.

As fuel-wood for domestic use became more and more inaccessible, tribal women turned to cow dung cakes, kerosene stoves, and thorny branches of *Gando Baval* (risky for women especially at night because of its thorns) as alternative sources of fuel. Alternatively, the women collected small branches, twigs, straw from plants of pulses and cotton from their fields. Those who did not have cattle at home requested others who owned cattle for the collection of animal waste to make cow dung cakes for fuel.

Changing Attitudes of Tribal Youth

Reasons for the changing attitudes among tribal youth are numerous and need to be investigated further. But, due to exposure to city life and the entering of tribal youth into the mainstream a definite change in their attitudes have been seen in our study. Tribal youth now celebrates more religious festivals and social occasions like marriages with great pomp and show.

Table 4.20 shows the changing patterns of expenses on marriages in our study. Seventy-three per cent, 72 per cent and 71 per cent of the total respondents from Zone III, Zone II and Zone IV respectively said that there was an increase in expenditure on marriages, while Zone I (54%) and Zone V (61%) have shown the same tendency towards display of wealth during weddings. Thirty-four per cent and 25 per cent of the total respondents in Zone I and Zone V also agreed on this aspect. It seems that the tendency of showing-off among the new generation of the tribal

Table 4.20: Zone-wise Distribution of Change in Pattern of Expenses on Marriage among the Respondents

Change in Pattern of Expenses on Marriage	*Zones*					*Study Area*
	I	*II*	*III*	*IV*	*V*	
Increased expenses on marriages	198 (54)	534 (72)	423 (73)	364 (71)	287 (61)	1806 (68)
Increased flaunting of wealth	125 (34)	111 (15)	81 (14)	92 (18)	118 (25)	527 (20)

Note: Percentages are given in parenthesis.

Table 4.21: Changes in the Pattern of Marriage among the Respondents

Changes in Pattern of Marriage	*Zones*					*Study Area*
	I	*II*	*III*	*IV*	*V*	
Inter-tribal marriages	117 (32)	245 (33)	238 (41)	266 (52)	226 (48)	1092 (41)
Marriages within the tribe	195 (53)	378 (51)	209 (36)	108 (21)	104 (22)	994 (37)
Considerable increase in love marriages	07 (02)	22 (03)	41 (07)	56 (11)	47 (10)	173 (07)

Note: Percentages are given in parenthesis.

communities led to increase in the expenses on marriages and flaunting of wealth during the religious and social ceremonies. It also seems the effect of sanskritization on the new generation of tribal communities.

The pattern of marriages among the tribal youth is given in Table 4.21. On the issue of inter-tribal marriages, respondents from Zone IV (52%), Zone V (48%) and Zone III (41%) agreed that inter-tribal marriages are now possible but only 32 per cent and 33 per cent of the total respondents from the Zone I and II agreed on this aspect. The tradition of marriages within the tribe is more prevalent among the respondents from the Zone I (53%) and Zone II (51%) than in the Zone IV (21%) and Zone V (22%). Love marriages showed a substantial increase in Zone IV (11%) and Zone V (10%) than in the other zones. It seems that these changes are due to additional factors like, exposure to films and television serials, and the migration into cities.

Traditionally, tribal communities in Gujarat have different traditions so far as marriages are concerned. We had seen during the field work some marriage practices in some specific tribal groups, in the Zones IV and V. A tribal boy usually got married to the daughter of the brother of his mother. This practice is now eroding drastically since the last two decades among the same particular tribal groups from the Zone IV and Zone V. Another traditional practice is such that the tribal boy has to pay all the expenses on marriage to the parents of the tribal girl whom he is to marry. The family of the tribal boy bears the expenses for things such as gold and jewellery, *mandap*, food, clothes, and related expenses.

Due to the exposure to the world outside their villages, increase in the level of education and impact of electronic media and films, inter-tribal marriages and love-marriages have increased drastically in last two decades, in Zones IV and V. As the level of education is low in Zones, I and II compared to Zones III, IV and IV, the changes are less among the tribals from Zones I and II.

Table 4.22: Zone-wise Distribution of Fragmentation of Family among the Respondents

Fragmentation of Family	*Zones*					*Study Area*
	I	*II*	*III*	*IV*	*V*	
Increased fragmentation	147 (40)	267 (36)	191 (33)	123 (24)	132 (28)	860 (32)
Increased family conflicts	73 (20)	186 (25)	215 (37)	225 (44)	99 (21)	798 (30)
Separation immediately after marriage	22 (06)	52 (07)	12 (02)	26 (05)	33 (07)	145 (06)
Separation due to economic conditions	07 (02)	15 (02)	12 (02)	10 (02)	33 (07)	77 (03)

Note: Percentages are given in parenthesis.

Table 4.22 shows the fragmentation of family among the respondents. Tribal families were more fragmented in Zone I (40%) and Zone II (36%) than in Zone IV (24%) and Zone V (28%); while conflicts within the family were more in Zone IV (44%) and Zone III (37%) than in Zone I (20%) and Zone V (21%). Separation was also because of economic pressures and 3 per cent of the respondents agreed to this factor.

We have mentioned above that tribal youth spent more on their marriages, in addition to this we have seen that film songs, religious songs and other melodies played or sung during religious and social occasions with the extensive use of Disk Jockeys (DJ) and music bands, have been introduced since the last one decade. Due to migration among tribals, easy accessibility to cities due to all weather roads and good road connectivity has led to more exposure to cities. It is felt that the increase in the level of education is also responsible for flaunting and showing off. Due to globalization, the impact of consumerism has also reached in the remote tribal areas of the state of Gujarat. The market is also playing its part in the changing patterns in the marriages or the celebration of religious and social functions.

IV

Concluding Observations

This chapter has dealt with the migration of tribal people from tribal to non-tribal areas of Gujarat. This migration has little to do with the degradation, regeneration or no-change in forests. But the point is that the seasonal migration has emerged as an important livelihood strategy for living in areas where there is a lack of livelihood sources in the local areas. Migration is mainly rural-urban to cities such as Vadodara, Surat and Ahmedabad in the State of Gujarat.

Despite substantial investments by the Government of India and the Government of Gujarat in watershed and rural development, over 30 per cent of tribal households were seen migrating seasonally. For an estimated 20 per cent of the households, money earned from migration is more important to their overall livelihood than agriculture. For almost all of them, migration is the main source of *cash* income (Jones and De Souza, 2004). During the dry season (November to June), when there is little or no work available in agriculture, large numbers of tribal people are seen migrating. Most migrants are single men or couples, at times with young children.

Migration is a problematic process, and this occurs mainly due to a combination of migrants being unaware of their rights; poor education and skills; a negative policy environment that aims to keep rural people in rural areas and actively discourages migration; monopsonistic behaviour among employers, contractors and labour market intermediaries and discrimination based on caste and gender (*ibid*). While away, migrants face many problems, including uncertainty in finding work and getting paid by contractors; insecurity, exploitation and harassment while travelling and in urban areas as well as difficulty in communicating with home folks and in remitting funds to their families.

But probably the most serious problem encountered by migrants is a lack of access to basic services such as the public distribution system which provides subsidized food; health and education.

is what the department has made. The Forest Department has been pushing through its approach of proprietary ownership of the forests, even after the introduction of the Joint Forest Management (JFM) through the Government Resolutions (GRs). The counter argument is that the dependent communities have been responsible for the illegal felling and destruction of the forests. The feeling is that the Forest Department being the owner has the authority to make revenue from the forest resources, which it feels right belongs to it (*Ibid*: 3).

I

Legal Interferences and Tribal Conflicts

Every successive forest policy and legislation formulated and adopted by the British Government resulted in increased restrictions on the tribals (See chapter 2). According to the Indian Forest Act, 1927 certain acts were prohibited in Reserved and Protected Forests. Acts prohibited in the Reserved Forests were as follows:

1. Any person who:
   (a) makes any fresh clearing prohibited by section 5, or
   (b) sets fire to a reserved forest, or, in contravention of rules made by the (State Government) in this behalf, kindled any fire, or leaves any fire burning, in such manner as to endanger such a forest; or who, in a reserved forest;
   (c) kindles, keeps or carries any fire except at such seasons as the Forest officer may notify in this behalf;
   (d) trespasses or pastures cattle, or permits cattle to trespass;
   (e) causes any damage by negligence in felling any tree or cutting or dragging any timber;
   (f) fells, girdles, lops, or burns any tree or strips off the bark or leaves from, or otherwise damages, the same;
   (g) quarries stone, burnt lime or charcoal, or collects, subjects to any manufacturing process, or removes, any forest-produce;

(h) clears or break up any land for cultivation or any other purpose;

(i) in contravention of any land for cultivation or any rules made in this behalf by the (State Government) hunts, shoots, fishes, poisons water or sets traps or snares; or

(j) in any area in which the Elephants' Preservation Act, 1879 (6 of 1879), is not in force, kills or catches elephants in contravention of any rules so made, shall be punishable with imprisonment for a term which may extend to six months, or with fine which may extend to five hundred rupees, or with both, in addition to such compensation for the damage done to the forest as the convicting Court may direct to be paid.

2. Nothing in this section shall be deemed to prohibit—
   (a) any act done by permission in writing of the Forest-officer, or under any rule made by the (State Government); or
   (b) The exercise of any right continued under clause (c) of Sub-section (2) of Section 15, or created by grant or contract in writing made by or on behalf of the Government under Section 23.

3. Whenever, the fire is caused willfully or by gross negligence in a reserved forest, the (State Government) may (notwithstanding that a penalty has been inflicted under this section) direct that in such forest or any portion thereof the exercise of all rights of pasture or to forest-produce shall be suspended for such time as it thinks fit.

   In Gujarat, this Section 26 has been amended as vide Gujarat Act 15 of 1960, sec. 6 (e) (w.e.f. 8-12-1960).

   (i) In Sub-section (1), for clause (b), substitute the following clause, namely:—
      (b) sets fire to a reserve forest or to the forest, land in respect of which a notification declaring the decision of the State Government to constitute it a reserved forest has been issued under section 4, or in contravention of any rules made by the Sate Government in this behalf, kindles in such

forest any fire or leaves any fire burning in such manner as to endanger such a forest; or who, in a reserved forest or forest, in a land notified as aforesaid, under Section 4.

(ii) after sub-section (3), insert the following sub-section namely:—

(4) When a person is convicted under clause (d) or (h) of sub-section (1)—

(a) a Forest officer not below the rank of a Ranger

(b) a Police officer not below the rank of a Sub-Inspector, or

(c) a Revenue officer, not below the rank of a Mahalkari may evict him from the forest or land in relation to which he has committed the offence.

Under the forest offences we have included the following types of activities which are considered to be an offence in the Indian Forest Act, 1927:

1. Illicit cultivation in forest lands.
2. Trespassing into the forest, cutting and cleaning the forest for cultivation.
3. Community cutting of trees and cleaning forest lands for cultivation.
4. Illicit cutting.
5. Grazing.
6. Fire.
7. Wildlife hunting.
8. Miscellaneous.

When our field team visited the offices of the Divisional Conservator of Forest of the areas under our study, some of the Divisions under the Forest Department of the Government of Gujarat presented only the total number of offences registered in that particular year without classifying it into different types of offences as classified in the Indian Forest Act, 1927. It can also be clearly seen that the highest number of offences registered is that of illicit cutting and felling of trees in most of the zones. Forest fires and grazing have also been quite high in most of the Divisions. The data of the Devgadh Baria Division and Godhra Division are not available in spite of repeated follow-ups.

Table 5.1 shows the cases detected for the period from 1960-61 to 2005-2006. Illicit cutting is the main offence which is detected in a large scale in the last 45 years of time. Illicit cutting was rampant between the periods 1970-71 to 1990-91. This offence was on a decreasing trend for over ten years starting from 1991-92 but once again it showed an upward trend from the year 2004-05. Table 5.1 clearly reflects the situation of different cases detected based on the data collected from the Gujarat Forest Statistics, Government of Gujarat, 1995 and 2006.

Table 5.1: Distribution of Cases Detected: 1961-2006

Cases	*1960-61*	*1970-71*	*1980-81*	*1990-91*	*2000-01*	*2005-06*
Fire	573	465	603	582	477	1,203
Unauthorized Grazing	621	1,652	2,802	2,119	1,619	1,409
Illicit Cutting	10,941	12,918	14,843	10,811	9,184	10,339
Other Cutting	3,036	7,120	14,587	4,101	1,537	2,109

Source: Gujarat Forest Statistics, Government of Gujarat, 1995 and 2006.

Analysis of the offence of illicit cutting by verifying the materials seized by the Forest Department can be seen in Table

Table 5.2: Distributions of Illicit Cutting Offences Booked and Value of Materials Seized

Year	*No. of Offences*	*Material Seized*				
		Teak Timber (qtl)	*Misc. Timber (qtl)*	*Fire Wood (qtl)*	*Charcoa (qtl)*	*Bamboo (No.)*
1990-91	8623	6085	NA	10724	2751	55682
2001-02	3961	4146	828	9311	989	17429
2002-03	4361	5750	962	20750	12201	36016
2003-04	4432	4559	1508	6482	2437	44518
2004-05	4373	4163	1680	7402	22209	13297
2005-06	4781	4314	999	7498	2297	17180

Source: *Gujarat Forest Statistics*, Government of Gujarat, 1995 and 2006.

5.2. Till the year 1990-91, bamboo was the main item for seizure where the illicit cutting offence was concerned. Fire wood seizure was also prominent till the year 2002-03. After 2002-03, the seizure of fire wood has decreased.

Table 5.3 shows the distribution of assaults on the forest officials by the local people living in and around the forest areas. Assaults on forest officials have shown a decreasing trend during the year 2004-05.

Table 5.3: Distribution of Assaults on Forest Officials

Year	*No. of assaults*	*Employees Received Injuries*			
		Minor Injuries	*Grievous Injuries*	*Deaths*	*Total*
1990-91	62	61	13	0	74
2000-01	52	32	7	0	39
2001-02	38	25	4	0	29
2002-03	31	30	4	0	34
2003-04	36	51	5	0	56
2004-05	30	22	3	0	25
2005-06	33	29	9	0	38

Source: *Gujarat Forest Statistics,* Government of Gujarat, 1995 and 2006.

From these tables we can clearly state that the different legislations on forests had a tremendous impact on tribal conflicts. It can be seen that the forming of the Forest Department and the forest legislations established authority over the tribals who were alienated from the growing powers of the Government meant increasing restrictions on the tribals. And increasing restrictions on tribals led to increase in tribal conflicts. When tribals were not allowed to take fodder for their animals and fuel for their domestic use and were caught and booked under the illicit cutting or under any other related offences, the tribals started assaulting the forest officials. Rampant corruption among the forest officials is also one of the main reasons for the conflict between the tribals and them. If the amount of money had not been resolved between the accused tribals and the forest officials, the forest officials would use their authority and power under different forest related legislation against the accused and that would generate conflicts between them. Hence, legal interventions always create conflicts if handled without people oriented rules and regulations. Legal interventions are needed to ensure strict and disciplined approach for the protection of the environment. However, to ensure success of such interventions the people should be involved; furthermore, their welfare should be kept in mind while framing rules and regulations. People-oriented and people-friendly environment policies and forest policies will ultimately lead to an improvement in the forests and environment.

II

Ethnographic Data on Conflicts

A continuous stay for over a month each in the following four villages in different zones of the study area gives us the character of conflicts in greater detail:

1. Nishana village of Naswadi taluka of Vadodara district of Zone II (A village where forest cover decreased (3%) for the period between 1971 and 2001 and also decreased (3%) between the years 2001 and 2009).
2. Chakaliya village of Jhalod taluka of Dahod district of Zone II (A village where forest cover decreased (1%) for the period between 1971 and 2001 but significant increase (24%) has been seen for the period between 2001 and 2009).
3. Galiba village of Jhagadia taluka of Bharuch district of Zone III (A village where forest cover remained unchanged for the period between 1971 and 2001 but significant reduction (16%) has been seen for the period between 2001 and 2009).
4. Moti Korwal village of Dharampur taluka of Valsad district of Zone IV (A village where forest cover remained unchanged for the period between 1971 and 2001 but significant increase (9%) has been seen for the period between 2001 and 2009).

In this section, we will discuss the different issues raised and seen in these villages, in relation to the conflicts between the Forest Department and the local tribal communities. From the ethnographic data, it has also been found that in most of the village people do not enjoy an amicable relationship with the Forest Department. Various causes and reasons are offered for the conflict between them, and we could present these instances from the study of four villages studied intensely.

Nishana Village of Naswadi Taluka, Vadodara District

One of the incidents which took place in the Nishana village was when the forest officials had come to dig pits for the plantation of trees on cultivated forest land. The villagers were annoyed with this gesture of the forest officials and got into a dispute with them; the consequence of this was that the officials were asked to leave the village.

In another incident, the forest officials came to check where the houses of the villagers had been constructed. The officials asked the villagers to shift their houses to the revenue land from the forest land or else they would be demolished. They also asked the villagers to leave the forest land on which they were cultivating as they claimed it to be Government property. The villagers argued with the officials and drove them out of the village. The officials came back later with reinforcements. The Rangers, Beat-Guards, and watchmen came and rebuked the villagers saying, "*Is this your father's land that you can construct your house anywhere you like?*" They continued saying, "*Stop cultivating in the forest lands and dismantle your houses therein or else you people will be dumped in the jail*". This set off an altercation between the villagers and the officials. The villagers claimed that they had been paying the fine imposed on them by the Department, but they were not given a receipt for it.

To avenge the insults meted out to the forest officials, the Beat-guard chopped the trees and accused the villagers of it. He reported this matter to the higher authorities and filed a case against the villagers. The authorities came and made the villagers take the logs on their shoulders and made them walk up to Ghata Amli village.

Some incidents of conflict and struggles of the Dungara Bhils of the Nishana village with the Forest Department have been listed below.

- In 1970, during the monsoon season, the forest officials came with Neem and Sisum seeds to be sown in the cultivated forest lands of the *Adivasis*. They sowed the seeds in some of the fields where the villagers had cultivated crops. Later the villagers confronted the officials.
- In 1975, the Forest Department officials came to the village and searched every household for stored wood. They came to take away the wood and those villagers who hoarded the logs were fined. But the officials did not give any kind of receipt that the villagers have been fined and that a certain amount had been taken away from them. The villagers gathered together to protest against the officials and also did not allow them to take the wood.
- In the year 2002, the Beat-Guard, Rangers and the watchmen came and asked the tribals to shift their houses from the forest land to the revenue land within a given period of time, or they threatened to demolish. The villagers united and drove them out for they had been living in the forests for generations.
- Again in 2002, the Forest officials came to the village and dug the cultivated area in the forest land to plant saplings for the Plantation Programme of the Department. Once again the villagers gathered together and objected and protested against the Department. In the same year, the forest officials came to the village to ask for land from the forest land cultivators for the plantation of trees in order to regenerate the forest. They also threatened to put the farmers in jail if their demands were not met with.
- In 2007, the Department took revenge on the villagers for not allowing them to continue with the plantation work on the cultivated forest land. So the Beat-guard brought labourers from outside the village and cut all

the trees and later blamed the villagers for it. The officials then came and asked all the villagers to gather and took them to prison without any inquiry being held. The villagers were also made to take the wood up to Ghatamal village. This subject also ensued in a clash between the Department officials and the villagers.

Chakaliya Village of Jhalod Taluka, Dahod District

The miscommunication between the forest officials and the tribals aggravated because the officials failed to convey to the tribals the different activities they held in the forest. In the past, the forest officer or the Beat-Guard used to come for inspection but never took any punitive action. The relations between the two deteriorated considerably making it antagonistic.

According to the villagers of Chakaliya, in the initial months of the current year, the Forest Committee took some 500 people from 12 *faliyas* of the village on a tour. The villagers visited Melol, Malav, Babroli, Shaktala, Old Bariya, Kanjeta and Van Kutir, where forests have been developed with the support of the people. Under this programme the villagers were also taken to area where the forest developmental programmes have been implemented. Demonstration and guidance about how the forests can be developed protected, and how water could be harvested, etc., with the support of the people was also demonstrated.

It could be said that there have been no conflicts or struggles between the tribals and the Forest Department officials. According to the villagers the Forest Department officials were afraid of the tribals. But according to the Acharya of the Ashram Shaala, the officials are not afraid of the villagers. The officials who are posted in the Division are here for 2-3 years of posting and then transferred to a new Division. So the officials prefer to be at peace with the villagers and let them be as they have been". This he felt had been misinterpreted by the villagers, as being afraid of them.

Usually *Nilgiri* trees are seen around in the villages where the

Forest Department had made plantation work. These trees are not of much of use to the villagers. The villagers suggest that if at all the Government would like to maintain the forests then it should implement the following suggestions.

- Destroy *Gando baval* and replace it by growing some good trees.
- *Ghavado, papal, Kanaj, Gundi, Dantiyo, Renjyo, Kaledo, Sadad, Subabul, Bor, Dudhi* (a kind of gourd), *Aankado, Kado* should be planted.
- Flowering trees like *Gulmohar, Khakharo, Keshuda, Shimalo, Kataro, Rayan, Garmalo, Saragavo,* etc. can be planted and forests can be produced with such flowering plants.
- The fruit giving trees like chikoo, mango trees, custard apples, *fanas* (jack fruit), *jambu, bedo, timru, billi, kaju* (cashew nut), etc. should also be promoted and grown.
- Growing *mahuda, timru, khakhara, sivam, nilgiri, deshibor, gundi,* coconut, *khajur,* etc. would also help to provide raw material for cottage industries.
- The land for grazing must be made available to all the villagers for grazing their cattle.

Galiba village of Jhagadia Taluka, Bharuch District

Ten years ago, Chaturbhai Shacharjang Vasava took his oxen to graze in the forest. While grazing, the oxen went into the forest coupe area. The Forest Department watchman who saw this beat up the animals. This led to a quarrel between the watchman and Chaturbhai.

Another incident took place in 2002 when the villagers were cleaning their fields the Beat-guard came and asked them for the permission that had been granted to them to clean the Forest Department's lands. Disputes continued for two days in the village between the Beat-guard and the villagers. Cultivation in forest lands was not permitted by the Forest Department. The farmers who cultivated in these forest lands were asked to stop their cultivation, and they also brought in the police force. The villagers opposed, argued and quarreled with the Forest Department officials. Once again on the third day the officials came back with seven jeeps, the SRP and the Police. They arrested people and put them inside the Netrang Police Station and later shifted to Valia. There were 44 villagers from Bilatha, Rupghat, Valpore and Galiba, and out of these 6 were from Galiba itself. People from the four villages formed a committee and protested in front of the Valia Police Station and demanded the release of the farmers who were arrested. Until the arrested farmers were released, they stayed there and threatened violence. The arrested farmers were finally released on bail and were sent home in the police vehicles.

In this incident women were also beaten up by the Forest Department officials. The victims filed cases against the Department, but after 2-3 hearings nothing more was heard.

Because of these incidents the villagers sowed their fields at night during the sowing season as they were afraid of the officials of the Forest Department. One of the tribals, Mathurbhai took seven to eight yoke-straps to plough his field at night. When the Forest officials came around midnight they fired at the farmers who ran for their lives leaving behind their yoke-straps. The Department filed a case against Mathurbhai, but he was later released on bail. Moreover, three years ago the forest officials sprayed some poison and damaged the standing crops of paddy, *tuar* and cotton. This caused the farmers to complain to the Forest Department and to the Rangers.

There seems to be not much of cooperation between the officials and the villagers. If the officials found any villager cutting trees or illegally cultivating forest lands they did nothing but took a chicken, money and let the people do whatever they wanted to. As long as the villagers provided chicken and liquor to the officials they allowed them to cultivate in the forests. If, however, the villagers did not pay the money or give the items formally or officially the officials did not give any kind of receipts to the people. Since, the Government acts on documents, which the villagers do not have, today they are in trouble for they do not have any evidence to claim that they have been cultivating in the forests land before1980. Now, some of them have been deprived the right to plough the land due to the lack of this evidence. People now think that the officials have deceived them.

Moti Korwal Village of Dharampur Taluka of Valsad District

The village has a *faliya* known as Satmali *faliya* for it is surrounded by seven hills. The other *faliya* is known as Karpunia because of the big tiger cave which is locally known as '*Kapar*', (take shelter).

Between the years, 1981-82 road and electricity were made available to the village when Shankar Navla was the Taluka (Block) President. But not much change or improvement was seen as regards education and employment. Not many have gained government employment. There are a few persons working as watchmen in the Forest Department and most people of this area are involved in wage labour.

Tribals could not cut even a few bamboos without the permission of the forest officers. If the potter needed to make tiles from clay, he had to take permission of the Talati and forest department by paying Rs. 100.

Before Independence people in the surrounding forests hunted animals like rabbit, deer, antelope, squirrel wild boar, etc. for food. They also hunted doves, pigeons, peacocks, etc. However, at present the state of the forests is such that the game seems to have all but disappeared. However, people continue to catch fish and crabs from the river.

About twenty years ago the village had 5o to 60 per cent of forested area. Women in this area did not face any difficulty for fuel, fodder and food. They collected fuel wood from the nearby areas. They also collected fruits, vegetables, roots and rhizomes to supplement their food. However, the forests have degraded, and this has led to many difficulties for tribal women folk who have to go deep into the forests in search of fuel wood. This implies that they have to leave their home for longer periods of time and walk longer. More time is spent for the collection of fuel involving physical fatigue, leading to anxiety and worry especially for their small children.

It was a known fact that some staff of the Forest Department involved in selling timber leading to the degradation of the forests.

The tribals offered the officers of the Forest Department money and fowls whenever, the officers demanded to be allowed to cut trees.

Over the past few years, relations have changed between the forest officials and the villagers. In the past, the Forest Department used to harass the villagers, but now relations have become more amicable. In the main village, forest committees have been established for creating community forestry and people get employment through this programme. The vast majority of the people work as labourers. Some villagers also get temporary employment in the Forest Department. Moti Korwal being a border village few villagers are involved in "purchasing" furniture wood from Maharasthra and selling in Dharampur and other cities.

III

Case Studies on Conflicts between Tribals and the Forest Department

There have been many incidents of the forests officials assaulting the villagers cultivating forest lands. In various places and at different times, there have been many disputes between the Forest Department and the villagers. Minor and major cases of conflict in the Dang, Sagbara and Antarsuba are presented below.

Dang

The district of the Dang is the richest in the state in terms of natural resources, and yet it is the poorest considering the parameters of human development. More than 90 per cent of the district has been declared either as Reserved or Protected Forests, while the tribals constitute more than 95 per cent of its people.

Forest area of Dang decreased by 4 per cent between the year 1971 and 2001, as per the Census report of 1971 and 2001. As per the satellite imageries prepared during the study, the forest has been increased by 5.3 per cent during the years 1990 and 2000 while the forest cover decreased by 8 per cent for the period between

2000 and 2007. As per the State of Forest Report of Forest Survey of India, the forest cover decreased by 2.2 per cent for the period between 2001 and 2009 while as per the Gujarat Forest Statistics the same was decreased by 2.5 per cent for the same time between 2001 and 2009. The following maps prepared from the satellite imageries also showed a decrease in forest cover between the year 1972 and 2007. 9.9 per cent forest cover decreased for the period between 1972 and 2007 in Dang as per the satellite imageries prepared during the study.

The Dang area remained under direct control of the British Raj. After Independence, it was handed over to the Bombay Presidency. Traditionally, the rights of the four Dang rulers and the tribals were recognized but slowly and gradually these rights were eroded after the declaration of large areas as forests under the Indian Forest Act 1927. Also, the rights of tribals were not settled, although this was mandatory by the Act of 1927. As a result, the four Dang rajas remained as pensioners, and the tribals as encroachers living at the mercy of the forest officials – with no land, no work and no development.

In the 1990s some movements were started by a few radical activists, and the tribals were organized and they made specific demands. But the Forest Department and the Government, instead of considering demands of the tribals, considered it a law and order problem created by the 'Naxalites'. A few were arrested under the National Security Act of 1980. Offences were registered; *lathi* charge and police firing were resorted to. The policy of divide and rule was adopted. The preventive detention of two main leaders under NSA (National Security Act) was challenged on several grounds, but the matter remained pending because of the large number of detention cases in the High Court. Ultimately, almost after six months, the petition came up for hearing and the detainees were ordered to be released. Two other petitions were filed, one against police atrocities and other for the demands of the tribals. The Government had to come forward with assurances for numerous welfare schemes, but they remained only on paper. The extreme radical posture of the leaders created a rift among the outside supporters on ideological grounds and eventually the movement fizzled out (Patel, G. 2009: 83). After Tarabai was shot dead in 1991 the government took steps to regularise the land cultivated by the tribals. The government did not take it lightly, nor did the forest department and police. "Till then, they were used to free meat, food, liquor and crops forcibly extracted from the locals. Bribery was rampant and so were beatings and assaults," says Pawar, "Most of us took it for granted that we have to pay the officials for cultivating our small piece of land" (http://m.hardnewsmedia.com/2009/01/2476). It is not surprising that, in 1991, when the tribals stopped paying bribes, the department reacted in a demonic manner. Curfew was clamped down and Tarabai, who had dared was shot dead. The killing was not a knee-jerk reaction of a nervous gun-toting forest guard. It was a message that was loud and clear. Surprisingly, the tribals reacted by burning down forest department offices. Heavy police reinforcements were rushed in. The crackdown followed. Over 400 people were picked up, thrashed and tortured. For more details, see Engineer (2002: 312 ff).

Sagbara (Narmada District)

The forest area of Sagbara taluka decreased by 18 per cent between the year 1991 and 2001 as per the Census 1991 and 2001. As per the satellite imageries, the forest area decreased very significantly between 1972 and 2007. Only extreme southern part of Sagbara shows increase in the forest area. The increase and decrease in forest areas of Sagbara are shown in Map 5.3.

A Public Interest Litigation by Arch Vahini was filed in the Gujarat High Court for prevention of the eviction of tribals in Sagbara Taluka in the Narmada District by the Forest Department. Here, the group had made good ground work and had systematically collected data, including documenting the history of this area during the Pre-British time. This was a typical case where tribals, legitimately entitled to hold and cultivate lands under *sanads* issued by the erstwhile rulers, were threatened with eviction on the grounds of unauthorized cultivation. The *sanads* were implemented during earlier times, and the Reserved Forest was declared only later under the Indian Forest Act of 1927. Although, the rights of the tribals were legally required to be settled under the Act before the final declaration, nothing concrete was done. The tribals were never informed as the areas were too remote and mainly inaccessible, and the Forest Department never bothered to visit the area. Practically it was not a declaration of public forest lands as Reserved/Protected Forest, where their preceding rights were never settled, though this was a requirement by the Forest Act and the Wild Life Act. The cultivating tribals are only treated as encroachers on their own lands and as unauthorized cultivators liable to be evicted. Their case is different from the case of those tribals who had no rights, but who had been cultivating the forest lands for many years and who claimed regularization. This distinction was deliberately and conveniently forgotten by the Forest Department, which resorted to large scale forced eviction after some interim order by the Supreme Court. A petition for the tribals of Sagbara and the PIL was admitted, and the interim order against eviction was passed by the High Court (Patel, G, 2009: 85).

Antarsumba (Vijaynagar-Sabarkantha)

The forest area of Vijaynagar taluka where Antarsumba falls increased significantly by 10 per cent between the year 1991 and 2001 as per the Census 1991 and 2001. As per the satellite imageries, the forest area increased very significantly between 1972 and 2007. The Maps 5.4 shows about the significant increase in forest areas of Vijaynagar.

If we look at the forest of Antarsumba, as per the Census 1991 and 2001, forest areas of Antarsumba have increased very significantly by 13.9 per cent between the year 1991 and 2001. Conflicting conditions developed in the month of February 2008 in the Sabarkantha district which left two persons dead and which were enquired into by two enquiry committees one by the Government of Gujarat, headed by Mr. P.K. Laheri (2008) and one by the Adivasi Maha Sabha, Gujarat, a right based organization which has been working among the *Adivasis* of Gujarat. The reports presented by both the Committees have been briefly presented here.

Newspapers reported the following incidents: two tribals

were killed on Wednesday in a clash with the police who opened fire when tribals reportedly attacked a police station. The police were trying to disperse a mob of 500 tribals who had attacked them and the forest officials in the Dholwani forest range near the Antarsumba police station. Three of the tribals were seriously injured and were brought to the Ahmedabad Civil Hospital. Police said they opened fire only after the tribals attacked them with bows and arrows, injuring nine forest officials and six policemen. However, the tribals said five of their men had been detained at the Antarsumba police station, and they had gone to release them. The officials said that the tribals gheraoed the police station around 3.30 am and started pelting stones. The mob paid no heed to the policemen's orders after which the SRP (State Reserve Police) fired (Paul and Panwar, 2008). But several activists and organizations claimed that the newspapers reported what the Government wanted to portray.

According to the report of the Committee headed by P.K. Laheri (IAS) which said that, on 5th February, 2008, complaints of illicit lopping of trees in different divisions of the Forest Department were reported. Sixteen villagers were named for illicit lopping in the division's nursery and Reserved Forest areas especially in the Vajepur and Abhapur villages of the Dholwani Range of Vijaynagar taluka. In the Vijaynagar police station names of these sixteen, persons were registered.

On 10th-12th February, 2008 some 250 people of BAMCEF (Backward & Minority Communities Employees' Federation) with weapons like *dhariya*, axe, sword, bows and arrows and threatened to kill the forest officials and did not allow the team to do their duties. The MLA (Member of the Legislative Assembly) of Khedbrahma and Vijaynagar, who met the BAMCEF people personally, reported that the forest officials had filed a case against the tribal people and that they have rights over the forest areas and that they would claim it. So, the case should be withdrawn, and any kind of struggle would not help.

The forest officials had asked the Collector in a meeting held on 11th February for help from the SRP (State Reserved Police); so an SRP company had arrived in Vijaynagar-Abhapur. In the wee hours of the 13th of that month the Sabarkantha district police in cooperation with the Forest Officials' arrested six persons. Around 9.30 a.m. the BAMCEF workers and the locals with the purpose of releasing their six comrades, gathered with different types of traditional weapons at the Antarsuba Ashram (Range Forest Office). Very soon a skirmish started between the workers and the SRP employees near the Range Office. The SRP personnel fired teargas shells to drive the away the mob, and they had to open fire to. Two people were killed in the firing incident.

The Committee members also visited the site where the incident took place, and met the officials and the villagers. The committee members also visited the Himmatnagar Civil Hospital where the injured people were admitted.

Recommendations of the Inquiry Committee Appointed by Government of Gujarat

- The Forest Rights Act, 2006 has been implemented from the 1st of January, 2008. The tribals and other beneficiaries of the forest dwellers would get their rights, and it was said that the authorities of the Forest Department should try to gain the trust of the people which would be helpful in the implementation of the Act. The Tribal Sub-Plan (TSP) and the Forest Department should come up with some decisions to train their officials and staff regarding the Forest Rights Act, 2006. The Act should also be translated in a language which could be easily understood by the layman so that they are informed about their rights and provisions of the Act. Committees at the level of the Gram Sabha, Sub-Division and the State Government should also be made.
- Individual claims should be filed according to the prescribed norms, rules and regulations of the Act in the prescribed form without any pressure on the claimant. It was also recommended that the processing of the forms should be decentralized.
- The Committee strongly noted that, the tribal areas of Gujarat state are calmer, unlike the other States. But they also mentioned that there have been many elements to

disrupt this peaceful existence of the tribals which the State Government, which should not overlook. To divert the tribals' care from such activities they should be involved in meaningful activities and provided with various developmental schemes through which income could be generated. It was also recommended that strict action should be taken up against any person or group liable of creating misunderstanding and confusion among the tribals.

- The conflicts and tensions which had come up between the Forest Department officials and the tribals during the implementation of the Forest Rights Acts should be discussed, and a peaceful solution should be sought for cordial relations in the future.
- The State Government should try to compensate for the death of the deceased in the incident so that the people of the area do not feel neglected.
- The Committee also recommended that the inquiry of this incident conducted according to the provisions of the Local Crime Branch would be better if managed by the Central Bureau of Investigation.

Another Fact Finding team comprising of twelve members was also made by the Adivasi Maha Sabha, Gujarat, and they submitted their reports too. They had also visited the sites, the victims' families and the doctors who attended them. According to them the tribals would not have resorted to violence if the enactment of the Scheduled Tribe and Traditional Forest Dwellers (Recognition of Forest Rights) Act, 2006 was launched. The claim made by the Forest Department with respect to large scale cutting of trees in the thickly wooded dense forest of teak in Vajepur was not true for there are no forests in Vajepur. Instead, there is a flat, fertile plain devoid of any trees except for about 200 to 250 trees of *mahuda*.

The Forest Department has also accused the tribals of destroying the irrigated plantations of *kher*, bamboo, *ambla*, teak, etc. planted three years ago in the area of Vajepur. But the report said that, in 2005-06, the Department did fence off approximately 7 ha and also dug pits and planted saplings which died due to neglect. The only thing that the tribals did on 7th and 8th February was to erect a wooden frame for a single small hut on this land as a symbolic gesture to display their claim to this land, and they wanted that their rights should be recognized along with others who were still in possession of the lands they were cultivating. But this was not needed as the Forest Rights Act had already recognized the rights of rehabilitation on the same or alternative land for all such persons who were illegally evicted in the past. Unfortunately, the tribals did not have this information about the provisions of the Act. Furthermore, the team also found that the forest offices below the Division Office did not have a copy of the Forest Rights Act and were not aware of the provisions of this Act.

During their visit, they could not see any fresh cutting of trees and fresh clearings for new cultivation in the Polo forests of Abhapur. Even if trees were cut it was only besides a *pagdandi* (footpath) without touching any other trees and only after leaving 1 or 2 feet of the trunk. This was done so that the trees could regenerate faster after the rains. The tribals had not resorted to wanton destruction but had come only to construct a hut to claim the right to protect and manage this forest and not for cultivation

The inquiry team also questioned the criminal complaint filed by the RFO (Range Forest Officer) of Dholwani on 8th February against 16 tribals. In the complaint, he said that on the 8th morning when he and the ACF visited plantation areas in Vajepur, the accused tribals made an unlawful assembly and prevented them from entering the plantation area of the forest land. They deterred them from discharging their duty, and threatened to kill them.

But in the complaint there is no mention of the issue of cutting of trees in Vajepur, which the Department talked about. The forest officials entering the area and the tribals preventing it is to be questioned, so also their threat to kill and their motive in doing so needs to be examined.

The only possible response could be that the forest officials on seeing a large gathering of tribals working in the area might have decided not to enter the area. It also reveals the peaceful and disciplined character of their protest and the total absence of violence—as they had peacefully prevented the officers from entering the area, without causing any bodily harm or injury. Even after the complaints, the police should have sent a message to the accused asking them to surrender and then release them on bail, and that would have been the end of the matter.

They also argued that if the tribals had come with the intention to attack and kill, they would have done so immediately after reaching the office and taking advantage of the element of surprise, besides no senior officers were present at that time. But they had gone there only to release their fellowmen. When they found the main gates of the compound closed, they stopped and started beating drums and dancing and shouting slogans for the release of their men. When the Deputy Superintendent of Police returned from Himmatnagar, people stopped his car and *gheraoed* him but no bodily harm or injury was inflicted on him. And yet after all this, without any provocation or warning, orders to fire were issued. Around 20 rounds, each of teargas shells and bullets was fired. Two persons lost their lives while three other tribals were seriously injured.

The inquiry team put down six recommendations for the Government to act upon after presenting their cases for argument. They were:

1. Both the criminal cases (FIR 16/08 and FIR 15/08) against these persons should be immediately withdrawn.
2. A criminal case of murdering and critically hurting these persons should be immediately filed against all those who ordered the firing and a high level Police probe, as well as a Judicial probe, be instituted.
3. A firm assurance to be given to these people that they shall get the land for which they shed their blood.
4. Compensation along with an unconditional apology should be given to these persons.
5. Strict action should be initiated against all those forest officials who spread false and grossly exaggerated stories about large scale destruction of forests by the tribals.
6. A firm commitment should be given to all the tribals of

Gujarat that the Forest Rights Act would be implemented in its true spirit and a time-bound manner.

The cases studied above demonstrate the source of conflicts viz., legal interventions. These three case studies point out that the officials and activists should work in a positive manner in the interests of the local tribal communities who are not able to understand the legality of the situations. Local tribal communities should be properly informed about the benefits available to them under different legislation.

An Explanation

Ashok Chaudhary, of the Adivasi Ekta Parishad, Surat expressed that the conflicts of the tribals with respect to forests have a particular historical background. Looking at it from a historical perspective, 'the outsiders' or the non-tribals, would be the Britishers, and other people started coming into the tribal community from different places at different points of time. Later conflicts between the tribals and the outsiders started due to the following reasons:

- Cultural differences between tribals and non-tribals, i.e., conflict of civilization, development, etc.
- Political set-up, i.e., the tribals' basic social group was a nation-state in itself where they had their own administrative system, customs and laws. But a new state and administration emerged in their society. As new administrations came up, their traditional administration was suppressed and slowly faded away.
- Territory being invaded—the new form of state was introduced, and people from outside their territory came and settled here. With the increase in population and the limited natural resources for livelihood which was solely used by the tribals, diminished. At that period of time they were ruled by kings, next came the Colonial State followed by the Democratic form of government and whatever laws were framed were in respect to the community and the tribals no more could lead a free life.

He further expressed, "We were thinking emotionally, but others were moving fast and taking our resources and utilizing it for their benefits faster and with a quick motion. Technology, industries and globalization speeded them to take away the tribal community's resources through the state, with all forms of Acts and laws framed by them and sometimes with violence, for they were an organized force. When this happened the tribals were confused and did not understand how a person could do this, how can one take away others' resources? It was out of their world and imagination. The other civilizations thought with speed, and we were thinking emotionally."

According to him individualism has become the principal factor of modern civilization. Its economic manifestation led to industries and personal property rights. All these led to the formation of capitalist society. Political manifestations lead to dictatorship which still continue even in the democratic governance of the country. Elections are conducted once in five years after which the people have no role to play. The State being the enforcer and protector of capitalism, personal and capitalist development, was in direct contrast to thinking in the tribal community, they never wished or prayed for personal development or benefits; any development or benefit has always been for the whole community, for the welfare of the village, he added.

Regarding the present situation of conflict, Chaudhary believes that, under the king and the Colonial rulers, the exploitation level of the natural resources and the tribals was very low. After Independence, these resources diminished. The tribals had to face injustice. No doubt developmental projects have come up in these areas, but it has also brought about mass marginalization of the tribals.

He added, "Forests were for the people. Later forests were for the Crown and exploitation began during this time. But since it was the initial phase the tribals were not that affected. That same Act is still followed by the Forest Department after independence. State became the owner of all the resources, and the exploitation of resources was speeded up. People's freedom and franchise decreased for the State is an organized machinery." The Britishers enacted and passed several Acts and Laws for their growing needs for the expansion of the Navy and the Railways and also claimed that they were preserving the forests "scientifically".

IV

NGOs Interventions in Tribal Rights

In this section, we will discuss the role played by some of the leading NGOs in the State for raising the tribal awareness for their rights as well as for joining their struggle for land and access to forest products.

A study by the Taleem Research Foundation of Ahmedabad (www.taleemindia.org) in 2008 showed that the lack of information is a major bottleneck in improving the outreach programme of Government schemes based on various laws applicable in the State of Gujarat. Since, the last two decades, different NGOs working in different parts of Gujarat are trying to create awareness of rights among the local tribal communities.

There are two different lobbies among these NGOs. These are the social activists for tribal communities and the environmentalists. Both have applied different approaches in creating awareness among the tribal communities. Environmental lobby always insists on the greening of the land including the degraded forest lands and waste lands and desire that community rights and not individual rights be given preference so that tribals could protect and maintain the existing forests and also the regenerate forests. They believe in alternate sources of livelihood through community rights over the forests. The lobby of the organizations of social activists who work for the tribal communities believe in fighting for the individual ownership of forest lands for tribals. They believe that tribals are the real owners of the forest lands and on this premise they need to hand over forests to the tribal communities for preservation and protection.

During the last two decades and particularly after the introduction of the concept of JFM, the two above-mentioned lobbies have gone about contacting and arranging tribals for their overall community development. When they came across a stretch of degraded forest land, they would talk about regenerating it during village meetings. If the tribals were willing and ready to take up the task, the NGOs would use their resources to get the work started on these degraded forest lands. The NGOs were fully convinced in their mission to carry out a nationally desirable mission of ecological, rural and tribal development—overlooking, however, the possible legalities involved in doing so. The local forest officials, however, objected to such activities, but would not really stop the work as they were unable to deny the fact that the forest was visibly improving with the support of local tribals, and this was wholly brought about by the intervention of the NGOs.

We will discuss the working of some of the social activists who are creating awareness on tribal rights for tribal communities in different parts of Gujarat. We will discuss the operations and modalities of campaigning of DISHA (Developing Initiatives for Social and Human Actions), GHADTAR, ARCH and RSSS (Rajpipla Social Service Society). Table 5.4 shows various details of the NGOs working for the tribal rights.

DISHA is a mass-based organization in Gujarat that started in 1985 whose aim is to alter societal power relationships in favour of the poor in order to produce social change. The organization believes that it is only through altering the power balance among different communities that our current society could be transformed into a more equitable one. DISHA espouses the ideals of self-determination that all individuals are entitled to control the natural, economic, political and other resources needed for them in order to determine the course of their own lives. In reality, however, the vast majority of people are deprived of the ability to choose for themselves, instead, economic hardships generally make the choices for them.

This organisation has successfully worked on forest land entitlement issues, atrocities and exploitation by forest officials, exploitation of women who collect minor forest-produce, inadequate employment/learning, exploitation of agricultural tribal labourers, severe lack of irrigation facilities and infertile lands, food insufficiency due to low productivity of land and the exploitation of forest labourers involved in nursery raising and watchmen. In a historic Supreme Court decision, DISHA won an eight year battle against the State for regularization of long-serving forest labour.

Activities of ARCH are different from those of DISHA. Health and education programmes in the tribal districts of the State of

Table 5.4: Details of Four NGOs Working for Tribal Rights in Study Area

	'DISHA'	*ARCH*	*GHADTAR*	*RSSS*
Established in	*1985*	*1989*	*1979*	
Founder	Mr. Madhusudan Mistry	Dr. Anil Patel Dr. Daxa Patel	Ms. Beena Dabhi	Late Fr. Joseph Idiyakunnel
Working Area	North Gujarat	Central Gujarat South Gujarat	Central Gujarat	Central Gujarat South Gujarat
Major Issues Undertaken	Forest Land Entitlement Exploitation of MFP Collectors Exploitation of Forest Labourers	Health Programme Campaign for Tribal Rights Primary Education Implementation of FRA	Developing Village-level Leadership Issues of Injustice Issues of Irregularities and Corruption in Tribal Welfare Schemes Legal Ownership of Forest Land	Legal Aid Legal Assistance Support Aid in NREGA Help in Getting Ownership of Forest Land using FRA
Awareness/ Movements	Gujarat Forest Produce Gatherers and Forest Workers Union Ekalvya Sangathan	Campaign on Effectiveness of NREGA Campaign for Effective Implementation of FRA by Pursuing Claims Training to Village-level Volunteers	TB Control Programme Campaign for Village-level Health Workers Health Awareness Campaign in Tribal Areas Campaign to Train Midwife	Legal Awareness Camp Training to FRC Members Jai Adivasi Maha Sangh (JAMS) Adivasi Maha Sabha
Achievements	Regularization of long-serving forest labourers with Supreme Court Judgement Implementation of FRA Forest Land Entitlement to Tribals Enforcement of Minimum Wages for Forest Labourers	Pursuing Claims under FRA Effective Implementation of NREGA	Balwadies and Training Centre at Dharampur Well-equipped Hospital at Mangrol and Dharampur Low Cost Diagnostic Services in Tribal Areas with Ten Mobile Clinics Implementation of FRA Publication of Health Education Booklet	Intensive legal support in implementation of FRA at village level Cases Settled Through Conciliations Legal Awareness Night Camps Legal Assistance in Tribal Areas

Gujarat are set up by ARCH. The main activities and programmes conducted by ARCH are health programmes, TB control programmes, advocacy and campaign for tribal rights, primary education to school children, arranging systematic training programmes for village health workers, publication of health education booklets to create information and the implementation of FRA.

Till date ARCH has published 24 booklets on different health topics in order to assist health education awareness campaigns and also to upgrade the experience of Village Health Workers and patients. ARCH has prepared audiovisuals, charts and power point presentations on adolescent education, pregnancy and post-pregnancy care.

Vadodara and Kawant Centres of ARCH remained heavily involved in the implementation of Forest Rights Act of 2006, in villages of the Eastern districts. ARCH is also helping the villages under their organization to claim community rights under the FRA. In collaboration with other organizations, ARCH conducted two series of training camps in the Eastern tribal belt, from the Dangs to the Banaskantha districts. The literature prepared by ARCH was widely used by other villages all over the State of Gujarat.

ARCH has helped 38 accused tribals in the Vijaynagar police firing case to get bail from the Gujarat High Court. Also, the imminent threat of 20 tribal families of Mudeti village has been successfully thwarted, as ARCH got a stay order from the Gujarat High Court against State Reserve Police (SRP) and the district administration to evict these tribal families.

GHADTAR (Community Education and Development Centre) works towards socio-economic and political changes in Central Gujarat. It addresses the issues of inequity, exploitation and social injustice. Developing leadership has been more effective in terms of taking up issues of injustice, corruption, and irregularity, atrocity, accessing resources of the Government and implementation of the welfare and developmental schemes of the Government intended for the tribal communities and also the implementation of the provisions of the FRA, NREGA and the RTI.

Through the leadership development in the area, it has been able to address issues relating to atrocity, exploitation; create employment through effective implementation of the National Rural Employment Guarantee Act (NREGA). GHADTAR has submitted claims for legal rights of the forest land and have been pursuing such claims through effective implementation of the Forest Rights Act (FRA). The organisation helps to follow up, to monitor, to pursue claims already filed and to ensure that these claims are approved and thus, help the claimants get the forest land rights; it also helps to file remaining claims and ensure their realisation and also helps people get benefits of community forest rights—these are some of the main activities of GHADTAR.

Fr. Joseph Idiyakunnel, known as "Father of Free Legal Aid in India" had established Rajpipla Social Service Society (RSSS) nearly thirty years ago at Rajpipla in order to serve the tribal and backward communities in the remote villages of the State of Gujarat. RSSS is active in Central and South Gujarat. Legal aid and legal assistance are the two major areas of the RSSS where they had done creditable work at the grassroot level. All their legal help and legal assistance centres play a very important role in coordinating and directing the activities in the villages falling in their respective block areas. In order to enhance the legal knowledge of the primary stakeholders concerning issues affecting their lives, legal awareness camps are held in the villages by the office managers. This helps them to be directly in touch with their office areas in additional related way.

The legal topics are decided on a need based situation as and when they emerge during the visit of people to the centre of their area. Many cases come to the legal aid and legal help centre in the block offices for guidance and legal support. RSSS office managers study the implications of each case, call the concerned parties and try to convince and reconcile the parties for mutual understanding and just settlement; if that fails, then through an advocate the matter is taken up in the appropriate court and pursued to its logical end. The organisation concentrates on reconciliation rather than confrontation.

All through the year, the main focus of the RSSS has been to enable people to fill up the claim forms for the forest land. This involved all the allied activities connected with the forest land claim, like ascertaining if the forms are filled correctly with all relevant proofs attached, site inspection, FRC meetings etc.

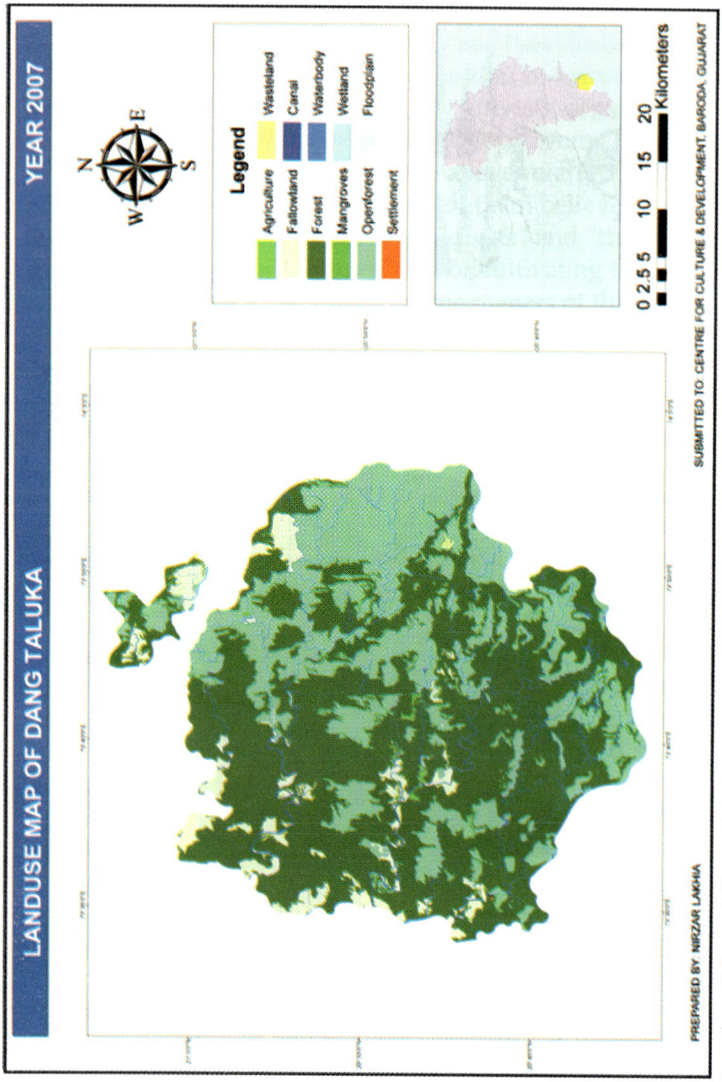

Map 5.2: Landuse Map of Dang Taluka

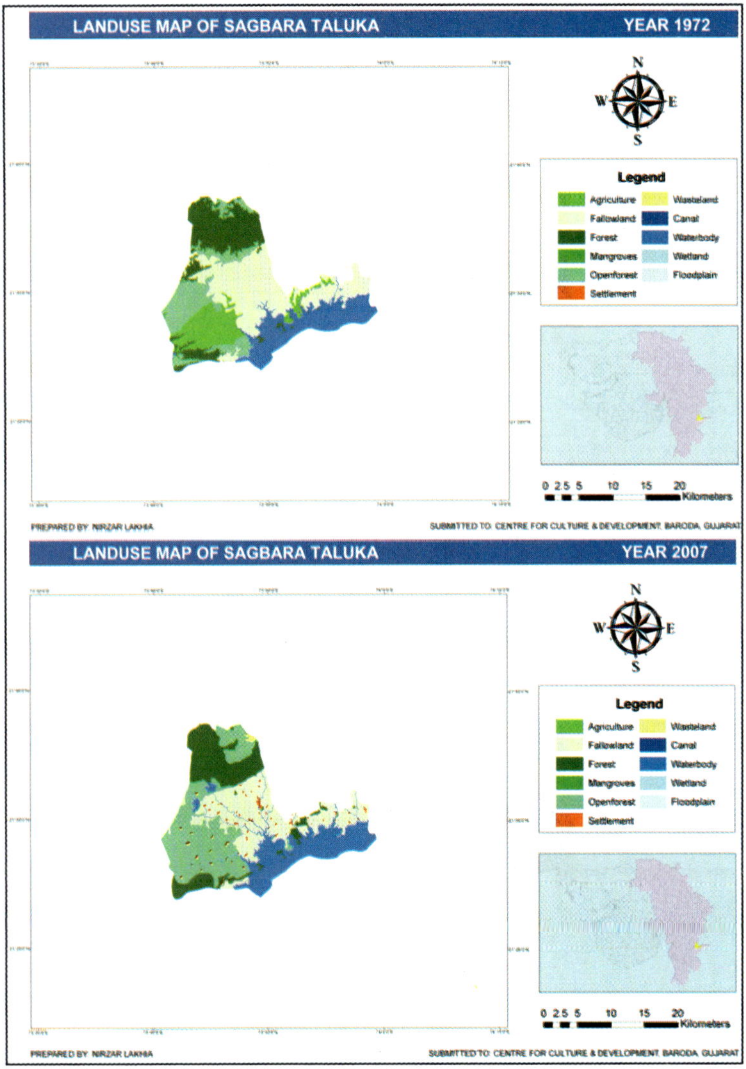

Map 5.3: Landuse Map of Sagbara Taluka

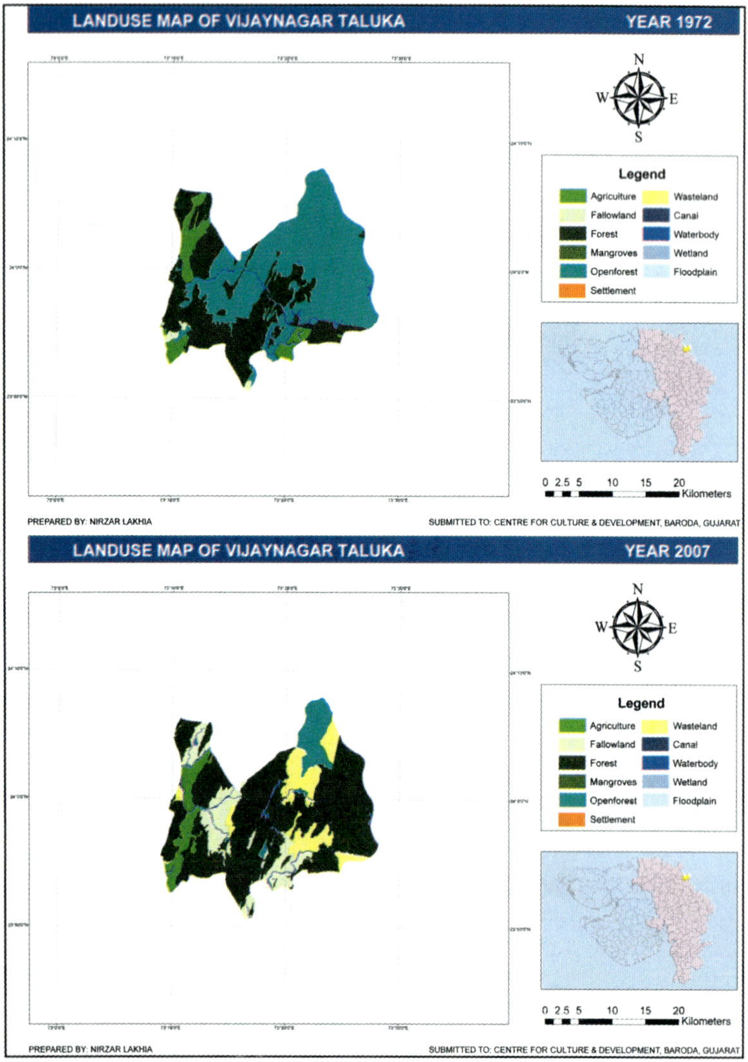

Map 5.4: Landuse Map of Vijaynagar Taluka

6
Profiles of the Villages
Respondents and Households

The village is still there, not merely as physical space, but with the population, possibly with a somewhat different social organization than before, and with its institutions like shrines, school, statutory Panchayat, the co-operative societies and the NGOs working in the village. The studies on villages brought out enormous diversity in village society and culture not only between various regions in the state but also within the region, which made anthropologists and sociologists extremely careful in making generalizations about village in terms of society and culture.

I

Profiles of Study Villages

During the field work, the team had generated village profiles. Table 6.1 shows that 92 per cent of the total study villages had provided with the profile.

Table 6.1: Study Villages and Village Profiles in Study Area

Zones	*Number of Study Villages*	*Village Profile Done*
I	28	28
II	52	47
III	49	43
IV	33	29
V	22	22
Total	**184**	**169**

A total of 169 village profiles were developed with information on basic facilities like education, health and irrigation. Profiles also covered the issue of migration. The Gram Panchayat office provided the data on the village profile. Table 6.2 shows the education facilities in the study villages.

Table 6.2: Education Facilities in Study Villages

Education Facilities (in number of villages)	*Zones*					*Study Area*
	I	*II*	*III*	*IV*	*V*	
Anganwadi	60	69	45	48	20	242
Primary School	49	73	47	38	22	229
Secondary School	04	06	07	02	06	25
Higher Secondary/Buniyadi School	02	04	03	03	00	12
Ashram Shala (Residential School)	03	07	04	07	02	23
College/ITI	01	01	01	00	00	03
No Education Facility	01	01	01	01	01	05

Ninty-seven per cent of the study villages has at least primary school facility in their respective villages. There are five such villages where there is no education facility at all within the village. All the villages have Anganwadi. Some villages with more households have more than one Anganwadi. Twenty-three villages have Ashram Shala, i.e., residential school for tribal children. Three villages have either college or Industrial Training Institute (ITI), and twelve villages have higher secondary school.

Table 6.3: Health Facilities in Study Villages

Health Facilities (in number of villages)	*Zones*					*Study Area*
	I	*II*	*III*	*IV*	*V*	
Public Health Centres	03	10	05	11	06	35
Maternity and Child Health Centres	08	12	09	14	07	50
Private Doctors (Allopathic, Ayurvedic and homeopathic)	03	14	06	16	12	51
Bhuva/Bhagat (Oracles/Healers)	114	149	64	68	22	417
No Medical Facility	22	25	30	15	11	103

Table 6.3 gives the details on the health facilities in the study villages. Fifty-six per cent of total study villages have no medical facilities within the village. Hardly 19 per cent villages have Public Health Centres (PHC). Twenty-eight per cent villages have the clinic or dispensary of private doctors. Most of them are either Ayurvedic or Homeopathic. Very few have the requisite qualification to practice as medical practitioners. Twenty-seven per cent villages have the facility of maternity home or child health care centre. If we look at the overall scenario, the health facility is very poor in the study villages.

Table 6.4: Irrigation Facilities in Study Villages

Irrigation Facilities (in number of villages)	*Zones*					*Study Area*
	I	*II*	*III*	*IV*	*V*	
River/Stream	10	17	14	15	09	65
Bore Well	06	07	14	09	06	42
Canal	01	00	07	00	00	14
No Irrigation Facility	12	22	16	09	08	67

Table 6.4 shows the irrigation facilities in the study villages. 36 per cent of total study villages have no irrigation facilities and are only dependent on monsoon. Thirty-five per cent villages are along the river. But many of the rivers are not perennial for the villagers for growing crops.

It is very interesting to examine the trend of migration in the study villages. Table 6.5 shows the migration from the study villages.

Table 6.5: Migration from the Study Villages

Zones	*Migration (No. of Villages)*	*No Migration (No. of Villages)*	*No. of Study Villages*
I	23 (82)	05 (18)	28 (100)
II	39 (75)	13 (25)	52 (100)
III	40 (82)	09 (18)	49 (100)
IV	27 (82)	06 (18)	33 (100)
V	19 (86)	03 (14)	22(100)
Total	148 (80)	36 (20)	184 (100)

Note: Percentages are given in parenthesis.

Practically 80 per cent of the study villages have migration. 25 per cent villages from Zone II have no migration while only 14 per cent villages from Zone IV have no migration. Table 6.6 shows migratory patterns in the study villages.

Table 6.6: Migratory Patterns in Study Villages

Migratory Patterns	*Zones*					*Study Area*
	I	*II*	*III*	*IV*	*V*	
Where (number of persons)						
Within District	2,625 (49)	6,918 (55)	4,135 (86)	3,692 (71)	2,487 (50)	19,857 (60)
Other Districts	2,760 (51)	5,600 (45)	680 (14)	1,475 (28)	2,085 (42)	12,600 (39)
Other States	25 (00)	25 (00)	00 (00)	30 (01)	390 (08)	470 (01)
Total	5,410 (100)	12,543 (100)	4,815 (100)	5,197 (100)	4,962 (100)	32,927 (100)
How Long (number of persons)						
Less than 3 months	1,105 (42)	4,309 (47)	1,957 (93)	3,240 (87)	1,067 (30)	11,678 (55)
3 to 6 months	1,150 (43)	2,050 (22)	140 (07)	500 (13)	662 (19)	4,502 (21)
More than 6 months	400 (15)	2,770 (31)	00 (00)	00 (00)	1,840 (51)	5,010 (24)
Total	2,655 (100)	9,129 (100)	2,097 (100)	3,740 (100)	3,569 (100)	21,190 (100)

Note: Percentages are given in parenthesis.

A migratory pattern in the study of these villages shows that 60 per cent of the tribals are migrating within the district while mere 01 per cent migrates to other states. Fifty-five per cent are migrating seasonally, i.e., for less than three months. Almost one fourth of the tribals are migrating for more than six months. Migration in the study villages of Zone III is more, but most of them are migrating to do work in the nearby industrial estates. Therefore, hardly 14 per cent of the tribals from the Zone III need to migrate into other districts. Fourty-three per cent of the tribals from the Zone I, are migrating for more than three months but less than six months. After further investigation, it is revealed that they migrate more if the monsoon is not good. As they do not have many industrial estates nearby their villages, they migrate to other districts for a longer period. They come back to their villages during the monsoon. 08 per cent tribals from the Zone V are migrating to other states. With further inquiry, they revealed that they go to cut sugar cane in bordering Maharashtra. Their duration depends upon the season of sugar cane. If the crop is good, people migrate for longer duration.

II

Profile of Respondents

After laying the ground with the profile of the villages under study, we will now analyze the respondents. Our team visited 2,672 households in 184 study villages and generated data based on a structured questionnaire. Due to the Parliament election in the year 2009, our team could not cover more respondents from Zone I as compared to other zones. Eighty-three per cent were male respondents, and the rest were female respondents. Table 6.7 shows the sex-wise distribution of the respondents.

Table 6.7: Sex-wise Distribution of the Respondents

Sex	*Zones*					*Study Area*
	I	*II*	*III*	*IV*	*V*	
Male	315 (86)	642 (86)	483 (83)	409 (80)	364 (77)	2,213 (83)
Female	52 (14)	100 (14)	97 (17)	103 (20)	107 (23)	459 (17)
Total	367 (100)	742 (100)	580 (100)	512 (100)	471 (100)	2,672 (100)

Note: Percentages are given in parenthesis.

Zone V had 23 per cent female respondents, while Zones I and II had merely 14 per cent female respondents. Zone's IV and Zone III had 20 per cent and 17 per cent female respondents respectively. Table 6.8 will show the age-group of the respondents from the study villages.

Table 6.8: Age-Group of the Respondents

Age-Group (in years)	*Zones*					*Study Area*
	I	*II*	*III*	*IV*	*V*	
18-25	17 (05)	33 (04)	25 (04)	18 (03)	24 (05)	117 (04)
26-35	144 (39)	247 (33)	198 (34)	176 (34)	161 (34)	926 (35)
36-45	101 (28)	221 (30)	211 (36)	188 (37)	147 (31)	868 (32)
46-60	85 (23)	182 (25)	119 (21)	106 (21)	121 (26)	613 (23)
More than 60	20 (05)	59 (08)	27 (05)	24 (05)	18 (04)	148 (06)
Total	367 (100)	742 (100)	580 (100)	512 (100)	471 (100)	2,672 (100)

Note: Percentages are given in parenthesis.

Almost two thirds of the total respondents were between the age 26 and 45 while nearly one fourth were between the age 46 and 60.04 per cent were between the age 18 and 25 while 06 per cent were more than 60 years. Table 6.9 will provide the information on the marital status of the respondents.

Table 6.9: Marital Status of the Respondents

Marital Status	*Zones*					*Study Area*
	I	*II*	*III*	*IV*	*V*	
Unmarried	05 (01)	05 (01)	18 (03)	07 (01)	06 (01)	41 (02)
Married	350 (96)	693 (93)	537 (93)	480 (94)	450 (96)	2,510 (94)
Widow/Widower	12 (03)	41 (06)	24 (04)	22 (05)	15 (03)	114 (04)
Divorcee	00 (00)	01 (00)	00 (00)	02 (00)	00 (00)	03 (00)
Abandoned	00 (00)	02 (00)	01 (00)	01 (00)	00 (00)	04 (00)
Total	367 (100)	742 (100)	580 (100)	512 (100)	471 (100)	2,672 (100)

Note: Percentages are given in parenthesis.

Most of the respondents (94%) were married while four per cent were either widow or widower. Mere two per cent respondents were unmarried. Table 6.10 will show the sex-wise literacy rate among the total respondents in the study villages.

Table 6.10: Sex-wise Literacy among Respondents

Literacy	*Zone I*		*Zone II*		*Zone III*		*Zone IV*		*Zone V*	
	Male	*Female*	*Male*	*Female*	*Male*	*Female*	*Male*	*Female*	*Male*	*Female*
Literate	161 (51)	20 (38)	218 (34)	07 (07)	323 (67)	37 (38)	188 (46)	40 (39)	244 (67)	38 (35)
Illiterate	154 (49)	32 (62)	424 (66)	93 (93)	160 (33)	60 (62)	221 (54)	63 (61)	120 (33)	69 (65)

Note: Percentages are given in parenthesis.

Out of total respondents (2,672) 48 per cent (1,276) were literate while 52 per cent (1,396) were illiterate. Out of total 2,213 male respondents, 51 per cent (1,134) and out of 459 female respondents, 31 per cent (142) were literate. Zonally, 67 per cent of male respondents from Zone's III and V were literate whereas literate female respondents included 07 per cent in Zone II. Sixty-six per cent male respondents from this Zone were illiterate. Table 6.11 will throw light on the level of education among the respondents from the study villages.

Table 6.11: Level of Education among Respondents

Level of Education	*Zones*					*Study Area*
	I	*II*	*III*	*IV*	*V*	
Illiterate	186 (51)	517 (70)	220 (38)	284 (55)	189 (39)	1,396 (52)
Primary	65 (17)	106 (14)	181 (31)	117 (23)	166 (36)	635 (24)
Secondary	58 (16)	72 (10)	90 (16)	75 (15)	69 (15)	364 (14)
Higher Secondary	47 (13)	29 (04)	48 (08)	12 (02)	24 (05)	160 (06)
Graduate and beyond	11 (03)	18 (02)	41 (07)	24 (05)	23 (05)	117 (04)
Total	367 (100)	742 (100)	580 (100)	512 (100)	471 (100)	2,672 (100)

Note: Percentages are given in parenthesis.

Respondents from Zone III and V were more educated compared to Zone II, IV and I. 38 per cent and 39 per cent respondents from Zone's III and V respectively were illiterate against 70 per cent, 55 per cent and 51 per cent respondents from Zone's II, IV, and I respectively fell in the same line. Zone III had the highest number of respondents who were graduates or beyond, while a mere 02 per cent and 03 per cent respondents from Zone's II and I respectively were graduates or beyond. Table 6.12 shows the family composition among the respondents across all the study villages.

Table 6.12: Number of Members in the Family of Respondents

Number of Members In Family	*Zones*					*Study Area*
	I	*II*	*III*	*IV*	*V*	
01-05	172 (47)	292 (39)	335 (58)	294 (58)	224 (48)	1,317 (49)
06-08	134 (37)	305 (41)	208 (36)	191 (37)	196 (42)	1,034 (39)
09-10	42 (11)	85 (12)	30 (05)	20 (04)	34 (07)	211 (08)
More than 10	19 (05)	60 (08)	07 (01)	07 (01)	17 (03)	110 (04)
Total	367 (100)	742 (100)	580 (100)	512 (100)	471 (100)	2,672 (100)

Note: Percentages are given in parenthesis.

Forty-nine per cent of total respondents had five or less than five members in their family while barely 12 per cent had more than eight members in their family. Fifty-eight per cent of the respondents from Zone's III and IV had five or less than five persons in their families. Thirty-nine per cent of total respondents had more than five but less than nine persons in their families. Twenty per cent of the respondents from Zone II had more than eight members in their families. Table 6.13 shows the age group of the family members of the respondents.

Sixty per cent of total family members of the respondents were less than twenty-five years of age while just 10 per cent were more than 45 years of age. If we consider the age 35, there are 78 per

Table 6.13: Age-Group of Total Family Members of the Respondents

(In Years)

Age Group	Zones					Study Area
	I	II	III	IV	V	
00-06	298 (13)	767 (16)	335 (11)	263 (09)	333 (12)	1,996 (13)
07-17	689 (32)	1,462 (30)	822 (26)	724 (26)	833 (30)	4,530 (29)
18-25	373 (17)	815 (17)	568 (18)	471 (17)	557 (20)	2,784 (18)
26-35	404 (18)	817 (17)	550 (18)	545 (20)	457 (16)	2,773 (18)
36-45	224 (10)	513 (11)	450 (14)	404 (15)	305 (11)	1,896 (12)
46-60	173 (08)	373 (07)	307 (10)	260 (10)	236 (09)	1,349 (08)
More than 60	43 (02)	113 (02)	80 (03)	72 (03)	49 (02)	357 (02)
Total	2,204 (100)	4,860 (100)	3,112 (100)	2,739 (100)	2,770 (100)	15,685 (100)

Note: Percentages are given in parenthesis.

cent of total family members below the age 35. Table 6.14 shows the relation of family members with the respondents.

Relation of family members with the respondents gives an interesting analysis. Forty-six per cent of total family members were either son or daughter, or both while mere 2 per cent was either father or mother or both. Hardly 01 per cent of total family members were either brother or sister, or both while 12 per cent of the total family members was either grandson or grand-daughter or uncle or aunt or all. Table 6.15 reflects the literacy level among the total respondents.

Thirty-eight per cent of total family members were illiterate, and 13 per cent were children below the school going age. Forty-nine per cent of total family members were literate. Zone III had higher literacy (60%) while Zone II lower (35%) as compared to other zones. Children below school going age were more in Zone II compared to all other zones. Table 6.16 will show the level of education among the literates of the total family members of the respondents.

Table 6.14: Relation of Family Members with the Respondents

Relation of Family Members with Respondents	*Zones*					*Study Area*
	I	*II*	*III*	*IV*	*V*	
Self	367 (17)	742 (15)	580 (19)	512 (19)	471 (17)	2,672 (17)
Husband/Wife	359 (16)	691 (14)	548 (18)	479 (17)	448 (16)	2,525 (16)
Father/Mother	39 (02)	73 (02)	108 (03)	115 (04)	53 (02)	388 (02)
Brothers/Sisters	11 (00)	80 (02)	27 (01)	22 (01)	21 (01)	161 (01)
Sons/Daughters	1,132 (51)	2,166 (45)	1,382 (44)	1,154 (42)	1,260 (45)	7,094 (46)
Sons-in-law/Daughters-in-law	125 (06)	357 (07)	179 (06)	169 (06)	183 (07)	1,013 (06)
Grand Sons/Grand Daughters and Others (Uncle, Aunt etc.)	171 (08)	751 (15)	288 (09)	288 (11)	334 (12)	1,832 (12)
Total	2,204 (100)	4,860 (100)	3,112 (100)	2,739 (100)	2,770 (100)	15,685 (100)

Note: Percentages are given in parenthesis.

Table 6.15: Literacy among Total Family Members of the Respondents

Literacy	*Zones*					*Study Area*
	I	*II*	*III*	*IV*	*V*	
Literate	1,094 (50)	1,690 (35)	1,863 (60)	1,467 (54)	1,500 (54)	7,614 (49)
Illiterate	812 (36)	2,403 (49)	914 (29)	1,009 (37)	937 (34)	6,075 (38)
Children (Below the School-going Age 06)	298 (14)	767 (16)	335 (11)	263 (09)	333 (12)	1,996 (13)
Total	2,204 (100)	4,860 (100)	3,112 (100)	2,739 (100)	2,770 (100)	15,685 (100)

Note: Percentages are given in parenthesis.

Twenty-nine per cent of total family members of the respondents from the study villages had obtained primary education while just 07 per cent had more than the secondary level education. Eleven per cent of total family members from the respondents of Zone's III and IV were educated more than the secondary level while the same is just 04 per cent in Zone II.

Table 6.16: Level of Education among Total Family Members of the Respondents

Level of Education	*Zones*					*Study Area*
	I	*II*	*III*	*IV*	*V*	
Illiterate	812 (36)	2,403 (49)	914 (29)	1,009 (37)	937 (34)	6,075 (38)
Primary	588 (27)	1,127 (23)	1,038 (33)	802 (29)	1,006 (36)	4,561 (29)
Secondary	300 (14)	372 (08)	501 (16)	380 (14)	325 (12)	1,878 (12)
Higher Secondary	156 (07)	114 (02)	190 (06)	156 (06)	91 (03)	707 (04)
Graduate and more	50 (02)	77 (02)	134 (05)	129 (05)	78 (03)	468 (03)
Children (Below the School-going Age 06)	298 (14)	767 (16)	335 (11)	263 (09)	333 (12)	1,996 (14)
Total	2,204 (100)	4,860 (100)	3,112 (100)	2,739 (100)	2,770 (100)	15,685 (100)

Note: Percentages are given in parenthesis.

The three main patterns of land ownership observed are Own Land, Joint Family Land and Shared Land. Individual land means that tribal households have land in their own name. Joint family land means that the land is owned by the head of the family and not given individually to the members of the family. Shared land is the land in which the tribal household gets to cultivate, but not

Table 6.17: Pattern of Land Ownership among Respondents

Land Ownership	*Zones*					*Study Area*
	I	*II*	*III*	*IV*	*V*	
Own Land	180 (49)	430 (58)	191 (33)	210 (41)	155 (33)	1,166 (44)
Joint Family Land	136 (37)	267 (36)	174 (30)	220 (43)	226 (48)	1,023 (38)
Shared Land	00 (00)	00 (00)	06 (01)	05 (01)	14 (03)	25 (01)
Landless	25 (07)	45 (06)	168 (29)	67 (13)	66 (14)	371 (14)
No Response	26 (07)	00 (00)	41 (07)	10 (02)	10 (02)	87 (03)
Total	367 (100)	742 (100)	580 (100)	512 (100)	471 (100)	2,672 (100)

Note: Percentages are given in parenthesis.

owned by them. They cultivate the land and divide the income between them and the owner of the land. There are a small number of tribal households that have no land, in other words we could say that they are landless tribals. Few respondents had not responded to issue on different patterns of land ownership. Table 6.17 shows the land ownership patterns among the respondents of the study villages.

Forty-four per cent of the total respondents had own land while 14 per cent were landless. Thirty-eight per cent respondents had land possessed jointly with their family members. Types of tribal land-holders in different zones have been categorized on the land-holdings in the following categories:

- Landless (having no land at all)
- Marginal (having less than 2.5 acres of land)
- Small (having land between 2.51 acres and 5.00 acres)
- Medium (having land between 5.01 acres to 10.00 acres)
- Big (having land more than 10.01 acres)

Table 6.18 shows the pattern of land holding among the respondents of the study villages.

Table 6.18: Types of Farmers among Respondents

Types of Farmers	*Zones*					*Study Area*
	I	*II*	*III*	*IV*	*V*	
Landless	25 (07)	45 (06)	168 (29)	67 (13)	66 (14)	371 (14)
Marginal Farmers	169 (46)	282 (38)	110 (19)	159 (31)	85 (18)	805 (30)
Small Farmers	92 (25)	208 (28)	122 (21)	128 (25)	84 (18)	634 (24)
Medium Farmers	22 (06)	82 (11)	46 (08)	46 (09)	61 (13)	257 (10)
Big Farmers	04 (01)	14 (02)	29 (05)	15 (03)	57 (12)	119 (04)
No Response	55 (15)	111 (15)	105 (18)	97 (19)	118 (25)	486 (18)
Total	367 (100)	742 (100)	580 (100)	512 (100)	471 (100)	2,672 (100)

Note: Percentages are given in parenthesis.

Fifty-four per cent of total respondents had five or less than five acres of land while mere 04 per cent had more than ten acres of land. Twelve per cent of the respondents from Zone V had more than ten acres of land while the same is just one per cent and two per cent from the Zones I and II respectively. Twenty-nine per cent of the respondents from Zone III were landless so also seven per cent and six per cent from Zones I and II respectively.

7

Changing Patterns of Tribal Livelihood and Literacy

Tribals whose traditional mode of livelihood in the remote past depended on hunting, gathering, fishing, shifting cultivation, have begun to settled agriculture and farming. Until recently, the dominant view was that the tribal residence necessarily implied reliance on farming agriculture and forests as a means of income. Tribal areas were seen primarily as a production site for agriculture and MFP, and tribal development was perceived as a derivative of agricultural development and MFPs. Policies for the development of tribal areas, when recognized as relevant policy domain, focused solely on agriculture, and neglected other economic activities. Policy perceptions and visions about agriculture and the development of the agricultural sector have been long dominated by the model of agricultural modernization, which advocates improving farm production through the use of improved technologies and more financial investments.

While agriculture is certainly an important factor in tribal economies, tribal areas contain a wide range of economic activities. It is only in recent years that a new model of tribal development emerged: one that takes a broader view on tribal economy, incorporating economic activities other than agriculture, while highlighting the broad diversity of tribal development methods. Generally, this is referred to as the diversification of tribal economy. In other words, heterogeneity, rather than homogeneity, is the dominant feature of tribal development. There is not one, but many, patterns of development (Carney, D., 1998: 132).

The livelihood approach provides an umbrella concept that meets two main objectives (Carney, D., 1998:149):

1. It holistically links the variety of ways by which tribal communities manage to make a living for themselves within the contexts in which they operate.
2. It is attentive to the processes that shape these endeavours, and to the activities of external institutions and individuals that can influence the way in which tribals can make a living.

Diversification at the individual or household level, 'supplementary livelihood', only means adding new activities. These can include agricultural or non-agricultural work, work for oneself or an employer, home based work or work at other places. Tribal livelihood diversification could be described as the process by which tribal households construct an increasingly complex portfolio of activities and assets, in order to survive and to improve their standard of living.

While tribals in the tribal areas gain their livelihood in a variety of ways, this range of income earning activities is often combined with, or linked to, agriculture and allied activities or forests and allied activities. The reasons why tribals diversify have been extensively debated. It is reasoned for countering their poverty or provide vent to their entrepreneurial strategy. The increased recognition that a tribal livelihood is multi-occupational and cross-sectoral (Frank and Biggs, 2001: 437), has become the fundamental starting point for critically reflecting upon tribal development policies of today.

It is important to make a distinction between intra-sectoral and inter-sectoral diversification strategies (*ibid*). Intra-sectoral (or agricultural) diversification, such as the introduction of new crops into farming systems or tribals investing in livestock have long been studied, and various policies and programmes have been designed to address and stimulate agricultural diversification. The notion of livelihood diversification focuses on inter-sectoral diversification, an expression of the fact that tribal communities' livelihoods straddle different economic sectors.

It can be said that an analysis of livelihoods needs to take into account the ways in which tribals use and organize access to resources, deal and negotiate with institutions, and live and work in a particular socio-cultural-economic and historical context, which in itself is the product of a particular configuration of global and local processes (Carney, D., 1998:162). Common household livelihood strategies in tribal areas include agricultural intensification (increasing farm yields); income diversification (through engaging in a range of off-farm economic activities); and migration (temporary or permanent, partial or with entire household). In this respect, the term livelihood enables us to see that tribal communities' income generating activities often involve migration, whether short or long-term, within the community or into cities.

'Supplementary livelihood', can include agriculture and allied additional sources and also forests and allied supplementary sources of livelihood for the tribals across a period of time and zones. Tribal livelihood diversification in agriculture, in our study areas, can be described as the live-stock properties, cultivating fruits or vegetables, cultivating on others' lands and working as agricultural labour in different agriculture farms. While diversification in forests and forest products can be described as bee-keeping, growing of income generating trees, furniture is made from the wood and fruits gathering from the fruit trees grown in the forests areas. Other than this one can see tribals taking to masonry, plumbing and other construction related activities.

Primary data from 184 study villages demonstrate the different additional sources of livelihood in the following sections. It shows the impact of land ownership and literacy on the livelihood of tribal communities. It will also look into the different kinds of assets held by the tribals to check the result of live-stock wealth, trees and wells and bore-wells on the livelihood of tribal households. It will analyze non-forest and non-agricultural sources of livelihood among the tribals and will also verify the dependency on forests for fodder, fuel and for other forest related products. Finally, it will give a detailed analysis of an inter-generational change in the patterns of additional livelihood among tribal communities. A pattern among landless tribals has been analyzed in a separate section. An attempt is also made to identify if differences in livelihood patterns exist in Zone II in three settings: where forests are degraded, where forests are regenerated and where they have remained unchanged.

I

Different Variables in Changing Patterns of Livelihood

(A) Agriculture as Livelihood

The three main patterns of land ownership observed are Own Land, Joint Family Land and Shared Land. Individual land means that tribal households have land in their own name. Joint family land means that the land is owned by the head of the family and not given individually to the members of the family. Shared land is the land in which the tribal household gets the land to cultivate, but not owned by them. They cultivate the land and divide the income between them and the owner of the land. There are a small number of tribal households that have no land, in other words we could say that they are landless tribals. Few of the respondents had not responded to the issue on different patterns of land ownership.

Table 7.1: Patterns of Land Ownership

(In Percentage)

Zones	*Own Land*	*Joint Family Land*	*Shared Land*	*No Land*	*No Response*
Zone I	49	37	00	07	07
Zone II	58	36	00	06	00
Zone III	33	30	01	29	07
Zone IV	41	43	01	13	02
Zone V	33	48	03	14	02

Table 7.1 provides a picture of the land ownership patterns among different zones. Respondents from Zone I (49%) and Zone II (58%) own more land than the respondents from Zone III (33%), Zone IV (41%) and Zone V (33%). One can observe the pattern of more land held jointly by the family in Zone IV (43%) and Zone V (48%) than in Zone I (37%), Zone II (36%) and Zone III (40%). The system of shared land, though very insignificant, is seen in Zone III (01%), Zone IV (01%) and Zone V (03%). This system of shared land farming is not seen at all in Zone I and Zone II. Landless tribal respondents were more in Zone III (29%) while a lesser number is found in Zone I (07%) and Zone II (06%). Zone IV (13%) and Zone V (14%) also have a substantial number of landless tribal respondents.

Types of tribal land-holders in different zones have been categorized on the land-holdings in the following categories:

- Landless (having no land at all)
- Marginal (having less than 2.5 acres of land)
- Small (having land between 2.51 acres and 5.00 acres)
- Medium (having land between 5.01 acres to 10.00 acres)
- Big (having land more than 10.01 acres)

Table 7.2: Types of Tribal Farmers

(In Percentage)

Zones	*Landless Farmers*	*Marginal Farmers*	*Small Farmers*	*Medium Farmers*	*Big Farmers*	*No Response*
Zone I	07	46	25	06	01	15
Zone II	06	38	28	11	02	15
Zone III	29	19	21	08	05	18
Zone IV	13	31	25	09	03	19
Zone V	14	18	18	13	12	25

Table 7.2 provides a detailed overview about the types of tribal land-holders among the respondents in the different zones. Twenty-five per cent of the tribal landholders are either medium landholders (13%) or big land-holders (12%), while only 36 per cent tribal land-holders are either marginal land-holders (18%) or small land-holders (18%) out of total respondents in Zone V. In Zone I, around 71 per cent tribal land-holders are either marginal land-holders (46%) or small land-holders (25%) out of the total respondents. Zone III has a maximum number (29%) of landless tribals. There is a significant number (i.e. 13% and 14%) of landless tribals, in Zone IV and Zone V respectively.

Cultivation on Forest Land

Cultivation on forest land is one of the major sources of additional livelihood sources among the tribal communities. Table 7.3 provides a detailed overview about the cultivation on forest lands among the respondents in the different zones.

Majority of the respondents had not responded to the question on the cultivation of forest land. In Zone V, 80 per cent of the total respondents refused to respond on the cultivation of forest lands.

Table 7.3: Cultivation on Forest Land

(In Percentage)

Zones	Marginal Farmers	Small Farmers	Medium Farmers	Big Farmers	Don't Want to Say
I	19	10	02	01	68
II	15	16	04	02	63
III	18	14	11	02	55
IV	27	13	02	01	57
V	05	05	08	02	80

But those who responded on the cultivated areas of the forest lands were mostly either marginal forest land-holders or small forest land-holders. In Zone IV, 27 per cent cultivated forest lands as marginal forest land-holders while 13 per cent were known to be small forest land-holders. In Zone III, 18 per cent cultivated forest lands were by marginal forest land-holders, while 14 per cent cultivated forest land were by small forest land-holders and 11 per cent by medium forest land-holders. In Zone I and Zone II, there are more marginal forest land-holders (19% and 15% respectively) and small forest land-holders (10% and 16% respectively) than medium forest land-holders (02% and 04% respectively) and significant forest land-holders (01% and 02% respectively). Zone V has a number of medium forest land-holders (08%) than marginal forest land-holders (5%) and small forest land-holders (5%).

Facilities of Wells and Bore-wells

The availability of wells and bore-wells play a vital role in the income generation from the agricultural land. Sufficient amount of water at the right time is a requirement for a good crop on

Table 7.4: Facilities of Wells and Bore-wells

(In Percentage)

Zones	Well	Bore-well
Zone I	38	19
Zone II	44	29
Zone III	30	17
Zone IV	53	42
Zone V	18	10

agricultural farms. Table 7.4 shows how many tribal have facilities like wells and bore-wells. When the irrigation facilities are not available, the wells and bore-wells are the only available sources for providing water to the crops and the livestock. Zone IV has the highest number of wells (53%) and bore-wells (42%) among all the five zones. Zone II also has a good number of wells (44%). But Zone V does not have such good wells (a mere 18%) and bore-well (a mere 10%) facilities. Irrigation facilities are also not good in Zone V.

The presence of bore-wells suggests good income among the tribal respondents. However, the installation of bore-wells needs money. And the presence of bore-wells in Zone IV (42% of the total respondents) show that the respondents earn a good amount of income, either from agriculture or from some other sources from which they are investing in order to earn more. A mere 10 per cent of the respondents from Zone V have such facilities like bore-wells; this implies that there are a lesser number of tribals who have enough income to create various facilities like bore-well for their livelihood.

Pattern of Cropping on Owned Revenue and Forest Land

This study found the changing pattern of cropping in the study area. Traditionally, the tribal communities across the study area were sowing the seeds and doing agriculture activities just for their subsistence. But since the last five years, we have seen a definite change in the cropping pattern and sowing behaviour, in the tribal areas across the state. Respondents' responses clearly show that they have moved from subsistence to the income generation. They still engage themselves in agricultural activities for subsistence, but they have also introduced new crops which can yield them a good amount of money. Table 7.5 shows a definite change in the cropping pattern.

The changing pattern of cropping has helped the tribals to generate income for the family. They moved to sow cash crops like cotton, groundnut, sugarcane, pulses and vegetables that can yield them good income. The experiment of sowing strawberry and cashew in Zones IV and V and I have yielded good results. Respondents from all the study areas responded that they were

Table 7.5: Change in Cropping Pattern in Study Area

Zones	*Name of the Crops Sown (Thirty Years Ago)*		*Name of the Crops Sown (During Last Five Years)*	
	Crops for Subsistence	*Income Yielding Crops*	*Crops for Subsistence*	*Income Yielding Crops*
I	• Juwar • Bajra • Rice • Pulses (*Udad*)	—	• Juwar • Bajra • Wheat • Rice • Pulses (*Udad*)	• Vegetables (Cabbage and Coli Flower, Potato, Pumpkin) • Fruits (Mango, Papaya, Water Melon, Guava, Banana) • Cotton • Pulses (*Udad*) • Wheat • Castor Seeds • Soya bean • Sesame Seeds
II	• Maize • Juwar • Bajra • Rice • Pulses (*Udad*)	• Papaya • Custard Apple • Mango	• Maize • Juwar • Bajra • Wheat • Rice • Pulses • (*Udad*)	• Vegetables (Tuver, Val-papdi, Gram, Cabbage, Coli Flower, Pumpkin, Gourd) • Fruits (Mango, Papaya, Water Melon, Sweet Melon, Custard Apple, Banana) • Cotton • Ground Nut • Pulses (Tuver, Gram, *Udad*) • Castor Seeds • Sesame Seeds
III	• Juwar • Rice • Maize • Pulses (*Udad*)	• Mango	• Juwar • Wheat • Rice • Maize • Pulses (*Udad*)	• Vegetables (Lady Finger, Val-papdi, Tuver, Green Peas, Gourd) • Fruits (Mango, Papaya, Banana) • Cotton • Sugar Cane • Pulses (Val, Tuver, Mag, Choli) • Wheat
IV	• Nangli • Rice • Juwar • Pulses (*Udad*)	• Mango	• Nangli • Rice • Juwar • Pulses (*Udad*)	• Vegetables (Lady Finger, Brinjal, Val-papdi) • Fruits (Mango, Banana, Strawberry, Cashew) • Pulses (Val, Tuver, Mag, Choli) • Sugarcane
V	• Nangli • Rice • Pulses (*Udad*)	—	• Nangli • Rice • Pulses (*Udad*)	• Vegetables (Lady Finger, Brinjal, Val-papdi) • Fruits (Mango, Strawberry, Cashew) • Pulses (Val, Tuver, Mag, Choli, Gram) • Sugarcane

now using better quality seeds and modern technology like drip irrigation to get better yielding crops.

(B) Minor Forest Products (MFP) as Supplementary Source of Income

The bulk of commercially important Non-Timber Forest Produce (NTFP), in the country comes from the forests, consisting of states like Madhya Pradesh, Chhattisgarh, Andhra Pradesh, Odisha, Jharkhand and Bihar while Gujarat and Rajasthan contribute a small portion of it. The rest of India produces a very small amount. Gujarat tribal communities always used MFP either for home usage (fodder, fuel, fish and other minor produces) or for generating additional sources of income. Tribals gather and collect honey, bam boo, gum , *timru patta*, fruits, *mahuda* etc. and sell them in the market to generate income. Tribals also collect *dodi*, bamboo, fodder and fuel for their home usage. Hence, MFP can also be considered at the time of seeing the patterns of livelihood among the tribal communities (see Table 7.6).

Table 7.6: Dependency on Minor Forest Produces

(In Percentage)

Zones	Before*	Now**	Before*	Now**
	MFP as Supplementary Source of Income		MFP for Home Usage	
I	15	19	09	05
II	33	42	14	15
III	26	21	21	12
IV	33	30	27	22
V	22	26	30	35

Note: *Before mean in the year 1999 (before 10 years of this study).
** Now means in the year 2009.

Forty-two per cent of the total respondents from Zone II are getting additional income from MFP. The same was only 33 per cent five to ten years earlier. Respondents from Zone III and Zone IV had shown a decreased dependency on MFP than five to ten years ago. It was 26 per cent and 33 per cent respectively for Zone III and Zone IV previously and now the same has decreased to 21 per cent and 30 per cent respectively. Respondents from Zone I are the least dependent on MFP if we compare with all other zones. Only 19 per cent of the total respondents from Zone I get additional income from MFP and the same was 15 per cent five to ten years ago. While in Zone V, 26 per cent of the total respondents use MFP as a supplementary source of income for their livelihood.

Except Zone V and Zone II, in the rest of the three zones, the respondents said that they had decreased their dependency on fodder and fuel from forests as compared to five to ten years ago. Twenty-one per cent of the respondents from Zone III depended on forests for their livelihood five to ten years before this study was carried out, currently only 12 per cent of the respondents depend on forests for the home necessities. The same was not true in Zone V where 30 per cent of the respondents depended on forests for their home use five to ten years ago while currently 35 per cent of the respondents depend on forests for the same.

(C) Other Supplementary Source of Income

Dairy Farming

The use of bullocks is an important part of agriculture, and the allied activities as most of the tribal families use bullocks for their farming activities. Except Zone V where only 52 per cent of the total respondents have bullocks, all other zones have a good number of bullocks available for their farming activities. Zone II was rated at the top with 72 per cent of the total respondents had bullocks. Out of total respondents from Zone I, Zone III and Zone IV, 67 per cent, 65 per cent and 61 per cent respectively used bullocks for their agriculture and allied activities.

The possession of cows and buffaloes plays an important role in providing additional sources of livelihood for tribal communities. On average, about 50 per cent of the tribal respondents own one or more than one cow or buffaloe. More and more tribal families are now keen on acquiring milk-bearing cattle as an additional source of livelihood. Respondents from Zone II held the highest number of buffaloes, i.e., 55 per cent while Zone I had the lowest, i.e., 42 per cent. Where, the possession of cows is concerned, Zone IV was at the highest with 54 per cent and Zone V was at the lowest with 41 per cent. The patterns of livestock rearing among the respondents are shown in Table 7.7.

Table 7.7: Live-stock Wealth

(In Percentage)

Zones	*Cows*	*Buffaloes*	*Bullocks*	*Goats Sheep*	*Hens*	*No Response*
Zone I	51	42	67	36	35	15
Zone II	46	55	72	49	40	14
Zone III	48	52	65	14	37	13
Zone IV	54	53	61	15	39	15
Zone V	41	48	52	09	47	35

It is imperative that the livestock holding requires a feeding system. The livestock feeding system is mostly that of semi-stall feeding, and the feed consists primarily of residues of sorghum, maize, paddy, wheat, groundnut and pulses. Livestock is fed green grass during the monsoon, small quantities of weeds from irrigated fields during the dry season, and limited quantities of spoiled grains. Cattle and buffaloes are grazed depending on the season.

Cultivation of green fodder is also very limited and is restricted to tribal land-holders who have access to irrigation facilities in the winter season only. Concentrates (compound feeds, produced commercially by co-operatives and private feed factories) are available where milk co-operatives are well established, i.e., in Zone II, Zone III and Zone IV. In some areas, limited quantities of a mix of home-made (mix of damaged grains and broken pulses) and compound feeds are offered to the cattle. But, in general, the amount and the quality of available feed resources are inadequate to meet the requirements of the animals. Some of the tribal land-holders depend on forests for fodder. Table 7.8 represents the dependency on forests for fodder among all five zones.

Table 7.8: Dependency on Forests for Fodder

(In Percentage)

Time	*Zones*				
	I	*II*	*III*	*IV*	*V*
Before*	22	18	30	34	19
Now**	20	17	33	36	24

Note: * Before means in the year 1999 (10 years ago).

** Now means in the year 2009.

Respondents from Zone III (30% and 33%) and Zone IV (34% and 36%) are more dependent on forests for fodder than respondents of Zone I (22% and 20%), Zone II (18% and 17%) and Zone V (19% and 24%). Dependency on forests for fodder has decreased in Zone I (from 22% to 20%) and Zone II (from 18% to 17%) over a period of time, but the same is not true of Zone III, Zone IV and Zone V where the dependency on forests for fodder has increased by 3 per cent, 2 per cent and 5 per cent respectively.

Income Generating Trees

Most of the tribals treet trees as source of their livelihood. Fruit trees like mango, chikoo (*achras sapota*), guava, *charoli* (*chirongia sapida*), custard apple etc.; *mahuda, tendu patta, saal* and teak are some of the trees which tribals hold and generate income from.

Respondents from Zone II (64%) and Zone IV (64%) have the highest number of income generated from these. Respondents from Zone V (35%) have the least number of income generating trees. Zone I (41%) and Zone III (43%) have a good number of income generating trees. The respondents collect the produces from these trees and create additional sources of income for their livelihood. In many of the tribal families, income from the trees is a major aspect of their livelihood. Respondents from Zone IV get a good income from chikoo and mango trees, while respondents from Zone II get a handsome return for the flowers gathered from the *mahuda* trees.

Other Supplementary Sources of Livelihood

The patterns of additional sources other than agriculture are as follows:

(i) Agriculture and allied activities which include cultivation on others' land and working as agriculture labour for various agricultural activities

(ii) Non-agriculture and allied activities which include working as a labour in industry, mines, quarry, construction, road, etc.; working as employees with several private companies and also working as government employees under different departments and working as a teacher, *gram-mitra*, bank employee, etc.

(iii) Artisan and miscellaneous skills which include mason, carpenter, black-smith, diamond cutter and diamond polishing, carpet maker etc. Miscellaneous activities include working in sugar cutting and sugar factory.

Tribals have now moved away from natal locations to elsewhere for additional sources of livelihood in greater numbers than they did five to ten years ago. Table 7.9 shows the real image of additional sources of livelihood as a whole for the current period and the period five to ten years ago.

Table 7.9: Supplementary Sources of Livelihood

(In Percentage)

Zones	*Zones*				
	I	*II*	*III*	*IV*	*V*
Before*	20	23	19	22	25
Now**	41	49	49	42	47

Note: * Before means in the year 1999 (10 years ago).
** Now means in the year 2009.

In Zone III, responses for supplementary sources of livelihood show an increase from 19 per cent (five to ten years ago) to 49 per cent. Zone III reflects the situation of other zones.

Table 7.10: Supplementary Sources of Livelihood for Tribals

(In Percentage)

Zones	*Before**	*Now***	*Before**	*Now***	*Before**	*Now***
	Agriculture and Allied		*Non-Agriculture and Allied*		*Artisan and Miscellaneous*	
I	29	23	69	69	1	6
II	31	34	59	44	7	24
III	21	33	71	53	4	12
IV	27	27	65	61	8	13
V	18	21	43	36	41	46

Note: * Before means in the year 1999 (10 years ago).
** Now means in the year 2009.

Respondents from Zone I have decreased their dependence on agriculture and allied (from 29% five to ten years ago to 23% now) and moved for artisan related sources (from 01% five to ten years ago to 06% now). Even among non-agriculture and allied sources of income, the trend shows a different picture. Previously, 69 per cent of the total respondents worked as non-agricultural labour but now this trend has decreased to 62 per cent and the rest 07 per cent moved from non-agricultural labour to government and private jobs.

Respondents from Zone II moved from agricultural labour to cultivation under our study of agriculture and allied sources of income. Decrease in agricultural labour showed that the trend is to a cultivated land owned by others on a sharing basis. Many a times, owners of the land do not cultivate the land, but give their agricultural land for cultivation to the tribals on the crop sharing basis. The tribals who cultivate the land of others need to give half the share of the crops. All the cost is shared by both, the original owner of land and the tribal who cultivate on the land of the owner. Five to ten years ago the cultivators were a mere 09 per cent of the total respondents, but this has now increased to 14 per cent, this trend leads to decrease in agriculture labour from 22 per cent to 20 per cent. Because of these trends the agriculture and allied source of income show an increase from 31 per cent to 34 per cent in Table 7.10. In the area of non-agricultural and allied sources, Zone II shows a decreasing trend (from 59% to 44%). Here too, the real non-agriculture labourers have decreased from 58 per cent to 40 per cent. Almost 04 per cent have started working either as government or private employees which was never a trend in this

Table 7.11: Agriculture and Allied Supplementary Sources of Livelihood

(In Percentage)

Zones	*Before**	*Now***	*Before**	*Now***
	Cultivation on Others' Land		*Agricultural Labour*	
I	12	11	17	12
II	9	14	22	20
III	8	15	13	18
IV	16	12	11	15
V	13	15	5	6

Note: * Before means in the year 1999 (10 years ago).
** Now means in the year 2009.

zone. Respondents have said that there has been an increase of artisans from a mere 07 per cent to 24 per cent. It was also noticed that respondents from this Zone II prefer to work as masons and carpenters than work in any other artisan fields.

The overall agriculture and allied sources show an increasing trend; that is an increase from 21 per cent to 33 per cent in Zone III. Respondents from this zone have shown an increase as cultivators and also increase as agriculture labourers. Cultivators have increased from 08 per cent to 15 per cent while agricultural labourers have increased from 13 per cent to 18 per cent. Non-agriculture and allied sources of income have shown a decreasing trend from 71 per cent to 53 per cent in this zone. Non-agricultural labour has decreased from 66 per cent to 46 per cent among the total respondents in Zone III and respondents who are working for Government, and private companies have increased from 04 per cent to 08 per cent in this zone (see Table 7.11). Respondents from this zone have said that there is a threefold increase in artisan and miscellaneous sources (from 04% to 12%) as additional sources of income. Most of them have moved from non-agricultural labour to the category of artisans (see Table 7.12).

Table 7.12: Non-Agricultural Supplementary Sources of Livelihood

(In Percentage)

Zones	Before*	Now**	Before*	Now**	Before*	Now**
	Labour (Non-Agri.)		Govt. Job		Pvt. Job	
I	69	62	0	3	0	4
II	58	40	0	1	1	3
III	66	46	0	3	5	4
IV	63	51	0	4	2	6
V	38	30	1	1	4	5

Note: * Before means in the year 1999 (10 years ago).
** Now means in the year 2009.

Respondents from Zone IV show different trends. Among the agriculture and allied sources of income, cultivators have decreased from 16 per cent (five to ten years ago) to 12 per cent (as of now) and agriculture labourers have increased from 11 per cent (five to ten years ago) to 15 per cent (as of now). Respondents from this zone show that non-agricultural and allied sources of incomes have decreased from 65 per cent (five to ten years ago) to 61 per cent (as of now).

Among this category, non-agricultural labourers have decreased from 63 per cent to 51 per cent over a period of five to ten years as stated by the respondents of Zone IV. Respondents who are working for the Government and private companies have increased from 02 per cent to 10 per cent over a period of time in this zone. Artisans and those working in assorted sources to generate income have also increased from 08 per cent to 13 per cent in this zone. In this category, artisans have increased from 02 per cent to 08 per cent in this zone as per the statements received from the total respondents of Zone IV (see Table 7.13).

Respondents from Zone V show particular trends. Under our study of agriculture and allied sources of income, cultivators have increased from 18 per cent (five to ten years ago) to 21 per cent (as of now) and agricultural labourers have increased marginally from 05 per cent (five to ten years ago) to 06 per cent (as of now). Respondents from this zone have said that non-agricultural and allied sources decreased from 43 per cent (five to ten years ago) to 36 per cent (as of now). Among this category, non-agricultural labourers have decreased from 38 per cent to 30 per cent over a period of five to ten years as per the responses received from the total respondents of Zone V. Respondents who are working for the Government and private companies have increased marginally from 05 per cent to 06 per cent over a period of time in this zone. Miscellaneous sources also play an important role in the additional sources of livelihood for this zone. Many of the respondents of this zone are regular workers in sugarcane fields and work as sugarcane

Table 7.13: Artisan and other Supplementary Sources of Livelihood

(In Percentage)

Zones	Before*	Now**	Before*	Now**
	Artisans		Other Job	
I	1	3	0	3
II	4	22	0	2
III	3	5	1	7
IV	4	5	4	8
V	1	2	40	44

Note: * Before means in the year 1999 (10 years ago).
** Now means in the year 2009.

cutters and in sugar factories as workers. This segment has increased from 40 per cent to 44 per cent over a period of the last five to ten years in this zone.

II

Patterns of Literacy and Sources of Livelihood

Land Ownership vs. Literacy

With the data on patterns of land ownership and types of land-holders we had seen in the earlier section, one can verify the rate of literacy with the patterns of land ownership in this section. One can see if there is any impact in the pattern of land ownership where educated tribals are concerned in different zones. The Table 7.14 gives us a detailed overview about the patterns of land ownership and the rate of literacy among the respondents in different zones.

Table 7.14: Patterns of Land Ownership *vs.* Literary

(In Percentage)

Zones	*L**	*I***	*L**	*I***	*L**	*I***	*L**	*I***
	Owned Land		*Joint Family Land*		*Shared Land*		*Landless*	
I	40	60	60	40	0	0	70	30
II	28	72	34	66	67	33	62	38
III	59	41	67	33	67	33	79	21
IV	38	62	48	52	67	33	67	33
V	48	52	67	33	64	36	77	23

Note: *L = Literate **I = Illiterate.

There is an upward trend in the rate of literacy among landless tribals. In Zone II, tribals possessing their own land and land held under the 'joint family' have 28 per cent and 34 per cent literate respondents respectively while, among landless tribal respondents, the rate is 62 per cent. More or less the same scenario has been seen in all the zones. We have observed that tribals who hold their own land tend to be less educated or almost illiterate. In Zone I and Zone II the tribal subjects in our study who own their land have 60 per cent and 72 per cent of illiteracy while the same is not true in Zone III where the rate of illiteracy among the respondent tribals is 41 per cent. The trend in Zone IV and Zone V also shows that there are more illiterate tribals where they own the land. The rate of illiteracy in Zone IV and Zone V is 62 per cent and 52 per cent respectively.

If we compare the responses given by the landless tribals with those who own land and land held by the 'joint family', the trend shows a high degree of difference in literacy level. In Zone I, if one combines the responses from the tribals owning land and those tribals having joint family land, the rate of literacy is around 50 per cent while in the same zone, the rate of illiteracy among the landless tribals is down to 30 per cent. In Zone II, 69 per cent respondents are illiterate having either their own land or joint family land while the rate of illiteracy is 38 per cent among the landless tribals of the same zone. Thirty-seven per cent of the respondents are illiterate who either own land or hold joint family land, while 21 per cent of the landless tribals are illiterate in Zone III.

In Zone IV, if one combines the responses from the tribals owning land and having joint family land, the rate of literacy is at 57 per cent while in the same zone, the rate of illiteracy among the landless tribals is down to 33 per cent. In Zone V, 43 per cent of the respondents are illiterate either owning their land or holding joint family land, while the rate of illiteracy is 23 per cent among the landless tribals of the same zone.

Literacy Levels among Landless Tribals

The rate of literacy among the total family members of the landless respondents of all the zones shows that the rate of literacy is high in Zone III and the lowest in Zone II. Seventy-seven per cent of total family members of landless respondents from Zone III are literate while mere 56 per cent of total family members of landless respondents from Zone II are literate. Zone V also shows good rate of literacy among the total family members of landless respondent tribals. In this zone, the rate of literacy is 62 per cent. Literacy rate in Zone I and Zone IV is 69 per cent.

Comparison of the rate of literacy between the total family members of overall respondents and total family members of landless respondents reveals that the total family members of landless tribals are more literate than the total family members of other respondents. Table 7.15 shows the trend of literacy between the total family members of the overall respondents and the total family members of the landless respondents.

Table 7.15: Rate of Literacy among Total Family Members of Overall Respondents and Landless Respondents

(In Percentage)

Respondents	*Zones*				
	I	*II*	*III*	*IV*	*V*
Overall Respondents	65	52	71	63	67
Landless Respondents	69	56	77	69	63

Comparisons reveal that, in Zone III, the rate of literacy (71%) is highest among all the zones with regard to the total family members (of the overall respondents); this zone also stood at the highest with 77 per cent of literacy among the total family members of the landless tribals. The same trend holds true in Zone II where the rate of literacy (52%) is the lowest among all the zones for the total family members of the overall respondents, the rate of literacy is 56 per cent among the total family members of the landless tribals. The literacy rate among the landless tribals in Zone IV is 6 per cent high when compared to the overall respondents of the same zone. In Zone I, 4 per cent are more literate than the total family members of overall respondents. Only Zone V shows a different trend in the rate of literacy for the total family members of landless respondents. The rate of literacy among the total family members of landless tribals in Zone V is 5 per cent less than the total family members of the overall respondents.

The trend in the level of education shows increased education between 6 to 15 years of age among the family members of the landless respondents. If we combine the level of education of the first three categories, that is, classes 1 to 5, classes 6 to 7 and classes 8 to 10, we can clearly analyze the rate of education among the age group—6 to 15 years. In Zone III, the literacy rate is high. In this Zone, the rate of education among the age groups—6 to 15 years is 57 per cent (classes 1 to 5–28%, classes 6 to 7–13% and classes 8 to 10–16%). In Zone II, the rate of literacy is the least,

Table 7.16: Level of Education among Total Family Members of Landless Tribals

(In Percentage)

Zones	*Level of Education*						
	1 to 5	*6 to 7*	*8 to 10*	*11 to 12*	*More than 12*	*Children*	*Illiterate*
I	18	12	16	6	3	14	31
II	21	7	9	2	0	17	44
III	28	13	16	6	3	11	23
IV	27	11	15	5	2	9	31
V	27	9	9	3	3	11	38

and the rate of education among the age group—6 to 15 years is 37 per cent (classes 1 to 5–21%, classes 6 to 7–07% and classes 8 to 10-09%).

In Zone I, the rate of education among the age group—6 to 15 years is 46 per cent (classes 1 to 5–18%, classes 6 to 7–12% and classes 8 to 10–16%); while in Zone IV, the rate of education among the age-group—6 to 15 years is 53 per cent (classes 1 to 5–27%, classes 6 to 7–11% and classes 8 to 10–15%). In Zone V, the rate of education is 45 per cent (classes 1 to 5–27%, classes 6 to 7–09% and classes 8 to 10–09%) (See Table 7.16).

If one looks into college education, technical education or professional education where one can study after class 12 among the total family members of the landless respondents, the trend for this level of education is seen more in Zone III (03%), Zone I (03%) and Zone V (03%) if we compare with Zone IV (02%) and Zone II (00%).

A comparison of the level of education from class 1 to class 10 among the landless in Zone III is 57 per cent which is highest among all the zones. While the total family members of the overall respondents of Zone III is 51 per cent. The same trend holds true even in Zone II where the level of education from class 1 to class 10 (34%) is the lowest among all the zones for the total number of family members of the overall respondents, the rate of literacy for the level of education from class 1 to class 10 is 37 per cent among the total family members of the landless tribals (see Table 7.17).

The literacy rate among the total number of family members among the landless tribals in Zone IV is 9 per cent higher when compared to the overall number of respondents in the same zone.

Table 7.17: Level of Education between Class 1 to Class 10 among Total Family Members of Overall Respondents and Landless Respondents

(In Percentage)

Respondents	*Zones*				
	I	*II*	*III*	*IV*	*V*
Overall Respondents	43	34	51	44	48
Landless Respondents	46	37	57	56	45

In Zone I, 3 per cent are more literate (for the level of education from class 1 to class 10) than total family members of overall respondents. Only Zone V shows a different trend in the rate of literacy for the level of education combining with class 1 to class 10 for the total family members of landless respondents. The rate of literacy for the level of education from class 1 to class 10 among total family members of landless tribals of Zone V is 3 per cent less than the total family members of overall respondents. If we look at the overall situation, it appears that the level of education is more among the landless as they have no other option to make livelihood sources. But still many of the landless tribals are migrating either for seasonal or livelihood as they have no land for their livelihood. That may be one of the reasons for low enrolment and high rate of school drop outs among their children.

III

Status of Landless Tribals in Changing Patterns of Livelihood

We studied landless tribals in different zones of our Study. Zone III seems to have the maximum number of landless tribals (29%) followed by Zone V (14%) and Zone IV (13%). Zone I (07%) and Zone II (06%) seem to have the least number of landless tribals.

Cultivation on Forest Land by Landless Tribals

We have observed and noted that though the landless tribals have no land either in their own possession or their possession as a joint family they are cultivating forest land on a large scale.

Table 7.18: Cultivation on Forest Land by Landless Respondents

(In Percentage)

Zones	*Size of Forest Land Cultivated*			
	Marginal	*Small*	*Medium*	*Big*
I	18	0	0	0
II	7	23	9	3
III	34	12	4	0
IV	41	15	5	0
V	10	10	30	0

Cultivation of forest land by the landless tribals is reflected in Table 7.18.

Forty-one per cent of the total landless respondents in Zone IV cultivate marginal sized forest land (it means they cultivate less than 2.5 acres of the forest land) while only 07 per cent of the total respondents in Zone II cultivate the same size of forest land. Twenty-three per cent of the total landless respondents of Zone II cultivate small sized forest land (this means cultivating forest land between 2.51 acres and 5.00 acres), while no respondents from Zone I cultivate the same size of forest land. In Zone V, 30 per cent of the total respondents cultivate medium sized forest land (this means cultivating forest land between 5.01 acres to 10.00 acres). While no respondents from Zone, I cultivate the same size of forest land. Three per cent of the total landless respondents from Zone II are the only people among all the Zones who cultivate big sized forest land (this means cultivating forest land more than 10.01 acres).

Table 7.19: Cultivation on Forest Land among Overall Respondents *vs.* Landless Respondents

(In Percentage)

Zones	*Size of Forest Land Cultivated by*							
	Overall	*Landless*	*Overall*	*Landless*	*Overall*	*Landless*	*Overall*	*Landless*
	Marginal		*Small*		*Medium*		*Big*	
I	19	18	10	0	2	0	1	0
II	15	7	16	23	4	9	2	3
III	18	34	14	12	11	4	2	0
IV	27	41	13	15	2	5	1	0
V	5	10	5	10	8	30	2	0

When one compares the total number of landless respondents with the overall total number of respondents, one can say that the landless respondents are not actually landless, but many of them cultivate on forest land. The Table 7.19 shows the overall comparison of cultivation on forest lands among the overall respondents and the landless respondents.

If one compares the marginal size of cultivation on forest lands in Zone III, Zone IV and Zone V, landless respondents cultivate more forest land. In Zone III, 18 per cent of total respondents cultivate marginal size of forest lands while 34 per cent of the landless respondents cultivate on the same size of forest land. In Zone IV, 27 per cent of the total respondents cultivate marginal sized forest lands while 41 per cent of landless respondents cultivate on the same size of forest land. In Zone V, 05 per cent of the total respondents cultivate marginal sized forest land while 10 per cent of the landless respondents cultivate on the same size of forest land.

Even if one compares the cultivation on small sized forest land in Zone II, Zone IV and Zone V, the landless respondents cultivate more than what the overall respondents cultivate small sized forest land. In Zone II, there are 16 per cent of the total respondents who cultivate on small sized forest land while 23 per cent of the landless respondents cultivate on the same size of forest land. In Zone IV, there are 13 per cent of total respondents who cultivate on small sized forest land while 15 per cent of the landless respondents cultivate on the same size of forest land. In Zone V, 05 per cent of the total respondents cultivate small sized forest land while 10 per cent of the landless respondents cultivate on the same size of forest land.

An analysis of cultivation on medium sized forest lands shows that landless respondents cultivate more than the overall respondents in Zone II, Zone IV and Zone V. In Zone II, 04 per cent of total respondents cultivate medium sized forest land, while 09 per cent of the landless respondents cultivate on the same size of forest land. In Zone IV, 02 per cent of total respondents cultivate on medium sized forest land, while 05 per cent of the landless respondents cultivate on the same size of forest land. In Zone V, 08 per cent of the total respondents cultivate on medium sized forest land while 30 per cent of landless respondents cultivate on the same size of forest land.

Live-Stock Holding by Landless Tribals

Holding of live-stocks particularly cows and buffaloes play an important role in providing additional sources of livelihood for landless respondents. In our study area on average nearly 46 per cent of the total landless respondents have one or more cows and 45 per cent of the total landless respondents possess buffaloes, one or more in numbers. More and more landless tribal families are now trying to hold milk-bearing cattle as their main source of livelihood. Table 7.20 shows the percentage of cows and buffaloes that the landless tribal respondents have in the different zones. Landless respondents from Zone II hold the highest number of buffaloes i.e. 50 per cent while Zone V has the lowest i.e. 38 per cent. Regarding the possession of cows among landless respondents, Zone IV stood at the top with 54 per cent and Zone V stood at the bottom with 36 per cent.

Table 7.20: Live-Stock Holding by Landless Respondents

(In Percentage)

Zones	*Cows*	*Buffaloes*	*Bullocks*	*Goat/Sheep*	*Hen*
I	49	45	49	58	24
II	47	50	58	36	33
III	43	48	53	23	31
IV	54	44	46	20	33
V	36	38	48	17	48

It appears that the landless respondents possess bullocks to either to cultivate on encroached forest land or to lease them out. Except Zone IV where 46 per cent of the total landless respondents have bullocks, all other zones have a good number of bullocks available for their farming activities. Zone II had the highest with 58 per cent of the total landless respondents possessing bullocks. Out of total landless respondents from the Zone I, Zone III and Zone V, 49 per cent, 53 per cent and 48 per cent respectively have bullocks for agriculture and other allied activities.

If one compares the total landless respondents with the overall total respondents, one can say that the landless respondents are not far behind in the holding of livestock. Table 7.21 gives a comparison on the holding of livestock among the overall respondents and the landless respondents. On average 48 per cent of the overall respondents and 46 per cent of the total landless respondents possesses, a cow, while 50 per cent of overall respondents and 45 per cent of total landless respondents own a buffaloe. However, 64 per cent of the overall respondents have bullocks while the landless respondents have only 51 per cent of bullocks, which could be because they do not own any land.

Table 7.21: Live-Stock Holding by Overall Respondents *vs.* Landless Respondents

(In Percentage)

Zones	O*	L**	O*	L**	O*	L**	O*	L**	O*	L**
	Cows		Buffaloes		Bullocks		Goat/Sheep		Hen	
I	51	49	42	45	67	49	36	58	35	24
II	46	47	55	50	72	58	49	36	40	33
III	48	43	52	48	65	53	14	23	37	31
IV	54	54	53	44	61	46	15	20	39	33
V	41	36	48	38	52	48	9	17	47	48

Note: * O = Overall Respondents ** L = Landless Respondents.

In some areas under our study, limited quantities of a home-made mix (of damaged grains and pulses) and compound feeds are offered to the livestock. In general, however, the quantity and quality of available feed resources are inadequate to meet the animal feed requirements. Some of the landless tribal respondents depend on forests for fodder.

Table 7.22 represents the dependency of the respondents and the landless respondents on forests for fodder. If we compare the total landless respondents with the overall total number of respondents, we can say that landless respondents (37%—five to ten years before and 34%—at present) in Zone II are more dependent on forests for fodder than the overall number of respondents (18%—five to ten years before and 17%—at present) of the same zone. This study reflects the dependency of the landless respondents in Zone II. The same is the case for dependency on the forest for fodder for the landless respondents in Zone IV where these landless respondents (43%—Five to ten years before and 50%—Now) are more dependent on forests for fodder than the overall Respondent (34%—five to ten years before and 36%—at present).

The situation in Zones III and IV is not very different from Zone II and Zone IV; but in Zone I, the dependency on forests for fodder is less among the landless respondents. The total number of landless respondents (12%—five to ten years before and 16%—at present) is less dependent on forest for fodder than the overall number of respondents (22%—five to ten years before and 20%—at present) in Zone I.

Table 7.22: Dependency on Forest for Fodder for Overall Respondents *vs*. Landless Respondents

(In Percentage)

Zones	*Overall Respondents*	*Landless Respondents*	*Overall Respondents*	*Landless Respondents*
	*Before**		*Now***	
I	22	12	20	16
II	18	37	17	34
III	30	29	33	33
IV	34	43	36	50
V	19	20	24	20

Note: * Before means in the year 1999 (10 years ago).
** Now means in the year 2009.

Income Generating Trees with Landless Tribals

Most of the landless tribals possess trees in the forest areas "under their family name" as a livelihood asset. Fruit trees like mango, custard apple, etc.; *mahuda, tendu patta, saal* and teak are some of the trees that the landless tribals hold in the forest areas for generations and from which they generate income by collecting and gathering fruits and produces.

Table 7.23 shows the possession of income generating trees among the overall respondents and landless respondents. Landless respondents from Zone I and Zone II who have income generating trees are not far behind the overall number of respondents. In Zone, I, the landless respondents have 38 per cent of these income generating trees, while the overall number of respondents have

41 per cent of income generating trees and in Zone II the same is the case with 59 per cent and 64 per cent respectively. But the scenario in Zone III, Zone IV and Zone V are different from that of Zone I and Zone II. Landless respondents have very less number of income generating trees than the overall number of respondents. Landless respondents in Zone III have 22 per cent of income generating trees against 43 per cent of the trees possessed by the overall respondents. In Zone IV the landless respondents have 35 per cent of income generating trees, while the overall numbers of respondents have much more, that is, 64 per cent of income generating trees and in Zone V the same is the case with 24 per cent and 35 per cent respectively.

Table 7.23: Possession of Income Generating Trees among Overall Respondents *vs.* Landless Respondents

(In Percentage)

Respondents	*Zones*				
	I	*II*	*III*	*IV*	*V*
Overall Respondents	41	64	43	64	35
Landless Respondents	38	59	22	35	24

Minor Forest Produces (MFP) as Supplementary Source of Income for Landless Tribals

Minor Forest Produce is generally used by landless tribals, either for home usage (fodder, fuel, fish and other minor products) or for generating additional sources of income. These landless tribals gather and collect honey, bamboo, gum, *timru patta,* fruits, *mahuda,* etc. and sell them in the market to generate income. They also collect *dodi,* bamboo, fodder and fuel for their home usage. Hence, we could also consider MFP as a measure of the livelihood status among the landless tribals.

Forty-two per cent of the total numbers of respondents from Zone II get additional income from MFP, and this was 33 per cent five to ten years ago among the overall respondents, while among the landless respondents the share remains static i.e. at 38 per cent in the same zone. The overall number of respondents, including the landless respondents from Zone III and Zone IV showed a decreased dependency on MFP than was the case five to ten years.

Table 7.24: Dependency on MFP as Source of Income among Overall Respondents *vs.* Landless Respondents

(In Percentage)

Zones	Before*	Now**	Before*	Now**
	Overall Respondents		Landless Respondents	
I	15	19	8	34
II	33	42	38	38
III	26	21	19	18
IV	33	30	55	48
V	22	26	32	41

Note: * Before means in the year 1999 (10 years ago).
** Now means in the year 2009.

It was 26 per cent and 33 per cent respectively for Zone III and Zone IV previously and now the same decreased to 21 per cent and 30 per cent respectively among the overall number of respondents; the same trend could be seen among the landless respondents also, that is, it decreased from 19 per cent to 18 per cent and from 55 per cent to 48 per cent respectively in Zone III and Zone IV. The overall number of respondents from Zone I was the least dependent on MFP when we compare all the other zones. Only 19 per cent of the overall respondents from Zone I get any additional income from MFP and the same was 15 per cent, five to ten years ago. But the situation is exactly the reverse among the landless respondents. Landless respondents from Zone I who get additional supplementary income from MFP have increased from 8 per cent five to ten years ago to 34 per cent now. Respondents from Zone V have MFP as a considerable source of additional income for their livelihood. 26 per cent of the overall respondents and 41 per cent of the landless respondents from Zone V use MFP as a supplementary source of income for their livelihood in recent times (see Table 7.24).

Other Supplementary Sources of Livelihood for Landless Tribals

The pattern of additional sources other than the cultivation on forest land for the livelihood of landless tribals shows different activities to generate income other than agriculture and forests such as: (i) agriculture and allied sources, (ii) non-agriculture and allied sources, and (iii) artisan and other jobs.

Table 7.25: Supplementary Sources of Livelihood among Overall Respondents *vs.* Landless Respondents

(In Percentage)

Zones	Overall Respondents	Landless Respondents	Overall Respondents	Landless Respondents	Overall Respondents	Landless Respondents
	Agriculture and Allied		Non Agriculture and Allied		Artisans and Misc.	
I	23	50	69	89	6	6
II	34	55	44	72	24	13
III	33	29	53	72	12	14
IV	27	27	61	74	13	17
V	21	26	36	35	46	63

Landless respondents (50%) are more dependent on agriculture and allied sources of income than the overall number of respondents (23%) in Zone I. Even among non-agriculture and allied sources the trend seems the same. 69 per cent of the overall respondents worked as non-agricultural labour, but 89 per cent of the landless respondents worked as non-agricultural labourers (see Table 7.25). In Zone I, landless respondents do not cultivate on others' lands while 11 per cent of the overall respondents cultivate on others' lands. Agricultural labourers are also four times more among the landless respondents (50%) than the overall respondents (12%) in Zone I. Landless respondents (10%) are involved in more Government jobs than the overall number of respondents (03%) in this zone. The same is the case with the artisans. Among the landless respondents, 6 per cent are artisans while, among the overall number of respondents, the artisans are only 3 per cent. The overall number of respondents is involved in other jobs (03%) while landless respondents do not have any other job at all in Zone I.

In Zone II the landless respondents (55%) are more dependent on agriculture and allied livelihood sources of income than the overall respondents (34%). Even among non-agriculture and allied sources, the trend shows the same picture. Forty-four per cent of the overall respondents worked as non-agricultural labour, but 72 per cent of the landless respondents worked as non-agricultural labourers. In Zone II, 15 per cent of the landless respondents cultivated others' lands while 14 per cent from the overall number of respondents cultivated on others' lands. Agricultural labourers are also twice the number among landless respondents (40%) than the overall number of respondents (20%) in this zone. Non-agricultural labourers are 61 per cent among the landless respondents against 40 per cent found among the overall respondents. Landless respondents (11%) are occupied in more private jobs than the overall number of respondents (03%) in this zone. Among the landless respondents, 13 per cent are artisans while, among the overall number of respondents, the artisans are 22 per cent. The overall numbers of respondents are involved in other jobs (02%) while landless respondents do not have any other jobs in Zone II.

Table 7.26: Agriculture and Allied Supplementary Sources of Income among Overall Respondents *vs.* Landless Respondents

(In Percentage)

Zones	*Overall Respondents*	*Landless Respondents*	*Overall Respondents*	*Landless Respondents*
I	11	00	12	50
II	14	15	20	40
III	15	05	18	24
IV	12	11	15	16
V	15	05	06	21

In Zone III; landless respondents (29%) are less dependent on agriculture and allied sources of livelihood than the overall number of respondents (33%). Among non-agricultural and allied sources, the trend shows the reverse picture. Fifty-three per cent of the overall respondents worked as non-agricultural labour, but 72 per cent of the landless respondents worked as non-agricultural labourers. In Zone III, only 05 per cent of the landless respondents cultivated on others' lands while 15 per cent of the overall number of respondents cultivated on others' land. Agriculture labourers are also more among landless respondents (24%) than among the overall number of respondents (18%) in this zone. Non-agricultural labourers are 62 per cent among the landless respondents against 46 per cent among the overall respondents. Landless respondents (10%) are involved in more private jobs than the overall number of respondents (04%) in this zone. Among the landless respondents, 07 per cent are artisans while, among the overall number of respondents, the artisans are 05 per cent. Seven per

Table 7.27: Non-Agriculture and Allied Supplementary Sources of Income among Overall Respondents *vs.* Landless Respondents

(In Percentage)

Zones	Overall Respondents	Landless Respondents	Overall Respondents	Landless Respondents	Overall Respondents	Landless Respondents
	Non-Agricultural Labourers		Government Job		Private Job	
I	62	79	03	10	04	00
II	40	61	01	00	03	11
III	46	62	03	05	04	10
IV	51	68	04	05	06	06
V	30	28	01	00	05	07

Table 7.28: Artisan and Other Supplementary Sources of Livelihood among Overall Respondents *vs.* Landless Respondents

(In Percentage)

Zones	Overall Respondents	Landless Respondents	Overall Respondents	Landless Respondents
	Artisans		Other Jobs	
I	03	06	03	00
II	22	13	02	00
III	05	07	07	07
IV	05	02	08	08
V	02	00	44	44

cent of the overall number of respondents and the landless respondents are involved in other jobs, in Zone III.

Twenty-seven per cent of the overall number of respondents and landless respondents are equally dependent on agriculture and allied jobs in Zone IV. Sixty-one per cent of the overall respondents worked as non-agricultural labour, but 74 per cent of the landless respondents worked as non-agricultural labourers. In Zone IV, 11 per cent landless respondents cultivated others' land while 12 per cent of overall respondents cultivated others' lands. Agriculture labourers are also slightly more among the landless respondents (16%) than among the overall number of respondents (15%) in this zone. Non-agricultural labourers are 68 per cent among the landless respondents against 51 per cent among the overall number of respondents. Among the landless respondents, 02 per cent are artisans while, among the overall number of respondents, the artisans are 05 per cent.

In Zone IV, landless respondents (26%) are more dependent on agriculture and allied sources of livelihood than among the overall number of respondents (21%). Among the non- agricultural and allied sources, the trend shows a slightly reversed depiction. Thirty-six per cent of the overall respondents worked as non-agricultural labour, but 35 per cent of the landless respondents worked as non-agriculture labourers. In Zone IV, mere 05 per cent landless respondents cultivated others' lands while 15 per cent of the overall number of respondents cultivated others' lands. Agricultural labourers are also more among the landless respondents (21%) than among the overall number of respondents (06%) in this zone. Non-agricultural labourers are 28 per cent among the landless respondents against 30 per cent among the overall number of respondents. Landless respondents (07%) generally engage in private jobs than the overall number of respondents (05%) in this zone. Forty-four per cent of the overall number of respondents and landless respondents are involved in other jobs, in Zone IV (see Tables 7.26, 7.27 and 7.28).

IV

Changes in Forest Cover and Tribal Livelihood: Some Emerging Trends

To get more focused observations on tribal livelihood, this chapter analyzes 53 villages (nearly 30% of the total study area), using three variables (20 villages where forest cover decreased, 13 villages where forest cover increased and 20 villages where forest cover remained unchanged).

Table 7.29 shows the land ownership distribution among the respondents of Zone II keeping the changes in forest cover as variable. Respondents from decreased forest cover areas (60%) own more land than the respondents from increased forest areas (58%) and unchanged forest areas (57%). One can observe that more land held jointly by the family in the areas where forest cover has been improved (37%). In unchanged forest cover areas landless tribal

Table 7.29: Distribution of Land Ownership among Tribals (As per Changes in Forest Cover)

(In Percentage)

Land Distribution Pattern	*Change in Forest Cover (1971-2007)*			*Total*
	Decreased	*Increased*	*Unchanged*	
Own Land	60	58	57	58
Joint Family Land	35	37	35	36
Shared Land	00	00	00	00
Landless	05	05	08	06
No Response	00	00	00	00
Total	100	100	100	100

respondents are more as compared to increased or decreased forest cover areas.

Table 7.30: Types of Tribal Farmers according to Changes in Forest Cover

(In Percentage)

Types of Tribal Farmers	*Change in Forest Cover (1971-2007)*			*Total*
	Decreased	*Increased*	*Unchanged*	
Landless Farmers	15	02	02	06
Marginal Farmers	32	39	44	38
Small Farmers	27	28	30	28
Medium Farmers	14	14	06	11
Big Farmers	03	03	01	02
Don't Want to Say*	09	14	17	15
Total	100	100	100	100

Note: * Respondents are apprehensive in replying this question.

For this table, landless means those who have no land at all, marginal farmers means those who have less than 2.5 acres of land, small farmers mean those who have land between 2.51 acres and 5.00 acres, medium farmers mean those who have land between 5.01 acres to 10.00 acres and big farmers means those who have land more than 10.01 acres.

Table 7.30 provides an overview about the types of tribal land-holders given changes in forest cover. Fifteen per cent are landless farmers in the decreased forest cover areas, in the Zone II while the same are just 02 per cent in the increased and unchanged forest cover areas. One can say that where the forest cover has decreased, the tribals might have to sell their land to maintain their livelihood or need to mortgage their land to the money-lenders. Money-lenders also include the wealthy tribals. In a surprising trend, 14 per cent are medium farmers in the areas where forest cover either increased or decreased. The same is just 06 per cent in the areas where the forest cover remained unchanged. This trend needs to be further investigated.

Table 7.31 provides an overview about the cultivation on forest lands among the respondents.

Table 7.31: Types of Tribal Farmers who Cultivate on Forest Land According to Changes in Forest Cover

(In Percentage)

Types of Tribal Farmers	*Change in Forest Cover (1971-2007)*			*Total*
	Decreased	*Increased*	*Unchanged*	
Marginal Farmers	18	16	12	15
Small Farmers	19	18	12	16
Medium Farmers	05	07	02	04
Big Farmers	01	03	02	02
Don't Want to Say*	57	56	72	63
Total	100	100	100	100

Note: * Respondents are apprehensive in replying to this question.

Majority of the respondents have not responded to question on the cultivation of forest land as they are apprehensive of retaliatory actions from the Forest Department. The trend is high (72%) in the areas where the forest cover remained unchanged. Medium farmers who are cultivating on forest land are more in increased forest cover areas (07%) while the same is just 02% in the unchanged forest cover areas. Surprisingly, there are large farmers who are cultivating on forest land in the areas where the forest cover has increased. This trend needs to be further investigated.

Table 7.32 gives an overview about the live-stock holding among the respondents. Except in the unchanged forest cover areas where only 55 per cent of the total respondents have bullocks, other two areas where either forest cover increased (79%) or decreased (83%) have a good number of bullocks available for their

Table 7.32: Live-stock Wealth according to Changes in Forest Cover

(In Percentage)

Live-stock Wealth	*Change in Forest Cover (1971-2007)*			*Total*
	Decreased	*Increased*	*Unchanged*	
Cow	48	39	52	46
Buffalo	49	55	62	55
Bullock	83	79	55	72
Goat/Sheep	48	52	48	49
Hens	33	34	52	40

farming activities. The possession of cows and buffaloes plays an important role in providing additional sources of livelihood for tribal communities. Cows and buffaloes (52% and 62% respectively) are more in the unchanged areas while buffaloes (55%) are more than cows (39%) in the areas where forest cover has increased. This trend shows that more and more tribal families are now keen on acquiring milk-bearing cattle as an additional source of livelihood.

Table 7.33 shows tribal respondents from the unchanged forest areas are having more facilities like wells (51%) and bore-wells (45%) than in the decreased forest cover areas (36% and 15% respectively).

Table 7.33: Facilities of Wells and Bore-wells according to Changes in Forest Cover

(In Percentage)

Time Period	*Change in Forest Cover (1971-2007)*			*Total*
	Decreased	*Increased*	*Unchanged*	
Well	36	46	51	44
Bore-well	15	28	45	29

The presence of bore-well suggests good income among the tribal respondents. However, the installation of bore-wells needs money. And the presence of bore-wells in the unchanged areas show that the respondents earn a good amount of income, either from agriculture or from dairy farming or some other sources from which they are investing in wells and bore-wells. A mere 15 per cent of the respondents from the decreasing forest cover areas have such facilities like bore-wells, this shows that there are a lesser number of tribals who have enough alternative sources of income to create different facilities like well and bore-well.

If one looks at the possession of income generating trees among the respondents in the Zone II with changes in forest cover, one can say that the respondents from unchanged forest cover areas (74%) have the highest number of income generating trees. Sixty-six per cent of the respondents from the increased forest cover areas have possessed income generating trees. Respondents from decrease forest cover areas (53%) have the least numbers of income generating trees like *mahuda* trees, gum trees, bamboo and other fruit trees. Respondents from Zone I have *mahuda, timru* and bamboo while respondents from Zone II have *mahuda, charoli,* custard apple and gum trees as income generating trees. Respondents from Zone III have *mahuda* and bamboo while the respondents from Zone IV and Zone V have *mahuda,* bamboo, gum and *timru* as income generating trees. The respondents collect the produces from these trees and create additional sources of income for their livelihood. In many of the tribal families, income from the trees is a major aspect of their livelihood. Mostly tribal women collect *mahuda* flowers, *dodi* and *timru* leaves from the trees, and they either sell them in the nearby market or to the depot of Gujarat Forest Development Corporation.

To summarize, one can say that tribals have started shifting their livelihood from the traditional hunting, fishing and shifting cultivation to the dairy farming and settled agriculture. Respondents from the unchanged forest areas have the highest number of cows (52%), and buffaloes (62%) also have the highest number of wells (51%) and bore-wells (45%). This suggests that the tribals with more live-stock get extra income, and they invest this income in the building of wells and bore-wells. Tribals from unchanged areas have also turned their attention to have additional income generating trees. The data suggests that 74 per cent of the respondents from the unchanged forest areas have said that they have income generating trees which give them extra income for their livelihood. Respondents from the regenerated or increased forest areas are also involving themselves in dairy farming and income generating trees (66%) to generate supplementary sources of livelihood.

V

Concluding Observations

One of the main advantages of thinking in terms of the changing patterns of livelihood is that it has directed our analysis away from narrow parameters of production, employment and income towards a much more holistic view which embraces social and economic dimensions. This approach stresses the importance of reducing vulnerability and enhancing environmental sustainability and building on local strengths and priorities. It recognizes that tribals are active agents of change and pursue a range of livelihood strategies. These changing patterns draw on different resources and different cultural repertoires. The ability to access different combinations of resources helps determine how vulnerable or robust a particular livelihood may be.

In contrast to the view of modernization and on change and development, the analysis on the changing patterns of livelihood in the previous sections takes note of diversity rather seriously. Various diverse practices are encountered and observed while analysing the inquiry on different activities of tribal communities. This diversity could be interpreted in different ways. For many it deals with and reflects the fact that tribals devise a variety of strategies to make ends meet. These strategies are increasingly built upon diversification and include and combine different economic sectors and places. The changing patterns of livelihood analysis capture this diversity and encourage practical strategies that build upon this.

The analysis on the changing patterns of livelihood has also helped to re-examine certain processes (Chambers, R., 1983). For instance, tribal migration has for a long time been perceived as negatively affecting rural and agricultural development. This focus on livelihood has actually opened our eyes to some of the more positive effects of migration on tribal poverty as well as on production and consumption.

The conditions that affect a tribal's livelihood are the mediating structures and processes, the shocks, trends and the seasonality, which are dynamic and change continually. Thinking in terms of livelihood sources allows a dynamic view of how social change proceeds. This provides a meaningful contribution to social analysis and promotes a debate on how things should change. Moving beyond structuralist interpretations of social change enables a more sophisticated understanding of how livelihood is affected by trends and changes over time and of changing opportunities and constraints for livelihood activities. Armed with the notion of agency, we have learnt that these mediating and structuring processes are subject to negotiation and political struggles and therefore are not immutable but can be changed.

The livelihood perspective for tribals is perceived as a useful role in the process of change, as it is tribal centered and takes the problems of tribal, and particularly the poorest, as a starting point for analysis and development planning. As mentioned by other writers, a livelihood framework 'puts tribal first' (Chambers, R., 1983). An important focus over here is on what kind of Government policies are needed to assist local tribal and less on the policies *per se*. The approach, therefore, enables a critical analysis of questions like the impact of building new roads, or the impact of higher education on career opportunities and its impact on different members in households and among tribal communities. Capability is interpreted as the human capacity to cope with shocks and stresses as well as the ability to recognize better, and act upon, different livelihood opportunities. Capability also refers to the way in which tribals use resources and negotiate accesses to them. The present study engages in an understanding of these conflicting tendencies among the tribals.

8
Findings of the Study

This chapter is devoted to the discussion on the summary of the findings of the whole study. The first section deals with the changing behaviour of forests and tribals in five zones. The second section constitutes the findings of the changes in the tribal livelihood patterns based on the primary data. Section three deals with the changing behavioural patterns of tribals. It also includes an analysis of the socio-cultural changes.

I

Changing Behaviour of Forests and Tribals in Study Area

The main observations from all the five zones of the study are as follows:

1. An overview from the forest change detection maps generated at zonal level from the satellite imageries showed that forest cover has significantly reduced at many places but in a few new areas it has increased since 1972. Table 8.1 shows the zonal percentage change in forest cover of the study area for the period between the year 1972 and 2007. Considering, the five categories of change in the forest cover, it can be seen that almost 22 per cent of the forest cover has an increasing, 41 per cent of reducing trend while another 37 per cent has remained unchanged. Out of total five zones, Zone II has shown almost 68 per cent of highly decreased to slightly decreased in the forest

cover, while Zone III has shown a 19 per cent decrease (highly decreased to slightly decreased) in forest cover. With almost 35 per cent increase, Zone I and II have shown a positive trend from slightly increased to highly increased forest cover.

Table 8.1: Zonal Percentage Change in Forest Area for the Years between 1972 and 2007

(In Percentage)

Categories of Change in Forest Area	*Zonal Percentage of Change*					*Change in Total Study Area*
	Zone I	*Zone II*	*Zone III*	*Zone IV*	*Zone V*	
Highly Decreased	06.57	18.51	05.94	06.63	04.19	10.65
Slightly Decreased	25.43	49.51	12.50	20.07	18.46	30.80
Unchanged	33.88	17.58	46.77	56.62	70.56	37.13
Slightly Increased	19.85	09.24	22.10	11.70	06.12	13.58
Highly Increased	14.27	05.16	12.69	04.98	00.67	07.84

Nearly 71 per cent and 57 per cent forest cover remain unchanged in Zone V and Zone IV respectively. If we look at the highly decreased category of forest cover in our total study area, Zone II has topped with 18.51 per cent followed by Zone IV with 6.63 per cent and Zone I with 6.57 per cent. Trends in slightly decreased forest cover category show that Zone II is leading among all the five zones with 49.51 per cent followed by Zone I with 25.43 per cent and Zone IV with 20.07 per cent. Among the slightly increased forest cover category, Zone III led the table among all the five zones with 22.10 per cent. Zone I also shows a slight increase in forest cover of 19.85 per cent. In the category of highly increased forest cover, Zone I led all the five zones with 14.27 per cent followed by Zone III with 12.69 per cent.

2. There has been a general perception that, on account of degradation of forests, there is a large scale migration of tribal populations. For this reason, we mapped the Census 1971 and Census 2001 data on village-wise tribal people of our study area.

   Table 8.2 shows the migration of tribal people in five zones. Zone II has the maximum migration from the tribal people

Table 8.2: Migration of Tribal Population for the Period between 1971 and 2001 in Study Area

(In Percentage)

Zones	*Percentage Shift in Tribal Population*
I	11.78
II	43.48
III	25.61
IV	16.87
V	02.26

(43.48%) over the period of thirty years, and Zone V has the minimum (2.26%). In Zone, I there does not seem to be a lot migration (11.78%) compared to Zone II, Zone III and Zone IV. Zone IV reflects considerable tribals migration (24.39%) over three decades. We analyzed the migration of tribal people with the changing character of forests in the State from 1972 to 2007; it was observed that the change in forest cover was not the only reason for this migration.

Our observations are that there are not many associations between changes in forest cover and migration of tribal communities in Gujarat. Despite an increase in forest cover, that is regeneration of forest covers, migration of tribals for livelihood purposes is a phenomenon that cuts across the five zones. Table 8.3 gives a clear picture of the zonal migration in tribal people between the years 1971 and 2001 with respect to change in forest cover.

Table 8.3: Zonal Migration in Tribal Population between the Years 1971 and 2001 with Respect to Change in Forest Cover

Zones/Shift in Tribal Population	*Forest Change 1972 to 2007*				
	Decreased	*Unchanged*	*Increased*	*Others*	*Grand Total*
Zone I	01.49	06.04	01.50	02.75	11.78
Zone II	16.74	14.25	04.93	07.56	43.48
Zone III	00.87	08.22	05.99	10.53	25.61
Zone IV	01.11	06.92	03.99	04.85	16.87
Zone V	00.00	02.26	00.00	00.00	02.26
Grand Total	20.21	37.69	16.41	25.69	100.00

20.21 per cent migration has been recorded in areas where there is a decrease in forest cover. The percentage of migration is 16.41 per cent in the areas where there is an increase in the forest cover. Even where there is no change in forest cover, 37.69 per cent migration in tribal population has been observed. Thus, migratory patterns are now not based on dependency on forests among tribal communities. Even where there is no change in the forest cover, migration seems to have doubled (37.69%) than in areas where forest cover has increased (16.41%) or decreased (20.21%). From this pattern, one may say that, in recent times, the tribals are not only dependent on forests or forest products. They are going for alternative sources of livelihood such as dairy farming, horticulture, agriculture besides opting for modern techniques in agriculture.

3. Increase in population among the tribal communities (which is always more than the general population growth rate) has also had an impact on tribal migration. Table 8.4 shows the decadal growth rate of tribal people in the State of Gujarat. Increase in population since the last four decades has created pressure on forests for additional food and the survival of families. Migration of some of the family members is also seen across the study area as small land holdings or insufficient forest produce does not support the survival of entire families.

Table 8.4: Annual Growth Rate of Tribal Population (1961-1991)

Decade	*Annual Rate of Increase (in %)*			
	Gujarat		*India*	
	Tribal Population	*Non-tribal Population*	*Tribal Population*	*Non-tribal Population*
1961-1971	3.6	2.8	2.7	2.5
1971-1981	3.0	2.7	3.6	2.0
1981-1991	2.7	2.0	3.1	2.7

Source: Census of India, 1961-1991

4. Virtually 3 per cent of forest land had been transferred for different development projects and other related purposes

out of the total land acquisition by the State of Gujarat. This 3 per cent of forest land covers a total 5.15 per cent of forest area in the State. Table 8.5 shows the forest land diverted by categories of projects. Out of the total forest land diverted for different purposes, 37.34 per cent have been diverted for agricultural purposes. 27.43 per cent of total forest land has been submerged for construction of dams in different zones of the State. 19.82 per cent of the total forest land diverted had been for the rehabilitation of displaced people in different developmental projects. The Gujarat Forest Statistics (May 1983) reveals that 56,214 hectares occupancy rights were given in the State and as, per estimates, the Forest Department had released 24,790 hectares for authorized cultivation to the tribals of the Dang. We observed that out of the total number of families displaced for developmental projects, almost 42 per cent were tribals. In other words, we can thus state that, since independence, almost 10 per cent of total tribal population of the State of Gujarat has been affected by such land acquisitions.

Table 8.5: Forest Land Diverted by Categories of Projects (1947-2004)

(In Hectare)

Categories of Project	*Land Acquired*	*% of Forest Land Acquired**	*% of Total Forest Area of Gujarat***
Agriculture	36,581	37.34	1.92
Submergence	26,880	27.43	1.42
Rehabilitation	19,414	19.82	1.02
Miscellaneous	12,276	12.53	0.64
Industries and Townships	1,684	01.72	0.09
Roads etc.	1,138	01.16	0.06
Total	97,973	100.00	5.15

Note * Total Forest Land Diverted is 97,973 ha.

** Total Forest Area of Gujarat is 1,892,750 ha.

Source: Gujarat Forest Statistics (as on 31/03/2006), May 2006.

5. During our field work, we asked many questions related to the information on forest laws and policies. We enquired about the tribal information on forest laws pertaining to

their basic requirements i.e., food, fodder, fuel and minor forest products.

- Of the total respondents in Zone I, 47 per cent responded that they have no problems in getting their daily requirement of fuel-wood for domestic use, while only 26 per cent of the total respondents in Zone IV responded, saying that they get their requirement for fuel wood very easily. While 31 per cent of the total respondents of Zone IV had shown a tendency in their responses that the tribal should get fuel-wood as per their requirement very easily.
- While on the issue of fodder, 48 per cent of the respondents of Zone I responded that the Forest Department allowed them to take fodder from the forest without any problem. But only 2 per cent of the respondents of Zone V responded positively, in favour of the Forest Department. While 26 per cent of the respondents from Zone IV responded that they should be allowed to take away enough fodder from the forest without the interference of the Forest Department.
- On the harvesting of Minor Forest Products (MFPs), 33 per cent and 34 per cent of the respondents from the Zone I and Zone II respectively, responded that the Forest Department allowed them to collect MFPs for their routine requirements, while only 20 per cent of the respondents from Zone III agreed to this response. While 30 per cent of the respondents of Zone IV had demanded that tribals should be allowed to get their MFPs regularly without any permission from the Forest Department or without any harassment by the Forest Department officials as they are collecting such produce undeterred since decades.
- When we asked about the suggestions of the tribal respondents in all the five zones on how to protect the rights of the tribals on forests and to check their knowledge regarding various laws applied on the forests, most of them were seen to be a lot more aware. Around 24 and 21 per cent of the total respondents from Zone II and Zone IV respectively demanded that tribals should get their rights over the forest as they were the original dwellers.
- In terms of the knowledge on forest laws and policies, the tribals in the areas of Zones III, IV and V seem more aware

than those of Zones I and II as more responses received from the Zones III, IV and V proposed the following:

(a) Forest regulations should be framed in such a way that they protect the tribals more than the Forests or the Forest Department,

(b) Forest policies and laws are not implemented properly,

(c) Tribals should be able to get their routine requirements from the forests without any harassment from the Forest Department.

- Respondents from Zones I and II were better informed regarding the forest laws and policies. When we asked for suggestions on modifications to the existing forest laws and policies, hardly 5 per cent to 7 per cent respondents from Zone I and II gave their many suggestions. But we received many more responses (about 15%) from the respondents of Zones III, IV and V. The following are the major suggestions given by the respondents on modifications to the existing forest laws and policies:

  (a) Government should not consider tribals as Naxalites if they start cultivating unauthorized forest lands. Government should take help from tribals for regeneration of forests where there is degradation of forests,

  (b) Government should provide either some piece of land or alternative sources for livelihood to those tribals who have no land,

  (c) Payments made by the Forest Department should be revised based on the rate of inflation,

  (d) There should be a change in the existing laws so that the traditional rights of the tribals over the forest could be protected, and

  (e) Laws and policies should be framed and implemented in such a way that the tribals should get their daily routine requirements from the forests without any harassment from the officials of the Forest Department.

When we asked about the question of co-operation between the Forest Department and the tribals (just to check their awareness about the JFM, Social Forestry and Agro Forestry), we were surprised seeing the number of responses we received from the different zones. As many as 59 per cent and 43 per cent of the total respondents from Zones I and II suggested that, with proper co-operation between the tribal communities and the Forest Department, new forests could be developed, and the degraded forests could be regenerated very easily.

While 25 per cent of the total respondents from Zone III suggested that the Government makes amends to the existing schemes in such a way that cordial relations between the Forest Department and the tribal communities could be ensured. We received thought provoking suggestions from all the zones in our area of study. If these suggestions are implemented, it will certainly improve the livelihood status of the tribals and provide for alternative livelihood support systems for them. Most of them also suggested that there should be an increase in tree plantation drives so that the planted trees could give handsome returns after some years which could also be beneficial to the tribals.

II

Changing Patterns of Tribal Livelihood in the Study Area

It was recognized that diversification at the individual or household level among the tribal communities, that is, 'supplementary livelihood', meant adding new activities. These could include agriculture and forest allied supplementary sources of livelihood for the tribal communities across the zones. We have described this in detail in chapter nine. In this section, however, we will discuss the important observations on the changing patterns of livelihood among tribal communities.

1. There are other additional sources of livelihood seen in our study areas which are neither connected with agriculture and its allied sources nor with forests and allied sources. Many of the literate tribals have developed artisan skills to earn their major share of income from these skills. In Zone II, we observed an increase in the number of masons during the last ten years. We have also seen an

increase in tailors, black-smiths, carpenters, barbers and carpet makers.

2. Tribal livelihood diversification in agriculture can be described as the live-stock holdings, *wadi* cultivation either for fruits or vegetables, cultivating on others' land and working as agricultural labourers; while diversification in forests and forest produce can be described as keeping honey bees, growing of income generating trees, furniture making and fruit gathering in forests areas.
3. Possession of cows and buffalos play an important role in providing additional sources of livelihood for tribal communities. On average, almost 50 per cent of the tribal respondents own one or more cows or buffaloes. Cattle rearing for milk seems to be on the rise as an additional source of livelihood. Respondents from Zone II possess the highest number of buffaloes (55%), while Zone I have the lowest number with 42 per cent. The possession of cattle in Zone IV seems to be high with 54 per cent, and Zone V stood at the lowest with 41 per cent.
4. Wells and bore-wells play a vital role in generating income from agricultural lands. Sufficient quantities of water at the appropriate time are necessary for a good crop. When irrigation facilities are not available, wells and bore-wells are the only available sources of water for crops and livestock. Zone IV has the highest number of wells (53%) and bore-wells (42%) in all the five zones. Zone II also has a good number of wells (44%). But Zone V does not have such facilities, and wells are a mere 18 per cent while there are only 10 per cent of bore-wells. Irrigation facilities are also not good in Zone V. The existence of bore-wells suggests good income among the tribal respondents as installing bore-wells require money. The presence of bore-well in Zone IV (42% of the total respondents) shows that the respondents earn a good income, either from agriculture or other supplementary sources. A mere 10 per cent of the respondents from Zone V have bore-well facilities which implies a lesser earning power among the population.
5. It was observed that tribals are now involved in different income generating activities other than agriculture and

forests. Non-agricultural and allied activities which include industrial labourers, workers in mines and quarries, on construction sites and roads, etc.; They are also now employed as workers with private companies, as government employees in different departments, as teachers, as *gram-mitra,* as bank employees, artisans and other trades like masons, carpenters, blacksmiths, diamond cutters and polishers, carpet weavers, etc. A comparison of the 1991 and 2001 census shows that the total scheduled tribal workforce participation rate in our study area increased from 51.94 per cent in 1991 to 67.45 per cent in 2001. The share of the workforce of scheduled tribes in the total scheduled tribe workforce has also increased marginally from 21.01 per cent in 1991 to 22.95 per cent in 2001, with the result that the main scheduled tribe workers declined marginally from 78.99 per cent in 1991 to 77.05 per cent in 2001. Non-workers among tribal communities have decreased drastically from 48.06 per cent in 1991 to 32.55 per cent in 2001—a decline of 15.51 per cent in just one decade. This data reveals that there is a definite shift in employment patterns among the tribal communities.

6. It was observed and analyzed that the tribals have now moved away from their areas in large numbers for other sources of livelihood than five to ten years ago. In Zone III, our data shows an increase from 19 per cent (five to ten years ago) to 49 per cent today. The same tendency seems to prevail in the entire study area. Respondents from Zone I have decreased their dependence on agriculture and allied activities (from 29% five to ten years ago to 23% now) and moved towards artisan related activities (from 1% five to ten years ago to 6% now). Even among non-agricultural and allied sources, the trend shows a different picture. Earlier 69 per cent of the total respondents worked as non-agricultural labour but now this has decreased to 62 per cent and the rest of the 7 per cent have moved from non-agricultural labour to Government and private jobs. Respondents from Zone II have moved from agricultural labour to cultivation under agriculture and allied sources. This move from agricultural labour has resulted in shared

cultivation of land owned by others. Five to ten years ago the cultivators were only 9 per cent of the total respondents, but the numbers have now increased to 14 per cent and this trend leads to a decrease in agricultural labour, that is, from 22 per cent to 20 per cent. This shows an increase from 31 per cent to 34 per cent in agriculture and allied sources of income earning. In the same domain, Zone II shows a decreasing trend (from 59% to 44%). Here, also actual non-agricultural labourers have decreased from 58 per cent to 40 per cent. Roughly 04 per cent have either been employed with the Government or work as private employees, which is a new trend in this zone. The percentage of artisans has increased from 07 per cent to 24 per cent. It was also noticed that Respondents from Zone II prefer to work as masons and carpenters.

7. An interesting observation was made on the working habits of tribals in different industries as unskilled labourers or as skilled labourers; they often remained absent at work. Our analysis show that this was occurring since their needs are limited and that once they got enough money for their survival, they remained absent for the remaining part of the month. This peculiar aspect needs to be studied in depth.
8. This study has also observed a particular shift in the attitude of educated tribal youth. On the one hand, graduate or post-graduate tribal youths avoid taking up traditional sources of income generating activities but on the other hand their employability is also of great concern as the education they have received does not create employment opportunities. We found that many prefer to be unemployed rather than take up traditional sources of income generating activities.
9. Our study on the changing patterns of livelihood has helped us to re-examine certain processes. For instance, tribal migration has for a long time been perceived as negatively affecting rural and agricultural development. The livelihood factor has actually enlightened us to some of the more positive effects of migration on tribal poverty as well as on the aspects of production and consumption. Similarly, increase in the levels of education among the

tribals has shown a positive trend and in some cases, the increase in education has also curtailed migration to an extent. We also found that literate sections of these tribals have taken advantage of various welfare schemes of the Government by living in the village.

10. The conditions that affect a tribal's livelihood which we refer to as "mediating structures and processes", *viz.*, the shocks, trends and seasonality, continually change. Changes in livelihood practices allows us to take a dynamic view of how social change proceeds. This provides a meaningful contribution to social analysis and promotes discussions and debates on social changes. Armed with the notion of agency, we have learnt that these mediating and structural processes are subject to negotiations and political struggles and therefore are not immutable but changeable.
11. The livelihood view is playing a useful role in this process of development, as it is tribal centered and takes their problems, and particularly of the poorest among them, as a starting point for analysis and development planning. The focus here is on the kind of government policies needed to assist local tribal and not on the policies *per se*. For example, the livelihood view can be used to look at the effects of different policies on tribal's livelihoods. The approach, therefore, enables a critical analysis on different perspectives, for example, the result of building new roads, or the impact of higher education levels on career opportunities etc. It focuses also on the human capacity to cope with shocks and stress as well as to better recognize, and act upon, different livelihood opportunities.

III

Socio-cultural Changes among Tribals

Tribal communities have suffered heavy losses due to deforestation and depletion of forests, raising monoculture crop, reduction of food sources (plant and wildlife). There has been an abrupt change in tribal population-environment relationship especially in a system which is sensitive to population density, or hunting and gathering. Increased migration has caused cultural heterogeneity. Owing to mining and other industrial activities in the vicinity tribals have been suddenly exposed to alter physical, chemical and biotic environmental stresses; the sudden change in their diet could have caused profound disturbance of water and electrolyte balance in the body causing various diseases. The migration to another environment might have a deleterious effect on social and cultural status of the tribals. We have dealt in detail in the chapter nine. Here, we will discuss the major socio-cultural changes in the tribal society in our study area.

1. Development of infrastructure like roads, concrete houses, railways, schools, colleges, and health centers, mineral and non-mineral mines, setting up of industrial areas, welfare centers etc. have affected the socio-economic and cultural scenario of the people. A large number of mines were opened up in many parts of tribal areas of Gujarat. This brought employment, improved communication system and welfare facilities which lead to a change in the pattern of living. The growth of the tribal community over the last four decades may have increased the demand of fuelwood, bamboo and timber which may have led to ecological depletion and dilution of diversity and density, which ultimately may have led towards an attitudinal change in the use of fuel-wood from forests. Shifting cultivation gave to sedentary cultivation mainly because of the schemes started by different organizations. Barren areas were brought under cultivation especially horticulture. The different schemes and development programmes commenced by the Government of India and the Government of Gujarat was to improve socio-economic conditions of the tribals community, which in turn has affected their society.
2. Ignorance due to illiteracy and lack of access to information and knowledge continues to be pervasive and challenging. But these areas seem to be improving in this respect especially in the last two decades. Table 8.6 shows the rate of literacy in 1991 and 2001. The data clearly reflects the increase in the level of literacy among tribals

in the five zones. An overall 10 per cent increase in literacy has been seen from 1991 to 2001. Zone III and Zone V show an increased literacy rate compared to the other zones. Zone I and Zone II show the minimal increase when compared with Zone III, Zone IV and Zone V during the same period.

Table 8.6: Literacy Rate among Scheduled Tribes in Study Area

Zones	*Literacy Rate (in %)*		
	1991	*2001*	*Change*
Zone I	30.22	36.85	+ 06.63
Zone II	23.22	31.80	+ 08.58
Zone III	32.01	43.91	+ 11.90
Zone IV	38.34	48.77	+ 10.43
Zone V	34.72	46.54	+ 11.82
Study Area	29.87	39.59	+ 09.72

Source: District Census Handbook 1991 and 2001.

3. With the increase in the level of literacy, we have seen a change in the clothing and food habits of the tribal communities. The women of Zones IV (28%) and V (28%) showed more change than the women in Zones I (18%) and II (9%). The low literacy rate among the tribal women in Zone I and Zone II could have been reflected in their changing patterns of clothing habits. The tendency among men as concerns the change in clothing habits shows more or less similar trends in the zones studied. Twenty-seven per cent of the total respondents said positively about latest fashions and its impact on clothing practices.
4. Compared to clothing habits, food habits have undergone more changes across the zones of our study. Fifty-four per cent of the total respondents said that they had introduced new food items in their daily diet. Respondents from Zone V (38%) seem to have introduced fewer new food items in their daily diet. However, the introduction of new food items seems less during their religious or social occasions. The correlation of food items with the literacy rate and the level of education seem to be interesting: when the rate of literacy is higher, the change in food habits is more. Hence, education plays a vital role in the shifting

attitude towards clothing and food practices of tribal communities.

5. Tribal women were earlier exploited, and the level of domestic violence was quite high. But increasing rate of education and generation of supplementary sources of income have empowered the women to some degree. Thirty-seven per cent of the total female respondents (17% of total respondents) responded that these women become smarter with education while 8 per cent from the same area said that tribal women become equal to men and took leadership roles at all community levels, i.e. village, taluka, district, state or national. These women now play an active role in SHGs and *Sakhi Mandalis* to create awareness on the necessity of saving money. Anti-liquor campaign by women especially belonging to *Sakhi Mandal* has been vigorous.
6. There is new trend emerging from the analysis of our primary data. 10 per cent of the respondents said that earlier tribal women went to work outside their village, which they have now stopped as their families do not seem to need the extra money.
7. Decrease in domestic violence and reduction in sexual exploitation of women in the tribal areas are two significant issues. Our study shows that there is a considerable reduction in domestic violence. Forty-one per cent of the respondents said a decrease in domestic violence while the same percentile of respondents said that there was no sexual exploitation in homes or villages. Thirty-two per cent of the total respondents said that there was greater awareness towards morality. When asked about these behavioural changes our field workers were told that education had made this difference. This factor seems to have given the tribal women dignity and self-respect. However, another important factor seems to be the improved economic situation of tribal families. As the economic situation of the family improves domestic violence, sexual exploitation and immorality decreases.
8. The exposure of the tribal youth to city life and their entry into the mainstream has caused a definite change in the attitudes of these youth. They have a tendency to celebrate religious festivals and social events like marriages in a

grand manner which was not the case in the past. In addition to these, loud playing of film songs and religious songs during these occasions have become the norm. Good road connectivity and better all weather roads have aided in tribal migration to cities.

9. Concerning inter-tribal marriages, respondents from the Zone IV (52%), Zone V (48%) and Zone III (41%) agreed that this was now possible, but our studies show that only 32 per cent and 33 per cent of the total respondents from the Zones I and II agreed unanimously on this issue. Marriages within the tribes are a prevalent tradition among the respondents from Zone I (53%) and Zone II (51%) than in the Zone IV (21%) and Zone V (22%). Love marriages or choosing of one's life partner have increased considerably in Zone IV (11%) and Zone V (10%), but this seems to be hardly possible in Zone I (02%) and Zone II (03%).
10. Lower females per one thousand males in many castes had led the tribal girls to get married to non-tribal boys. Table 8.7 shows the sex-ratio (number of females per one thousand males) in the study area. Surat district has just

Table 8.7: Ranking of Districts by Sex-Ratio, 2001 and 2011

Zones		*Sex- ratio (Number of Females per 1000 Males)*	
		2011	*2001*
I	**Banaskantha**	**936**	**930**
	Sabarkantha	**950**	**947**
	Mehsana	925	927
	Patan	935	932
	Ahmedabad	903	892
	Gandhinagar	920	913
II	**Panchmahal**	**945**	**938**
	Dahod	**986**	**985**
	Kheda	937	923
	Anand	921	910
	Vadodara	934	919
III	**Narmada**	**960**	**949**
	Bharuch	924	921
	Surat	*788*	810
IV	**Tapi**	**1004**	**996**
	Navsari	**961**	**955**
	Valsad	926	920
V	**The Dang**	**1007**	**987**

Source: Census 2011.

788 females per one thousand males. There are several districts in the study area which have less than 925 females per one thousand males.

There seems to be a tendency now among the tribals to get married to non-tribals. There are many reasons why tribal girls are getting married to non-tribal boys. Increased migration of tribals into urban spaces seems one of the reasons that led to such marriages.

11. Exposure to cinema and television, increased interaction with the cities, has made a difference in the lifestyles of tribal youth, who imitate the patterns they have seen and apply them within their families. Tribal families are more fragmented in Zone I (40%) and Zone II (36%) than in the Zone IV (24%) and Zone V (28%) while conflicts within the family is more in Zone IV (44%) and Zone III (37%) than in Zone I (20%) and Zone II (21%).
12. Two important facts emerged from the analysis of our primary data. They are: (i) tribal youth no longer like to live in their villages, but look for new avenues and opportunities, and (ii) an indifferent and rebellious attitude of the educated youth towards their villages and their fellow villagers seem to have increased. We feel that there is a need for social scientists to study these aspects in-depth.
13. We also observed that the *nouveau riche* in the tribal communities have now become the new oppressors. Earlier *sahukars* (money-lenders) exploited them by lending money at high interest rate of 24 per cent. But now it is mostly the new rich of tribal government servants, tribal politicians and tribal businessmen who lend money at high interest rates.

IV

Other Findings

In this section we have considered additional findings regarding forest related laws, role of the forest department, role of the princely states and British Rule; especially the effect of British Rule on the forest and tribals.

1. The formation of the Forest Department, imposition of various Forest Acts and their implementation by way of day-to-day administration has had an unprecedented and lasting impact on the tribal communities. Due to the implementation of certain Forest Acts, the symbiotic relations between the tribals and the forests have been severely disturbed. These Acts secured a permanent settlement of the Reserved Forests, whereas, in the protected forests, the existing rights were recorded but not settled. The role of the Forest Department was less of a facilitator and more of an enforcer. A conciliatory approach was always avoided by citing different rules and regulations. The natural result of the various forest related Acts was the alienation of the tribal communities from their traditional means of subsistence. Increasing commercialization of forests and other forest products, replacement of species useful to the tribals with commercially viable species (along with several restrictions) made matters worse.
2. The situation was not very different in the princely states of Gujarat. Progressive princely states like Baroda and Rajpipla had passed laws to take control over the forests. Hunting in these dense forests was prohibited to all except to the Royalty. Most of the princely states had imposed restrictions on the collection of Minor Forest Products from the forests controlled by them. At the time of handing over these forests to the Government of India, many princely states had handed over the forests to the Indian Union after extensive cutting of trees.
3. The Indian Forest Act of 1927 has not been redrafted even after eighty three years of its implementation. The draconian Indian Forest Act of 1927 needs to be redrafted looking to the current situation of the environment and the needs of the tribals. Many forest related Acts have been passed and implemented after Independence, but reforms that are departmentally centered and dependent on the "go-ahead" from top-politicians and top-bureaucrats who, rarely rely on inputs from individuals outside the Government, either from the scientific community or the NGOs. It is important to note that the whole area has attained a certain rationality,

consensus and aloofness which are associated with the world of high level politicians, bureaucrats of superior status and intellectuals. There is an absence at the central and state levels of tribal or other political parties representing the interests of forests-dwellers, the lack of green or environmental parties, and the lack of strong organizations of forest workers and forest industries. This has made it possible and necessary for the bureaucrats and politicians to take policy decisions in conjunction with NGOs which perform as "macro" actors, with informed and educated public, and the judiciary.

4. Despite significant resource flow and national concern, the potential of forests to reduce poverty, realise economic growth, and their contribution to the national and global environment has not been fully realized. A combination of market and institutional failures have led to forest failing to contribute as significantly to rural incomes and poverty alleviation and economic growth as would be possible under good economic management.
5. Most of the bamboos have been cut for the paper mills in the tribal belt. Due to the telecommunication market penetration in the tribal areas, the uses of mobile phones have become common among the tribal communities. Timber and bamboo mafias are using this facility to remain in contact in such a way that they can avoid the raids by the Forest Department.
6. Our findings from the study include lack of knowledge on the part of the government about the multiple roles and benefits of forests, especially its role in drought proofing and prevention of soil and water run-off, linkage between management and livelihood security of the forest-dwellers, low level of technology, and inadequate research and extension. Other problems are weak planning, wastage in harvesting and processing, market imperfections, over-emphasis on Government involvement and control, low level of people's participation and NGO involvement, lack of inter-sectoral coordination and weakness and conflicting roles of forest administration.
7. After globalization, the market has entered the tribal areas and has changed the tribal identity by changing their

traditional living practices. Tribal areas are getting more and more exposure to the latest trends of the market due to the arrival of satellite television, migration and their visits to the nearby city areas. Tribal males and females have changed their clothing patterns and also begun using cosmetics which were never used previously. Tribal males and females never used under-garments traditionally, but younger generations are using them. Many new food items have entered the tribal homes even in the remotest villages in the State. Pharmaceutical companies have also entered the area and penetrated and exploited the untapped market using the local so-called 'medical practitioners' (as most of them are practicing without valid certificates). More and more tribal people have started visiting medical doctors instead of using their traditional knowledge to cure the diseases. Our findings confirm the impact of these changes among the tribal communities in the study area.

8. Impact of Hinduization and Sanskritization has been clearly visible among the Gujarat tribal communities with the increase in education. Growth of infrastructural facilities has also played a role to bring tribals into the mainstream. Hindu nationalists have also made missionary efforts to speed up Sanskritization of tribals through a variety of means. A number of sects from Hindus and Jains are active in tribal areas gaining followers. Christian missionary intervention especially in education has also speeded up Sanskritization. Educated tribals looking for jobs would prefer to hide their identity and pass off as Hindus to gain respectability in places wherever they go especially the cities and towns. Different schools have viewed the tribals differently in India. The British colonial view saw the tribals in India being isolated from Indian civilization and living in inaccessible areas and having their own religion and culture. A few anthropologists and missionaries like Verrier Elwin have subscribed to this view. The opposite view is that tribals were part of Indian civilization, and there were links between both. G.S. Ghurye the noted sociologist argued though most of them lived in hilly and forest areas and their technology and economy were poor, they are primary

"backward" Hindus in religion. The debate revolved around whether to keep them isolated in their habitats or to integrate and assimilated them? A.M. Shah (2010:206 ff) has observed that the Gujarat tribals were never isolated even though they lived in hills and forests. Pilgrim areas, travel and trade routes, exchange of forest products with non-forest dwellers, quarries and surface mining have all connected the tribals with non-tribals. Findings of our study confirm Shah's observations.

9. Although the environmental lobby is against the FRA, but if well implemented it could be a golden opportunity for tribal communities to get substantial supplementary sources for livelihood. The only aspect to be looked into during implementation of the FRA is the safety of the land which has been given to the tribals under the FRA. A continuous monitoring over the ownership of land would keep at bay money-lenders and land *mafia* who are only too quick to look for opportunities to grab land from the tribals.
10. The State of Gujarat has invested heavily in afforestation programmes on private and common lands often with substantial foreign support particularly with the help of the JBIC. This has benefited a large number of villages both directly and indirectly, but social forestry and farm forestry tend to ignore tribal forest-dwellers who have little access to land. Social forestry has made the forests "slide from the hills to the plains". The response to this has been the JFM and similar schemes which seek to combine the profit motive, sustainable management, state control and local support. What is needed is a reform of the 1927 Indian Forest Act to provide an overall framework for controlling access, but allowing people to satisfy their economic needs.
11. Ordinary forest-dwellers and tribal farmers are the major groups with economic interests in the forests and forest products, as they cultivate in forest areas as well as grow, collect and sell large quantities of fuel wood and other forest products including timber. This group has rarely participated in the policy-making process. One reason for the lack of support is that a major portion of the economic activities of the forest-dwellers is illegal. Another reason

> is that they, like many other groups, have concentrated on influencing the implementation of Government policies through what Grindle and Thomas call "informal and non-public channels" rather than on policy formulation (Grindle and Thomas, 1991: 62-63). The forest-dwellers are often represented through NGOs and social activists instead of being represented through organized pressure groups. The NGOs and social activists do not generally portray these groups as economic interest groups, but impute environmentalist rationality to them. This is problematic, as economic rationality "only incidentally coincide with ecological rationality" (Herring, 1994a: 24).

The major conclusion drawn from this study is that the tribal communities are fast changing. Their dependence on forests has been changing. The belief that tribals are frozen in time and are living in isolation is not true. Integration of tribals with non-tribals is picking up at a more rapid pace than in the past. Sanskritization and Hinduization appears to be speeding up in the last decade through Hindu sects, Gandhian institutions and Sangh Parivar outfits. The decennial census has already labelled them as Hindu Gamits, Hindu Vasavas, Hindu Koknas and prefix of Hindu is found attached to all the tribals in Gujarat.

9

Contours of Long-term Policy Implications

'What does the forest bear?
Resin, timber and foreign exchange, so said the forest officer
The women instantly replied, with their own slogan
What does the forest bear? Soil, water and pure air
Those are the basis of human life'
—A slogan from the 'Chipko Movement'

The present ecological crisis is primarily a result of the conflict between greed and need, luxury and survival, growth and sustainable development. The Governments, particularly those in the developing countries and more specifically India, are caught in this dilemma. They try to reconcile the two conflicts by enacting more laws and policy resolutions that deal with slogans and promises to ignore the root causes associated with this global crisis. This game of running with the hare and hunting with the hounds is clearly difficult and impossible. The history of forests and tribal related legislation and policies in India and the resultant plight of tribals and other forest dwelling communities highlight this conflict which in turn needs urgent and effective solutions.

This chapter is an attempt to visualize the possibility of developing forests with the help of tribal communities. The subject of forests was included in the State list in the Seventh Schedule of the Constitution (Item 19) of India. During the period of Emergency (1975-77), the subject was transferred from the State list to the concurrent list through the 42nd Amendment to the Constitution (Item 17 A) of India. As the subject 'forest' included in the concurrent list while suggesting for the long term policy implication, we are looking to the country as a whole and not limiting to the state of Gujarat.

The long-term policy implications will ensure the required forest cover and tree cover, and at the same time, assure a steady supply of raw materials to the industries. In this manner, it would also provide supplementary sources of livelihood for the tribal communities. We have also interrogated the works of some renowned environmentalists and conservationists with a view to see what is most appropriate in Indian conditions. For instance, work of the Nobel Laureate Elinor Ostrom (1990) has been studied for the long-term policy implications. In the next few sections, several revolutionary changes are proposed in the forest and tribal related laws and policies.

I

Review of National Forest Policy along with Forest Laws on Scientific Lines

We propose that the National Forest Policy of 1988 be reviewed. The following paragraph has been taken from this National Forest Policy:

> "The national goal should be to have a minimum of one-third of the total land area of the country under forest or tree cover. In the hills and mountainous regions, the aim should be to maintain two-third of the area under such cover in order to prevent erosion and land degradation and to ensure the stability of the fragile eco-system."

This paragraph (4.1) of the National Forest Policy, which has become a mandate for the Forest Department, but, in fact, it has no scientific basis. We will discuss the proposal for the whole of the country citing Gujarat as an example. One has to take into account the altitudes and slopes in scientific procedure which is followed globally for effective afforestation and agricultural development and growth.

Gujarat has different geophysical and eco-climatic features with eco-systems ranging from different types of grasslands, wetlands and water bodies. Study of meteorological and hydrological conditions with the role of biodiversity needs to be taken into account for considering the changing behaviour of forests in the state. Study of altitude and slopes in the development of forestry and agriculture is also required as the state has varied patterns in altitude and slopes. One needs to analyze the natural conditions like agro-eco sub-regions, soil types, meteorological and hydrological conditions, influence of altitude and slopes affecting the behaviour of forests in Gujarat before making policy implication argument.

Various attempts have been made to characterize Gujarat's diversified ecosystems for different purposes. Agro-eco region classification is the latest to emphasize moisture availability and indices, which will be useful for determining limiting factors to establish forest vegetation in the State of Gujarat. These varying agro-eco conditions in the State of Gujarat have resulted in a greater variety of soils. Therefore, the systematic appraisal of agro-ecological regions has tremendous scope in grouping relatively homogenous regions in terms of soil, climate and physiographic and conducive moisture availability periods (length of growing season) in planning appropriate land use either for agriculture or forests.

The study area has been grouped into four agro-eco sub-regions depending upon the soil, bioclimatic type and physiographic conditions. Each agro-eco sub-region has further been classified into agro-eco unit at district level. Agro-eco sub-regions distributed are summarized in Table 9.1.

Soil Types

As a result of mixed parent rocks, slopes, rainfall patterns, geophysical locations, wind velocity and direction; different types of soils have been formed in the State of Gujarat. The soils of Gujarat are usually classified (based on soil classification prepared by Gujarat Agriculture University and National Bureau of Soil Survey and Land Use) into the following nine types: (1) black soils, (2) mixed red and black soils, (3) residual sandy soils, (4) alluvial soils, (5) saline-alkali soils, (6) desert soils, (7) lateritic soils, (8) hilly soils, and (9) forest soils.

Based on the above classification of soils, different types of

Table 9.1: Agro-eco Sub-regions in Study Area

Agro-eco Sub-regions		*Location (Districts)*	*Zones of Study Area*
Name	*Type*		
North Gujarat Plain	Hot, Typical Arid	Palanpur in Banaskantha and Western Mehsana	Zone I
North Gujarat Plain (inclusive of Aravali Range and Eastern Rajasthan Uplands)	Hot, Dry, Semi-Arid	Sabarkantha, Eastern Mehsana and Ahmedabad	Zone I
Eastern Gujarat Plain	Hot, Moist, Semi-Arid	Panchmahal, Dahod, Vadodara, Kheda and Anand	Zone II
		Bharuch, Narmada and Surat (North and Central)	Zone III
North Sahyadris and Konkan Coast	Hot, Humid	Surat (South and South-West)	Zone III
		Tapi, Navsari and Valsad	Zone IV
		Dangs	Zone V

Source: Agro-ecological Sub-regions of India for Planning and Development, National Bureau of Soil Survey and Land Use Planning, 1999.

soils occurring in different agro-climatic zones of the State of Gujarat are indicated in Table 9.2.

Black cotton soil is the predominant soil type in Gujarat covering approximately 38 per cent of the state followed by sandy soils (including sandy-clay loam soils) covering approximately 33 per cent of the state distributed mainly in the North and North-West zones. On the other hand, coastal alluvial soils and saline-alkali soils are distributed in the coastal area of the state, while desert soils are restricted to Kutchch only. Hill and forest soils are confined mainly to the Eastern Gujarat.

Soil in the state varies in its manifestation across the region. Deep black cotton soils of South Gujarat are neutral to alkaline; hilly soils of Dang show slightly acidic reaction; whereas they are sodic in the Bhal region. There are no true lateritic soils, but some soils nearing lateritic nature have developed in high rainfall areas of Dang from basalt rocks. The irrigation projects have raised water tables in districts of Kheda, Anand, Ahmedabad, Surat, Tapi, Navsari and Valsad. The salt contents in such soils vary from 1.5 per cent to 5.7 per cent. The main categories of problematic soils

Table 9.2: Distribution of Soils in Different Agro-climatic Zones (Unit 1,000 ha)

Types of Soils	*Zone IV Zone V*		*Zone III*		*Zone II*		*Zone I*		*Spreading in All Five Zones*	
	South-south Gujarat Heavy Rainfall Zone		*South Gujarat Zone*		*Central Gujarat Zone*		*North Gujarat Zone*		*Bhal and Coastal Zone*	
	Area	*%*	*Area*	*%*	*Area*	*%*	*Area*	*%*	*Area*	*%*
Deep Black Cotton Soils	484	55	542	53	327	15				
Mixed Red and Black Soils					845	38	296	13	296	31
Lateritic Soils	160	18								
Hilly/Forest Soils	109	12	117	11	355	15	122	05		
Residual Sandy Soils							1260	55		
Sandy-Clay Loam Soils					659	30	621	27	249	26
Coastal Alluvial Soils	137	15	291	28	36	02			59	06
Desert Soils										
Saline-alkali soils	15	00	79	08	09	00			364	37

Source: Natural Resources of Gujarat 2005: 65.

of the state are waterlogged soils, sodic soils, sandy soils prone to soil erosion and low fertility soils found in hills.

Meteorological and Hydrological Conditions

Temperature, rainfall patterns with distribution of rainfall, humidity, aridity, and river discharge for major rivers and soil and moisture conservation play a vital role in land use. Great part of our study area lies between 35°C to 45°C isotherms. The highest temperature is recorded in the month of May, when the mean maximum temperature reaches as high as 45°C in Zone I, Zone II and some part of Zone III whereas coastal areas where sea breeze penetrate have a lower mean maximum temperature of 34°C compared to the inland areas. The mean minimum temperature in January ranges between 10°C to 14°C. Zone I had experienced the coldest and hottest temperatures.

Gujarat receives an average annual average rainfall of 972 mm with average rainfall of 35 days (average rainfall for the period between the years 1998 to 2007). However, there is a large variation in annual rainfall within the State of Gujarat ranging from 647 mm to 1291 mm. Chart 9.1 shows the average rainfall between the years 2001-2002 to 2008-09. High rainfall received in Eastern hilly areas of Dang (Zone V), Valsad, Navsari and Tapi (Zone IV) and Surat (Zone III) districts. Number of rainy days also varies from 30 days in Zone I to 76 days in Zone V. There is high seasonal variation in the distribution of rainfall with more than 90 per cent of annual rainfall falling between June and September during the South West monsoon rains. Monsoon breaks in June and reaches its maximum intensity in July and August, which are the rainiest months of the year and tapers off towards the end of September with marginal rainfall. The rest of the year is dry except for occasional showers.

Humidity and aridity are mainly influenced by rainfall and its distribution with intensity and also by evapotranspiration which determine the type and distribution of natural vegetation. A large number of area in the State of Gujarat falls under arid, semi-arid and desert conditions where aridity is very high. Some areas in Gujarat receive low and erratic rainfall. Even during monsoon,

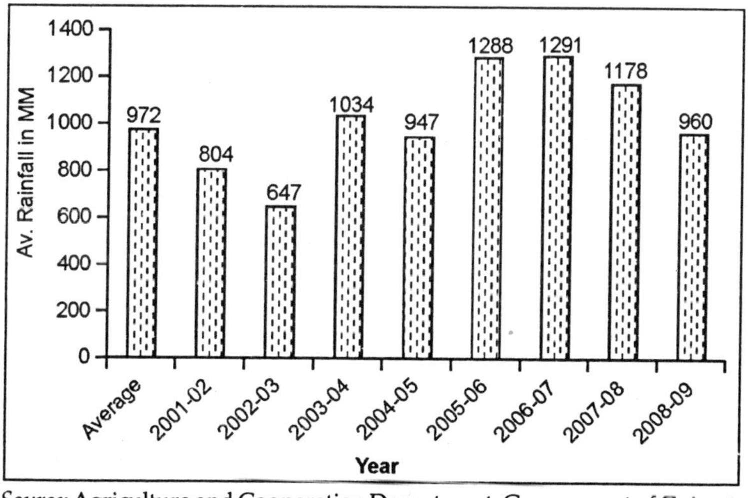

Source: Agriculture and Cooperation Department, Government of Gujarat.

Chart 9.1: Average Rainfall in Gujarat (2001-02 to 2008-09)

dry spells are common. Due to this nature, the general humidity in the state is low. During the summer (April-May), relative humidity recorded in most of the areas of Gujarat is between 70 per cent to 80 per cent, and in coastal areas it is as high as 90 per cent, while, in winter (November to February), the atmosphere is dry for the most of the places. The relative humidity varies from 40 per cent to 50 per cent except on the coast where it is higher all year around.

Soil and moisture conservation works are carried out by Rural Development Department, Gujarat Land Development Corporation and Forest Department in the State of Gujarat. Soil and moisture conservation work include line treatment through series of check dams, afforestation on river banks, pasture development through silvi-pasture work, farm ponds, percolation tanks, terracing, contour bunding and water harvesting.

All these meteorological and hydrological conditions affect the conservation and preservation of forests in the State of Gujarat. Change in any of these conditions will automatically lead to the change in the forests behaviour. Then of course legal and illegal felling of trees also affects forest behaviour.

Gujarat has a striking diversity of ecosystems which endows the state with a rich and diverse fauna and flora. The biodiversity-rich Western Ghats terminate in the South Eastern tip of Gujarat while further to North, on the Eastern edge taper out the Satpura and Vindhya mountains, with the North Eastern corner composed of the Western end of the Aravali mountain range. These striking distinct physiographic features together with varying climatic profile mark the state as the home for a special biodiversity assemblage. Corresponding to the variety of ecosystems, the state has rich and varied floral wealth. The behaviour of forest can change over a period of time even without human intervention if associated flora has not been developed or disappeared. Every forest has its own family of associate trees e.g. *tectonia grandis* (teak) should grow together with its associates such as *terminalia crenulata* and *dendrocalamus strictus*.

Importance of Altitude and Slope in Forests

The Land Capability Classiiication (LCC) allocates lands to different sustainable uses based on slope, soil and rainfall. According to LCC the following are the major guidelines based on the gradient of the land for proper land use under which the fertility and condition of the land is maintained over a long time with good returns from the land (Matela, 1984):

1. **Flat Land**: For agriculture crops
2. **Gentle Slopes**: Up to 7° (12%). For agricultural crops; planted with simple agronomic conservation measures, i.e. contour and close planting, strip cropping, vegetative barriers, etc.
3. **Moderate Slopes**: 7° to 25° (12-47%). For agricultural crops; planted on a variety of terracing systems, i.e. hillside ditches, intermittent terraces, bench terraces, etc.
4. **Steep Slopes**: 25°-30° (47-58%). For agro-forestry and orchard crops; planted with individual basins, orchard terraces and/or the establishment of proper vegetative cover for erosion control.
5. **Very Steep Slopes**: 30°-40° (58-84%) for forestry.

Maximum Slope (%)		Conservation Treatment	Crop type
	0.35 per cent	Contour Cultivation	Any Crop
	3.5-12 per cent	Ridges or Bunds	Any Crop
	27 per cent	Step terraces on hillsides	Close cover, crops, bushes, perennials
	36 per cent	Step terraces on hillside ditches	Trace crops with ground cover
	47 per cent	Orchard terraces on hillside ditches	Trace crops with ground cover
	65+ per cent	Forests only	

Chart 9.2: Category of Slopes and Crops

6. **Cliff and Non-operable Slopes**: 40° (84%) and over for Protected Forest.

The slopes suitable for each category of land use may vary according to the type of soils on different sites. The important thing is the relative position of the different types of land use along the contour. Categories (1), (2) and (3) are to be listed for use as pasture lands when the soils are shallow or have other limitations.

According to the LCC, lands above 35° slopes should be under forèsts. The adoption of this scientific criterion would release substantial lands—most of these would be degraded forest lands near villages—to meet the needs of the tribal communities. Our argument is that the focus of the Forest Department and the conservationists should shift from quantity to quality. The most important benefit and the one that cannot be fulfilled by any other means are the quality of life that forests can give us—clean water and help in cleaning the air. A healthy forest with several canopies of trees, shrubs and ground cover of grasses and a thick layer of humus alone can do a great job in the area.

Influence of Altitude

The primary consequence of altitude is the decrease in air pressure with the increase in elevation. Only in exceptional cases—as in the Himalayan States of India—this phenomenon has some agricultural value since the results of decreased pressure are usually observed only above considerably high altitudes at which climatic controls such as temperature, precipitation, etc. limit agricultural land utilization (see Annexure 4 for Altitude Zone-wise Forest Cover in India). At the same time, at the height of 3500 m and above the decreased atmospheric pressure causes nausea and agricultural activities cannot be carried out despite conditions being favourable to numerous domesticated plants. Usually the rarefied air of the high mountains increases transpiration rates of plants, which, unfortunately, restricts growth.

In the tropics, altitude is of special importance for utilization of land for agriculture. Modification in temperature associated with increasing elevation make these areas habitable (Klages, 1958) for farming communities. Coppock (1964) has emphasized that there is an upper limit to the area of favourable land for agricultural pursuits and that very often does not occur at a fixed elevation everywhere. At times, the optimum altitude varies with economic conditions—falling in times of agricultural depression and rising when the prices are high and production costs relatively low. Or it may reflect the long history of agricultural colonization of the upland margins. Broadly speaking, the locational height of the improved land varies with the size of the upland mass, with its latitude, and with its climate. However, the important secondary consequences of increasing elevation, both agronomically and economically significant, are: (i) decreased temperature, (ii) increased precipitation, (iii) increased wind velocity, (iv) poor soil, and (v) rugged relief. The following is the altitude map of the study area, the map suggests that the high altitude areas are present as one moves away from the coastal area.

Influence of Slope

The slope of the land is also an important physiographic aspect influencing the agricultural land-use of an area. The effects of gradient on agriculture may be both direct and indirect. The most obvious direct impact of the slope is in the form of the restraint on cultivation and accessibility of land use. The indirect effect of slope manifests itself in pedagogical and climatic modifications including the position of the water-table, the development of soils, air drainage and the relative freedom from frost. However, data on slope is available only in a generalized form in view of the fact that it is obtained from contoured maps. For practical purposes, especially for agricultural land-use hardly any data is available from which the importance of the slope can be known. One can never ignore the fact that very steep sloping areas cannot be brought under cultivation because of inherited limitations (Singh and Dhillon, 2006).

The gradient map of the study area suggests that the forest cover increases as we go on higher grounds which justify the LCC we discussed earlier. When the slope becomes steeper, the area is good for dense forestry while a lesser slope is good for agriculture. The LCC allocates lands to different sustainable uses based on slope, soil and rainfall. According to the LCC, land gradient beyond 35° should be under forests. Adoption of this scientific criterion will make available substantial lands—most of these would be degraded forest lands near villages—to meet the needs of the tribal communities.

Our argument is that the focus of the Forest Department and the conservationists should shift towards quality reforms and its implementation. The most important benefit and which cannot be replaced by any other nor fulfilled by any other means is what good quality forests can give us. A healthy forest with its tree canopies, shrubs and ground cover of grasses and the thick layer of humus alone can do a great job in the area helps a great deal in conserving the environment. Also measuring soil erosion levels, and slope and altitude analysis of land by the Forest Survey of India would be more beneficial to society at large than by just measuring top canopy density levels.

It is recommended that Gujarat should move away from the "33 per cent areas under forests syndrome" and prescribe to the quality of forests and not the quantity. Gujarat has 9.67 per cent of the total geographical area as forest area. As per the current status (Refer Table 9.3), there is only 0.06 per cent and 03.07 per cent of total geographical area for the state of Gujarat is covered under very dense forest and moderately dense forest respectively.

Table 9.3: Forest Cover of Gujarat State

Forest Cover	*Forest Cover in Ha*	*% against Total Forest Cover*	*% against Total Geographical Area**
Very Dense Forest	11,400	00.8	00.06
Moderately Dense Forest	602,400	40.9	03.07
Open Forest	857,700	58.3	04.38
Total	1,471,500	100.0	07.51

Note: * Total Geographical Area of Gujarat is 19,602,200 ha.
Source: Gujarat Forest Statistics, 2006.

From our study, we have suggested that 8 per cent of the total land in the State of Gujarat should be converted into very dense to dense quality forests based on agro-eco sub-regions, soil types, meteorological and hydrological conditions, impact of altitude and slopes with the help of the latest technology like the GIS and satellite imageries. The remaining 1.67 per cent of the degraded forest land (9.67% forest area – (minus) the 8 per cent forest area as per our suggestion) should be handed over to the respective

Gram Sabha (as conceptualized in The Panchayats Extension to Scheduled Areas (PESA) Act 1996) in the region of the respective village with full rights over the use of degraded land in the following manner:

(a) There should be scientific demarcation on the degraded forest lands that, after two to three years, these lands should be handed over to the nearest village *Gram Sabha* for regeneration keeping in mind the livelihood of tribals living in the region of the forest area. They should start getting returns from these forests by way of fodder, fuels and other income generating products. These forest areas can be named as "Village Forest".

(b) The demarcation should be based on four phases:
   (i) First phase plantation should be made in such a manner that the tribals should be able to get their basic needs for fuel and fodder.
   (ii) Second phase plantation should be planned in such a manner that the tribals should get monetary returns in the first year e.g. plantation of lemon trees, vegetables, flowers etc.
   (iii) Third phase plantation should be made in a manner that the tribals can start getting monetary returns after three to five years depending upon the soil types, agro-climatic conditions and considering other related factors e.g. mango trees, cashew trees and other fruit trees.
   (iv) Fourth phase plantation should be made in a manner that the tribals with the help of the Gram Sabha could grow trees like *mahuda*, teak, sal, *tenduva* etc. so that these trees can give financial returns after 10 to 15 years or later.

(c) There should be a joint effort by all the four stakeholders—the Government, the tribal people, the *Gram Sabha* and the NGOs. There should be an apolitical committee to manage the affairs of these lands in the villages. Leading environmentalists and conservationists should also be involved in these efforts so that the improvement in the quality of air and water is achieved at a desired healthy level. There should be a mandatory provision that all these committees should be registered either under the Bombay Public Charitable Trust Act or the Societies Act, so work is done in a proper and legal manner. The provision should also extend to investment of surplus money and creation of a market to create alternative employment schemes with the support of Government intervention and the support of NGOs. Income Tax Act should take care to exempt the income generated through these types of activities.

(d) Government of Gujarat should carry out survey on the current status of the forest land given to the forest dwellers since 1960. If the actual situation (not the legal status or the status on paper) shows that the forest dwellers do not have real possession of that particular forest land which had been given to them in different time-period, the Government of Gujarat should make it mandatory that such forest lands should be handed over to the respective Gram Sabha under (a) above.

(e) There should be an increase in the tree cover from 839,000 ha (4.3% of total geographical area for the State of Gujarat) in the rural, urban and semi-urban areas. We recommend for 8 per cent of total geographical area for the State of Gujarat should be included under the tree cover in next ten years. Social Forestry Programme can be useful in increasing tree cover. Trees can be planted on both the sides of the national as well as state highways and all along the railway lines. Trees can also be planted on both the sides of the irrigation canals and riverbeds. Local people should also encourage to plant income generating trees. Anand and Kheda District in Zone II are the best example of urban forestry. Anand and Kheda have as such no forest at all. But Anand occupies 71 trees per ha and are generating income worth of Rs. 140 crores from the timber. Earning from tree cover is the concept of Kheda model. It keeps the carbon balance and also locks the carbon. Tribal areas can also adopt Kheda Model and can produce the alternative source of livelihood.

(f) We also suggest that there should be an increase in the mangrove cover from 104,600 ha (0.53% of total geographical area for the state of Gujarat) in the coastal areas. We propose for 5 per cent of the total geographical area for the state of Gujarat should be covered under mangrove cover in the next ten years as Gujarat has more than 1,600 km coastal line.

(g) All forest villages need to be converted into the revenue villages. The open forest land other than the newly converted revenue area should be handed over to the respective *Gram Sabha* under (a) above.

Every community has an inherent right to use the natural resources around its settlement. This is done by urban and rural populations when they take up industries or agriculture where most of the land is in private ownership. With the implementation of these suggestions, tribal communities thus, would be empowered with better livelihood, can get better infrastructure and educational facilities, all with their own resources. Migration could be controlled as the tribal communities will get recourse to supplementary source of livelihood within the village or in the vicinity of their own village.

But, all this is denied to the tribal communities when large areas of forests are made the property of the State. Table 9.4 shows the global distribution of forests and the reason to the idea that a qualitative forest cover is better than a quantitative area of 33 per cent of the total land area should be under forest cover. The Table 9.4 also shows that Asia has only 18.5 per cent, and Africa has 21.4 per cent of forests from its total land area. Oceania has about 24.3 per cent forest cover, while America has 32.7 per cent of forests from its total land area. We can clearly observe that the temperature and rainfall pattern play a vital role in the development of forests and the regeneration of forests. In Europe and Latin America where the temperature and rainfall patterns is very much conducive for the growth of forests, the forested areas are 44.3 per cent and 47.3 per cent respectively.

The weather in India and particularly in most of the parts of Gujarat is not conducive for the afforestation programme. Hilly areas of the Eastern part of Gujarat are the best areas for forestation. All other degraded areas should be handed over to the *Gram Sabha* as per our proposition so that they can ultimately develop a green belt if not the dense forest for livelihood.

Table 9.4: Distribution of Global Share of Forests over Land

Area	*% of Forest over Total Land*
Central Africa	44.6
East Africa	18.9
Northern Africa	08.2
Southern Africa	29.0
West Africa	14.9
Total Africa	**21.4**
Central Asia	03.6
East Asia	21.3
South Asia	19.2
South East Asia	46.8
Western Asia	04.3
Total Asia	**18.5**
Total Europe	**44.3**
Caribbean	26.1
Central America	43.9
South America	47.7
Total Latin America And Caribbean	**47.3**
North America	32.7
Total America	**32.7**
Total Oceania	**24.3**
Total World	**30.3**

Source: State of the World's Forests 2007, FAO, Rome, 2007.

The Indian Forest Act, 1927 and the Forest (Conservation) Act, 1980

The Indian Forest Act of 1927 which enabled the Government to proclaim any piece of land as forest and claim it as a Government land was intended to safeguard the interests of commercial forestry and ensure a regular supply of timber based on *eminent domain*. As a result of blanket notifications, the land inhabited by tribals for generations was converted into reserved forests. Tribals were considered encroachers by government officials as the legal record of rights did not exist in tribal areas. The Indian Forest Act of 1927 needs to be discarded completely and it is time to introduce a totally new comprehensive Forest Act.

Though Mr. Jairam Ramesh, the former Minister of State for Environment and Forests of the Government of India had stated that "the Forest Conservation Act, 1980 is sacrosanct. That's the Bible for me. Naturally, there is a significant lobby for liberalizing this Forest Conservation Act, 1980 under any pretext. I cannot be party to any decision that allows for significant diversion of forest land" (Bindra 2009: 56), but according to us, The Forest Conservation Act of 1980 is not a practical and scientific proposal with "33 per cent areas under forests syndrome" (Rao and Sankaran, 2003), and this has been reflected in the National Forest Policy of 1988. Hence, this Act needs to be reviewed fully, keeping in mind the LCC, rainfall patterns, soil types and the needs of the tribal communities of the country.

Explanation in Section 2 of the Forest (Conservation) Act, 1980 has been substituted by an amendment in 1988 and now read as follows:

> "***Explanation***: For the purpose of this section "non-forest purpose" means the breaking up or clearing of any forest land or portion thereof for—
> (a) the cultivation of tea, coffee, spices, rubber, palms, oil-bearing plants, horticulture crops or medicinal plants;
> (b) any purpose other than reafforestation, but does not include any work relating or ancillary to conservation, development and management of forests and wild-life, namely, the establishment of check-posts, fire lines, wireless communications and construction of fencing, bridges and culverts, dams, waterholes, trench marks, boundary marks, pipelines or other like purposes."

This interpretation is very restrictive. The building of dams, culverts or bridges or laying of pipelines for the use of local tribal communities would constitute a non-forest purpose and would not be entitled to an exemption under this details. This Act was intended to check the diversion of pristine forest land for non-forestry purposes except by the concurrence of the Central Government. It was envisioned to provide a legal remedy for the settlement of rights of the tribals. But instead, it aggravated the plight of tribal communities by causing further evictions in the name of conservation and denying their legal rights.

The National Forest Policy of 1988 created a jubilant mood among activists and Non-Governmental Organizations (NGOs). Various NGOs began to plan numerous development projects for the betterment of the tribal communities and were sure that they would be permitted to use degraded forest lands. But the Amendment of the Forest (Conservation) Act of 1980 in the year 1988 dissipated all the euphoria created. The cost of conservation has soared high, and social conflicts have threatened the very objectives of conservation. The amendment was made only to achieve the arbitrary target of 33 per cent forest cover set by the Forest Policy of 1988, despite the fact that there were high discrepancies between the forests on paper and the ground realities regarding forest, large tracts of non-forest lands were converted into forest land by 'blanket legislation'. As far as Gujarat is concerned, 33 per cent of land as forest area can never be a reality.

The need of the hour is to have a new comprehensive Forest Act as the country is heading towards a developed economy with the growth rate of more than 6 per cent of GDP. But, unfortunately India lacks the political will to bring into force a comprehensive Forest Policy.

It is proposed that, current environmental problems and the problems of the tribal communities in the country need a total review with scientific and systematic outlook. There is a crying need to review the current status of forest-dwellers and forests as a whole need to do away with the Indian Forest Act of 1927 and The Forest (Conservation) Act of 1980 and bring in new comprehensive Forest Law which looks after the environment, the forests and the forest-dwellers.

Forest Rights Act, 2006

The Scheduled Tribes and Other Traditional Forest Dwellers (Recognition of Forest Rights) Act, 2006, known as Forest Rights Act (FRA), needs minor amendments in the Act for effective implementation at the ground level. There is no doubt that there exists genuine problems of the forest dwelling tribal communities, who, due to the multiplicity of factors could not get their rights recognized under the law and consequently come across harassment at the hands of the Government Departments. The recognition of the *right to the land* where tribal communities have lived for generation is not just basic human right but is also a constitutional right. In view of these concerns, the Supreme Court of India is still determining the lawsuit concerning the settlement of rights in the case of the Centre for Environmental Law *vs.* the Union of India in W.P. 337 of 1995 and also in the case of Mr. T.N. Godavarman Thirumulpad *vs.* the Union of India in W.P. 202 of 1995.

Unfortunately, despite its wide ranging implications, it seems that the whole process of drafting the FRA Bill was undertaken in haste. It is still not known as to whether the Technical Sub-committee represented any group with "rich experience and deep association" keeping in mind environmental protection and its impact on human beings. Further, it has been determined that no public consultation had ever taken place. It was clearly stated that the subject matter of the FRA was clearly not an issue concerning national security, so there was no reason to keep out public discussion. The FRA Bill was made available for comments only for a brief period, which was clearly insufficient time to comment on the Bill with wide reaching implications.

The FRA aims to correct a "historical Injustice", however, in its current form it is bound to create more confusion than rectification. We think that many of the issues relating to the non-recognition of rights could be dealt through procedures prescribed in our suggestions, mentioned previously. These should be followed in a time bound manner; there is, therefore, an urgent need to bring into the discussion a cross section of people, including diverse tribal communities so that a viable, realistic and ecologically sustainable solution can be worked out on the issues concerning the rights of the forest dwelling Scheduled Tribes.

We propose the formation of a Tribal Forest Land Commission at the national level having offices in all the States of India on the lines of the Election Commission, comprising of a multi-disciplinary team of tribal representatives, experts in the field of forest and wildlife and representatives of the various NGOs headed by a Judge of the Supreme Court. The State office of the proposed Tribal Forest Land Commission should be headed by a Judge of the respective High Courts of the State. The Commission should be entrusted the task of monitoring the successful implementation of FRA based on practical, but scientific approaches and also monitor the post-implementation phase for at least a decade.

The Commission should study the following points at the time of strictly implementing the various provisions under the FRA:

(a) Aspirations of tribal and the socio-economic status of the tribals,
(b) Current livelihood status of beneficiaries,
(c) Number of beneficiary nuclear families, and their intention towards adult children who need their own land and dwellings,
(d) Record current forest cover of the area which is to be transferred to them, and
(e) Perception of tribals towards wild and other ferocious animals which inhabit that forest, and recent changes in perception as opposed to historic and romantic perceptions.

This general perception is based primarily on conjectures although there is no denying the fact that community participation is essential for successful conservation. Yet security of tenure by itself will not lead to conservation. Examples are the forests in most of the North Eastern States governed by Sixth Schedule of the Constitution wherein security of tenure did not lead to the conservation of biodiversity. This point was highlighted in the Report of the Expert Committee of the North East (also called the Rajamani Committee Report 2.5.1) which observed that:

> The Government owned Reserved and Protected Forest areas are generally being conserved and worked under the prescription of working plans...but rest of the forests are being subjected to heavy and unregulated felling at the pleasure of the owners or contractors working in the area after taking lease from the local owners, tribal chiefs and the District Council Authorities. The Arunachal Permit system in un-classed forest also follows the same procedure. As no scientific silvi-cultural or yield control is developed, the best seed bearer trees are being removed without any effort or investment for regeneration or seeding or planting of the areas....this is the main reason for a fall in the forest cover in the North Eastern States.

Security of tenure and title deeds transferred to the tribal families would not be the primary solution. On the contrary, if the forest lands were given to the tribal family as per the FRA, then there needs to be a guarantee for the security of the title deed. Money-lenders in the tribal areas are one of the main culprits for the poor economic conditions of the tribal communities. The Government of Gujarat has been giving *Adhikar Patra* (Authorization Letter), which gives cultivation rights to the tribals but not the ownership rights to the land.

Here, instead of individual deeds, as, per our proposal under National Forest Policy of 1988 above, we propose; the forest land should be allotted to the village level committee comprising of tribal representatives, *Gram Sabha,* Panchayat representatives, representatives of the NGOs working for the welfare of the tribals in the area and other influential experts who can provide their expert services in the areas of agriculture, horticulture, silviculture and soil conservation along with the knowledge of all the latest development in these areas.

II

Review of the Draft of National Tribal Policy 2005

The Draft of the National Tribal Policy of 2004 presented by NDA (National Democratic Alliance) Government has been replaced by a fresh Draft formulated by the UPA (United Progressive Alliance) Government called the National Tribal Policy (NTP) in July 2006. The following excerpt from 1.2 of the NTP, 2006 needs to be carefully read:

> ...are known to dwell in compact areas, follow a community way of life, in harmony with nature, and have a uniqueness of culture, distinctive customs, traditions and beliefs which are simple, direct and non-acquisitive by nature...

This excerpt from the NTP, 2006 is a clichéd picture of the tribal community in India. Contrary to this, empirical studies and our own current study points out that the tribal community is no longer in 'compact areas'. The 'community way of living' has also broken down; tribal families are moving out of their areas in search of jobs and for the betterment of the lives of their families. The traditional hold of the respective communities over the lives of these tribals has weakened, for it is unable to protect their interests and provide them a living with dignity. We deeply desire that the Draft of the NTP should include terms currently used for tribal communities and their way of life and not from a historical perspective. The NTP Draft should also have thought about migrant tribal people, whose numbers are multiplying every year in the metropolises, but no census records are available on them. It is unrealistic to assume that tribal habitations, their habitats and way of life would remain as they were in the past. In the name of 'development for national interest', the tribal communities have been the biggest losers and mute spectators in this whole saga of development. Now, our metropolises are swelling with the unremitting streams of tribal migrants who are attracted like moths to the bright city lights; it then becomes all the more imperative that the interests of these people are protected. It is our opinion that there will be changes when tribal communities are acknowledged as dynamic and changing rather than as closed and frozen entities in time. This can be only ensured by special schemes and laws to safeguard their interests. Neither are tribal traditions and beliefs 'simple' nor are they 'direct', as stated in the Draft. Tribal social structures are highly complex, requiring an intensive anthropological study. Srivastava (n.d.:13) has seen, "It seems to me that those who have characterized tribal beliefs as 'simple' have at the back of their minds the evolutionary ideas—the tribal societies are 'simple' and in the course of time, become 'complex'."

This Draft also notes that the alienation of land is the '...single most important cause of pauperization of tribals...' The Draft has indeed used the right word—'pauperization'— to describe the conditions of the tribal communities. It also rightly states that the migration of non-tribals into tribal areas has been of great disadvantage to the local people. These outsiders have not only usurped the land, but also exploited these tribals, reducing them to slavery. Against this backdrop, we think that two steps need to be urgently taken. Firstly, all illegal transfer of tribal land should be checked stringently and secondly, the alienated land should be restored to the tribals. The problem of land alienation demands urgency, not only because it has jeopardized the lifeline of tribals, making them perpetually live on the doles that Governments and NGOs give them, but because it is the prime cause of many violent manifestations of tribal interests in various parts of India. We would also like to suggest that anthropologists should give more importance to the study of issues that are impoverishing tribal communities. They should also take up critical issues of the different legislation and their effectiveness in these conditions.

The Draft NTP of 2006 has fortunately addressed the entire process of displacement; it states that only if it is absolutely mandatory should displacement take place, and that if so it should be made in a 'more humane' manner (8.6 of Draft NTP, 2006). In this regard, we would like to raise many questions—as to how this will actually be made, the kinds of attitudinal changes that would be introduced among the officials working in the tribal areas, who often look down upon the tribal communities, and how the support of tribal communities would be ensured in the development project. These concerns need to be discussed not just debated but should be demonstrated in practical terms, as well.

The Draft also notices that tribal people over a period of time have started feeling a 'deep sense of exclusion and alienation' (11.2 of Draft NTP, 2006). With respect to this, we would like to draw attention to the fact that unscrupulous elements, invariably from outside, posing as the messiahs and problem-solvers of tribal people, play upon the gullibility of the tribals. They are also known to spread the culture and ideology of violence among them. These facts have been observed during our field work. The sequence of events in some States has been so bad that all development programmes have been virtually halted. The situation of tribal communities is alarming because of their exploitation by the 'perpetrators of violence', on the one hand, and their interrogation by law-enforcing agencies, on the other. The truth is that the tribals are caught in the crossfire and are confused about what to believe. We would like to suggest that money being spent to fight the tribal violence should be diverted to tribal development programmes. The rights of tribals over natural and financial resources should be restored, and issues of economic deprivation should be addressed through NTP.

This Draft has also many regressive features. The proposal to reinstate the 'single line administration' (5.1 of Draft NTP, 2006), for example, would lead to a concentration of powers in the district officials instead of fostering real decentralization at the grassroot level (Roy Burman, 2006). Single line administration was developed in Africa and India during the colonial era and was used at the local level. In this system, any semblance of local self-government was out of the question. If a partnership approach was intended, the contents in the Draft would have been different. There is not a single sentence, apart from mentioning the unfortunate aspects of Naxalism, about what the tribal people are doing for their advancement in education, health, gender rights, human rights, cultural rights, environmental securities and so on. It is necessary to see to what extent partnership programmes could be found with the tribal communities especially with its march towards social transformation and in close alliance with other progressive sections of Indian society. All these issues need to be addressed while redrafting the NTP.

III

Stakeholder Council—A Local Tribal Community Responsibility

Stakeholder Councils are called by many names and are created for a variety of specific purposes. Whatever, they are called, and whatever the stated purpose for which they are created, they all have many common features, and they all have a universal goal (The Consensus Process: Developing an Appropriate Response http://). To develop an effective local response in the State of Gujarat and particularly in our study area, it is necessary to understand the objectives, the processes, the techniques, and the players. The general objective of all stakeholder councils is to promote three primary values:

- Environmental Protection
- Equity
- Sustainable Economic Development

A comprehensive "community" plan must be developed which promotes, links or "integrates," above mentioned values. In some areas under tribal communities, stakeholder councils are formed to work on a single component of a comprehensive plan that is to be combined with the work of other councils that may be working on different components and in different geographical areas of the same community. The various councils may or may not know about the work of other councils that are underway simultaneously.

Currently in the USA, the most common programmes are related to the "visioning" process to create "Sustainable Communities;" Ecosystem Management Plans; Heritage Area or Corridor Plans; River Protection Plans; Biosphere Reserves; and Economic Renewal Plans. Almost always, the plan will encompass more than one political party.

The stated purpose of the stakeholder council may be related to environmental protection only, which is usually referred to as *natural resource management*. It could be related to any one of many other individual objectives such as economic renewal, education, emergency response, or transportation. Or, the stated purpose could be to develop a comprehensive plan that addresses all the issues. Whatever, the stated purpose, it will attempt to integrate environmental protection, equity, and sustainable economic development. We desire to suggest similar programmes on the same pattern for the State of Gujarat. We had made the following suggestions for National Forest Policy 1988:

> There should be joint efforts of all the four pillars—Government, people, Gram Sabha and Non-Governmental Organizations. There should be a political committees which will manage all the affairs of these lands in villages. There should be a mandatory provision that all these committees be registered either under the Bombay Public Charitable Trust Act or the Societies Act so that the committee can get the work done in proper and legal manner and can invest the spare money and can create a market or generate alternative employment with the support of the governmental interventions in support of leading NGOs...

Our suggestion is based on the current Indian scenario. The stakeholder councils in the USA and the formation of committees, as recommended by us have more or less the same goal and objectives, that is, environment protection, equity and sustainable economic development. The other major goal for the formation of the committee as per our suggestion is to move from *conflict to co-*

operation, as we strongly feel that in today's world nothing can be achieved by conflicts and confrontations.

The idea of sustainable development for the betterment of the local tribal communities would be extremely positive and would be also well received by many communities. We believe that the use of different means like, boycotting, misinterpreting different Government schemes and laws and protesting against Government procedures would not be effective. In fact, such actions could be counter-productive, and reduce the credibility of those who engage in these activities. We strongly feel that, in tribal communities, involvement is the better course of action. Here, we propose "collaborative decision-making", which is a process that begins with a predetermined outcome.

IV

Role of NGOs and Social Activists

It is not quite right to generalize the activities of NGOs and social activists. It is not right to assume that all NGOs and social activists are 'do-gooders', who have a magic wand to remove all the ills of society. At the same time, it is also not right to generalize that all NGOs and social activists are corrupt or their programmes mis-managed. In Gujarat, there are a number of NGOs and social activists 'floating around' in the name of people's development; even the most corrupt politicians have registered NGOs. There is a need to discern good from bad Government officials, bureaucrats, NGOs and social activists.

While making the distinction about the role of NGOs and social activists, we will confine ourselves to Non-Governmental Organizations and social activists who have come through the test of fire; organizations which have grown with a genuine commitment and appreciation for social welfare and justice. We speak about those who are aligned to the interests of the marginalized tribal communities and strive to demonstrate professional and ethical values in their work; those who are driven by a vision and mission and not by funds alone.

As we are well aware that today there are no forest lands and by extension there is no aspect of tribal life that does not come under the asphyxiating jurisdiction of the Government. It would, in fact, be in the best interests of the Government, the tribal people and the environmental health of forests, to work out a profit sharing and land maintenance agreement for all timber and other forest produce. Tribal people who have lived on the land for centuries have a higher stake in protecting and maintaining forests than the business and administrative interest groups who currently control it.

Here, the root of the problem is not so much in the concept but the delivery mechanism. Consider the example of watersheds, the 'in-thing' in development work with the Government these days. While, in principle, the approach is ideal to harness the natural and physical capital of the tribal areas, the gaps are in the design and the implementation processes. It is the landed that will benefit the most by developing the land. Most watershed programmes, today, need to have contributions made by the people as a pre-requisite. In real terms, the danger is that the big landlords would be back in business, forcing the landless, marginal and small tribals to do free labour for them in return for small favours. The land will belong to the big farmers, their incomes would increase; but what of the poor tribal, what of equitable land distribution? In the overall analysis, we have to ensure that the poorer sections of the tribals do not become more marginalized and poorer than what they already are. Here, we need to question the sensitivity of the Government towards social equity in the implementation of such programmes.

The Government needs to be conscious of its social obligations, in ensuring adequate efforts to make necessary products and services available to the poorer tribals in rural areas, and ensuring that development does not happen at the cost of social equity. The need of the hour is to have a Government that does not consider NGOs to be handmaidens, nor as adversaries. Where, the interests of the impoverished tribals are in question, the Government and NGOs could certainly come together and have a dialogue to ensure that social justice and equity are upheld. We need an administration that is vigilant and conscientious and an administration that works for the upliftment of the poor.

In effect we have proposed the following points that should be the broad objectives of the NGOs and social activists so that the tribals living in remote areas as well as the marginalized tribal families could derive the desired benefits:

- To explain and discuss the general characteristics of different systems functioning in the given socio-economic, socio-cultural, political and ecological settings
- To highlight and delineate crucial factors responsible for several reforms and to make effective and efficient management and quality service provisions in the community
- The fundamental goal is to act as a catalyst in bringing about local initiative and community participation in the overall improvement in the quality of life
- To develop civic and environmental consciousness among the tribal communities so that the organization of civic amenities and sanitary facilities on a self- help basis can be established. Awareness campaign could be generated for the enactment of suitable legislation for the betterment of civic standards and environmental protection.
- Mobilization of service to all segments of society like the poor, women, children and youth, through various schemes like drug and alcohol addiction programmes, organization of rallies against child labour, medical camps, blood donation camps, etc. could be made. This also includes the protection and preservation of nature, wildlife, historical and heritage monuments.

A common platform for detailed interaction between academicians, researchers and the representatives of NGOs and social activists is the need of the hour and requires immediate attention. This study brought forth a number of issues that helped to understand NGOs and social activists as organizations and comprehend academic processes and practical utilities. Issues like developing a common platform for NGOs, social activists and academicians, difficulties that NGOs and social activists' face while interacting with academicians and *vice versa*, the question of accountability of the two, issues of sustainability, of empowerment etc. were raised and discussed extensively. While it was felt that academicians were more theory oriented, NGOs, and social activists have a micro perspective. NGOs and social activists deal with the everyday realities of life, the nexus of power structures and issues of sustainability of projects. Therefore, their intervention strategies need to be culturally appropriate. The role of caste, class and regional differences in the formulation of policies and development work has not been given its due recognition by the Government. It is suggested that such issues be brought into the limelight through public forums like conferences where people from different segments of society can meet and discuss issues of relevance. NGOs and social activists have produced an alternative to the development strategies of the Government and at the same time, supplemented the programmes of the Government.

There are many other suggestions for NGOs and social activists that have emerged from our study; however, some important ones have been delineated below:

- For a better understanding of tribal communities and better policy-making and implementation of development programmes, it is needed to study tribes and the local communities from their point of view.
- More general spaces have to be carved out for the meeting of the different segments within society.
- For ethnographers, the contributions made by NGOs and social activists (as facilitators and as professional organizations) are difficult to ignore. NGOs and social activists also need to adopt a similar attitude towards research.
- A review of the power equation, attitude of the so-called 'mainstream' towards tribes as passive subjects, issues of welfare, governance, development, empowerment and approaches to tribes are what need attention in the policies formulated.
- Participation of the tribals in the developmental processes and the formulation of policies is very important.
- The national policy on tribes should specifically mention the actions that the State plans to adopt for the upliftment of tribal communities.
- NGOs and social activists play an important role in mobilizing people by creating awareness among them to protest against fallouts in situations of displacement and rehabilitation; thus their role needs to be enhanced.
- Women's issues need to be concretized into measures for empowerment through economic development and public forums.

- In terms of health and population, many times traditional knowledge is brushed aside on pretexts of primitiveness. National policy has to be evolved within a fully integrated planning framework that seeks to provide universal, comprehensive primary services, relevant to the actual needs and priorities of the local communities at a cost that people can afford.

The general feeling was that all those working for the welfare of the tribals should come together more often to elicit different points of view and move towards a better, more integrated approach towards tribal issues. At this stage, we recommend that looking to the value of the print and electronic media; the involvement of media in the process of dialogue between the NGOs, social activists and the academicians is highly desirable. Whatever, transpires in the dialogue should be informed to the general public. Media can play a very vital role in raising particular issues by telecasting documentaries and stories on the success and failure of the various projects and developmental programmes administered by various NGOs, social activists and academicians.

V

Forest Management by State

The general practice of the Forest Department is to prepare a working plan to recommend 10 to 20 years of effective forest management. These working plans pull together all the basic data of the existing state of particular forests and plan for its future management. Although, in recent years, forest protection is an impending issue, the working plans prepared in a routine way, have continued to take a casual approach and not a scientific approach. It is, therefore, necessary that a proper attention be given to the forest protection at the time of preparation of these plans.

Officers responsible for drafting these should not wholly rely on data collected by the concerned Deputy Conservator of Forests, but they should independently obtain necessary data using the latest technology like satellite imageries, GPS and GIS systems. The working plans, suggest the future management of forests, but no suggestions on how to control the degradation or destruction of forests is given. It is essential for officers who prepare these plans to give adequate importance to the serious issues of degradation and destruction of forests and make a detailed recommendation to resolve these problems efficiently. They should have provisions for hiring the required staff, buying the necessary equipments and the vehicles to control this menace. The size of beats and rounds should also be redefined keeping in view the problems of degradation and destruction of forests areas.

While suggesting the management systems and the regeneration plans for the forests, it is advisable to keep the people in mind. It is observed that trees that are directly beneficial to the people are not damaged by them. One good example is *"Mahuda"* trees. Regeneration plans to keep people in mind yields high success. Officers who are preparing the working plans need to take this into consideration for better implementation of their management plans. Regeneration of forests on dry hills is an uphill task for the Forest Department and also for the people residing in the nearby villages. We recommend that there should be check dams or ponds all along the hillside. When rain water remains stored over three years, the hilly tract would automatically get the required moisture and the soil would start generating plants. After about five years, the process of regeneration of forests even on those hillsides traditionally and historically known to be barren could be achieved.

Apart from the revisions needed in the Working Plan the following points also need to be addressed for effective forest management:

1. For effective functioning of the Forest Department, we recommend that the training of the forest personnel up to Beat Guard level should include courses on tribal dialects, culture, traditions, rural development, community participation, etc. The present negative attitude of the Forest Department needs to undergo a change.
2. As the forests need to be conserved and regenerated, with the support of the local tribal communities, establishing a close rapport between the officials and the supporting staff of the Forest Department and the local tribal communities is highly desirable.
3. It is recommended that the size of the jurisdiction should

not be based on the area but should be based on the different problems the forests areas are facing. We are of the opinion that the officials start losing the battle and are demoralized and do not give proper fight to tackle the problems facing in their jurisdiction. As a policy matter, after every three years, a small exercise to find out how much area one can manage successfully to fix the size of the beat, round, range and division should be undertaken.

4. We suggest that using the latest technology like satellite imageries to take stock which includes the type of trees, age of trees, cash value of trees, annual return available from the trees etc. under different categories— beat wise, round wise, range wise and division wise.
5. We recommend that there should be a special protection force for the protection of forests wealth. A Forest Protection Force (FPF) should be created on the lines of diverse security forces created by the Government for internal peace and safety to preserve the 8 per cent forest (as per our suggestion) (Refer 2 above) of the total geographical areas of the state of Gujarat.

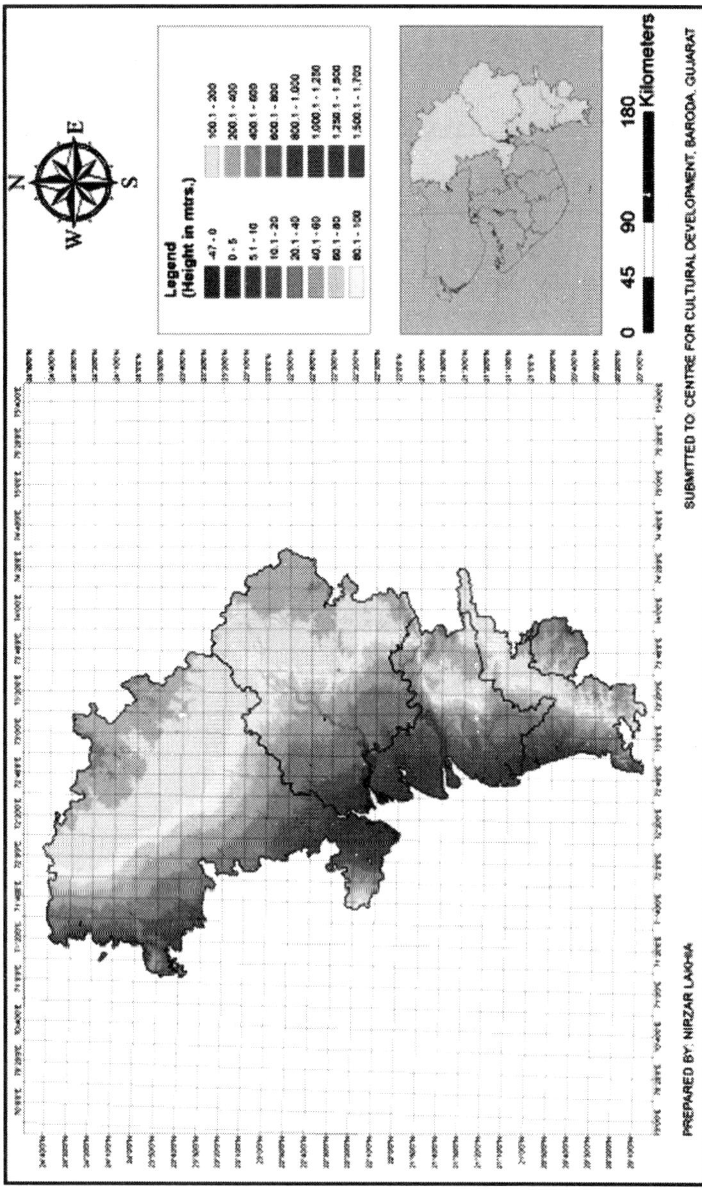

Map 9.1: Altitude Map of Study Area

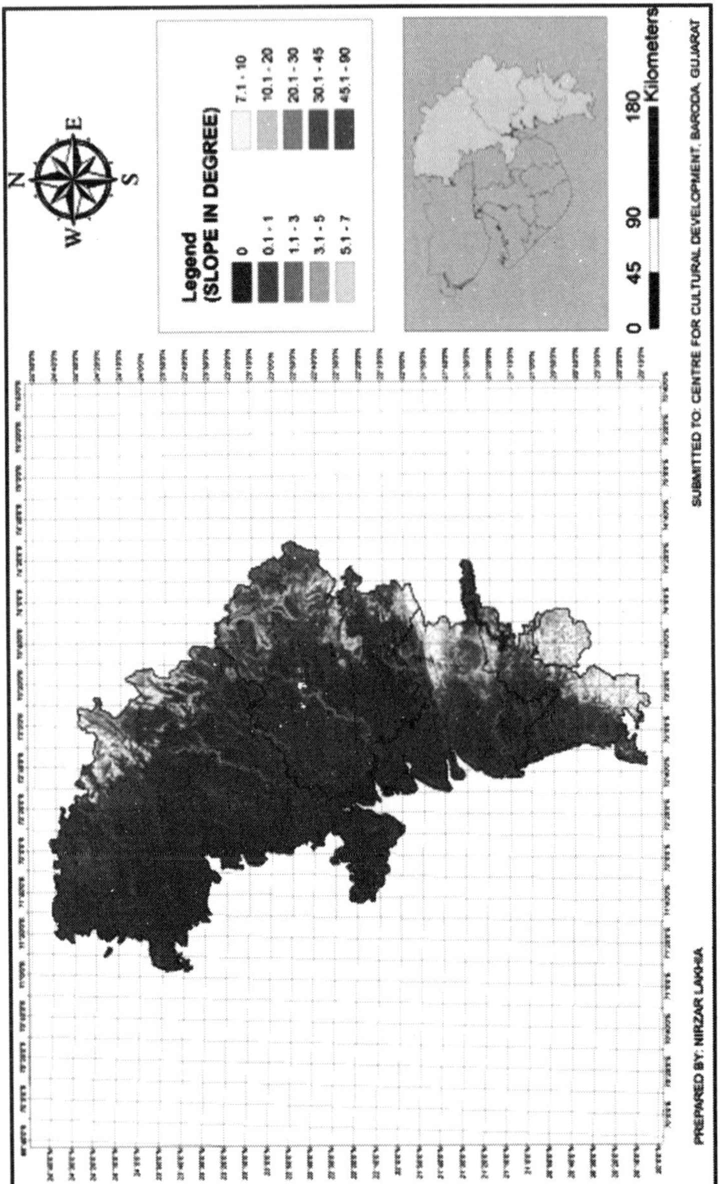

Map 9.2: Slope Map of Study Area

Annexure-1

Sampled Villages Taluka and District-wise from Eastern Gujarat

Region-I (A, B, C, D)

District	*Taluka*	*Villages*			
Sabarkantha	Vijaynagar	*Cluster A*	*Cluster B*	*Cluster C*	*Cluster D*
		1. Kelava			
		2. Chitariya			
		3. Jaleti			
		4. Gadi			
		5. Navagam (Dhanela)			
		6. Vireshwar			
		7. Zer			
		8. Bhakhara			
		9. Antarsumba			
		10. Kherwada			
		11. Dagla			
		12. Saroli			
		13. Vanaj			
		14. Aabhapur			
Sabarkantha	Khedbrahma		1. Mama Pipla		
			2. Chandrana		
			3. Bora (Rajasthan)		
			4. Ganer		
			5. Padapat		
			6. Matarwada		
			7. Dantral		
			8. Ganva		
			9. Chhatrang		
			10. Kalikankar		
			11. Demti		
			12. Ajavas		
			13. Vinchhi		

Annexure-1 (*Contd.*)

Region-II (A, B, C, D)

District	*Taluka*	*Villages*			
Chhota Udepur	*Vadodara*	*Cluster A*	*Cluster B*	*Cluster C*	*Cluster D*
		1. Tundeva 2. Singla 3. Dhadagam 4. Kunbhali 5. Koli 6. Ambala 7. Kevdi 8. Jamli 9. Gandiya			
Pavi Jetpur	**Vadodara**	1. Boddha 2. Raipur 3. Zal 4. Kosam 5. Mudhiyari 6. Bandi 7. Degla			
Dahod	**Dhanpur**		1. Bhindol 2. Harakhapur 3. Panam 4. Gumli 5. Kejera 6. Vankota 7. Rachhava 8. Khajuri 9. Kanakhunt 10. Mendhri (Limdha)		
Dahod	**Dhanpur**			1. Kanakuva 2. Udar 3. Sajoi 4. Amli Menpur 5. Bhindol 6. Panv 7. Kantu 8. Bilia	
Panchmahal	**Ghoghamba**			1. Kharod 2. Simaliya 3. Kanpur 4. Gamirpura 5. Uncha Beda 6. Ambakhunt 7. Bor 8. Boria	

(*Contd.*)

Annexure-1 (*Contd.*)

District	*Taluka*	*Villages*			
Chhota Udepur	*Vadodara*	*Cluster A*	*Cluster B*	*Cluster C*	*Cluster D*
Panchmahal	**Halol**				1. Bapotiya 2. Navi Bhat 3. Champaner 4. Moti Umarvan 5. Kanteli 6. Dharia 7. Talavdi 8. Shivrajpur 9. Ved 10. Vadatalav

Region-III (A, B, C)

District	*Taluka*	*Villages*			
Surat	*Mandvi*	*Cluster A*	*Cluster B*	*Cluster C*	*Cluster D*
		1. Ladkuva 2. Patal 3. Kolkhadi 4. Paravat 5. Kasal 6. Choramba 7. Balethi 8. Ishar 9. Kalmoi 10. Petarkui 11. Piplaval 12. Limdha 13. Picharvan 14. Amli 15. Lundha 16. Jamkui 17. Gangapur (Devgadh) 18. Tuked			

(*Contd.*)

Annexure-1 (*Contd.*)

District	*Taluka*	*Villages*			
Surat	*Mandvi*	*Cluster A*	*Cluster B*	*Cluster C*	*Cluster D*
Narmada	**Dediapada**		1. Mal 2. Mota Sukamba 3. Kaltar 4. Nana Sukamba 5. Samot 6. Bhatpur 7. Gadi 8. Dhonkhetar 9. Piplod 10. Morjadi 11. Dantawadi 12. Godda 13. Zarnavadi 14. Kunbar 15. Gangapur 16. Jambar		
Bharuch	**Jhagadia**			1. Kantol 2. Vishalkhadi 3. Movi 4. Koliyapada 5. Kund 6. Bhalod 7. Dholi 8. Vali 9. Vandarveli 10. Shankoi 11. Dabhal 12. Razalwada 13. Jamoli 14. Vankol	

Region-VI (A, B, C)

District		*Taluka*		*Villages*	
Valsad	*Dharampur*	*Cluster A*	*Cluster B*	*Cluster C*	*Cluster D*
		1. Kangvi 2. Shishumal 3. Tamachhadi 4. Penadha 5. Dhamni 6. Laheri 7. Mankadban			

(*Contd.*)

Annexure-1 (*Contd.*)

District	*Taluka*	*Villages*			
Valsad	*Dharampur*	*Cluster A*	*Cluster B*	*Cluster C*	*Cluster D*
		8. Hanmatmal 9. Avadha 10. Rajpuri Dungar			
Navsari	**Vansda**		1. Ghodmal 2. Khatamba 3. Lachhakdi 4. Bartad 5. Mankuniya 6. Boriachh 7. Ambapani 8. Kandha 9. Ravaniya		
Tapi	**Vyara**			1. Kalamkui 2. Besania 3. Padam Dungri 4. Kevdi 5. Takiamba 6. Chunavadi 7. Dhogiamba 8. Ambapani 9. Dholka 10. Dhangdhar 11. Dhamandevi 12. Raigadh 13. Pipalwada	

Region-V (A, B, C, D)

District	*Taluka*	*Villages*			
		Cluster A	*Cluster B*	*Cluster C*	*Cluster D*
Dang	Dang (Ahwa)	1. Bardipada 2. Mahal 3. Savarda Kasad 4. Savarkhadi 5. Chikhla 6. Wankan 7. Dardi	1. Kalamvihir 2. Vanzar Ghodi 3. Padalkhadi 4. Kirli 5. Dhavli Dod	1. Diwandemrun 2. Jamlapada 3. Isdar 4. Gadhavi	1. Gavdahad 2. Javtala 3. Jamanyamal 4. Baj 5. Girmal

Annexure-3

Forest Flora of Gujarat: Trees, Shrubs and Herbs, Climbers, Bamboo and Grasses and Twinners

List of Trees

Local name	*Botanical name*	*Family*
Aduso	*Ailanthus excelsa*	*Simaroubaceae*
Arduso	*Ailanthus excelsa*	*Imaru aceae*
Agathio	*Sesbania grandiflora*	*Leguminosae*
Agathiyo	*Sesbania grandiflora*	*Fabaceae*
Alan	*Elaeodendron roxburghii*	*Celasteraccae*
Alan	*Elacodendron glaucum*	*Celastraceae*
Aladi, Al, Allori	*Morinda tinctoria*	*Rubiaceae*
Al	*Morinda tomentosa*	*Rubiaceae*
Ambo	*Mangifera Indica*	*Anacardiacoae*
Ambedo, Ambadi	*Spondias pinnata*	*Anacardiaceae*
Ambadi	*Spondias pinnata*	*Rubiaceae*
Ambedo	*Spondias mangifera*	*Anacardiaceae*
Amla	*Emblica officinalis*	*Euphorbiaceae*
Amli, Ambli	*Tamarindus indica*	*Caesalpiniaceae*
Aniyar or Rinjado	*Acacia leucophloea*	*Mimosaceae*
Anjan	*Hardwickia binata*	*Caesalpiniaceae*
Ankal, Ankol	*Alangium salvifolium*	*Alangiacoae*
Ankal	*Analgium salvifolium*	*Cornaceae*
Aritha	*Sapindus emarginatus*	*Sapindaceae*
Asitari, Asintro	*Bauhinia racemosa*	*Caesalpiniaceae*

(*Contd.*)

Local name	*Botanical name*	*Family*
Bakam Limdo	*Melia azedarach*	*Meliaceae*
Baval, Deshibaval	*Acacia nilotica*	*Legriminosae*
Deshibaval	*Acacia nilotica*	*Mimosaceae*
Bahedo	*Terminalia bellirica*	*Combretaceae*
Bhangro	*Erythrina suberosa*	*Papilionaceae*
Bhongaro	*Erythrina suberosa*	*Fabaceae*
Bili	*Aegle marmelos*	*Rutaceae*
Bilior Bel	*Aegle marmelos*	*Rutaceae*
Biyo	*Pterocarpus marsupium*	*Papilionaceae*
Biyo	*Pterocarpus marsupium*	*Fabaceae*
Charoli	*Buchanania lanzan*	*Anacardiaceae*
Chani bor	*Zizyphus nummularia*	*Rhamnaceae*
Dantio, Asan	*Bridelia retusa*	*Euphorbiaceae*
Dhaman	*Grewia tiliaefolia*	*Tiliaceae*
Dhavdo	*Anogeissus latifolia*	*Combretaceae*
Safed Davdo	*Anogeissus latifolia*	*Combretaceae*
Dhau	*Anogeissus pendula*	*Combretaceae*
Dheki	*Diospyros cordifolia*	*Ebenaceae*
Dudhi	*Wrightia tinctoria*	*Apocynaceae*
Dudhi, Kalo Kudo	*Wrightia tomentosa*	*Apocynaceae*
Ganda Baval	*Prosopis juliflora*	*Mimosaceae*
Garmalo, Bahva	*Cassia fistula*	*Caesalpiniacea*
Ghatbor (Ghunt)	*Zizyphus xyloeyrus*	*Rhamnaceae*
Gol	*Trema orientalis*	*Ulmaceae*
Gol	*Trema orientelis*	*Urticaceae*
Gol	*Randia brandisii*	*Rubiaceae*
Gorad	*Acacia senegal*	Mimosaceae
Gugal, Saledi, Salaz	*Boswellia serrata*	*Burseraceae*
Gundi/Gundo	*Cordia dichotoma*	*Ehretiaceae*
Gundi	*Cordia dichotoma*	*Boraginaceae*
Goras Amli	*Pithecellobium dulce*	*Mimosaceae*
Haldarvo, Hed	*Adina cordifolia*	*Rubiaceae*

(*Contd.*)

Local name	*Botanical name*	*Family*
Ingoria, Hingori	*Balanites aegyptica*	*Balanitaceae*
Jambu	*Syzygium cumini*	*Myrtaceae*
Kadaya, Kadai	*Sterculia urens*	*Sterculiaceae*
Kadvai	*Hymenodictyon excelsum*	*Rubiaceae*
Kagar, Kanti	*Acacia ferruginea*	*Mimosaceae*
Kaju	*Anacardium occidentale*	*Anacardiaceae*
Kakad	*Garuga pinnata*	*Burseraceae*
Kakadio, Bondaro	*Lagerstroemia parviflora*	*Lythraceae*
Kalam	*Mitragyna parvifolia*	*Rubiaceae*
Kanaji	*Holoptelea integrifolia*	*Ulmaceae*
Karanj	*Pongamia pinnata*	*Leguminosae*
Karanj	*Pongamia glabra*	*Caesalpiniaceae*
Karanj	*Pongomia pinnata*	*Papilionaceae*
Karanj	*Pongamia pinnata*	*Fabaceae*
Karvali	*Streblus asper*	*Moraceae*
Karvali	*Streblus asper*	*Urticaceae*
Kasid	*Cassia siamea*	*Caesalpiniaceae*
Kasid	*Cassia siamea*	*Leguminosae*
Khair	*Acacia chundra (catechu)*	*Mimosaceae*
Khakharo/Kesudo	*Butea monosperma*	*Leguminosae*
Khakhro/Kesuda	*Butea monosperma*	*Papilionaceae*
Khakhro, Kesudo	*Butea monosperma*	*Fabaceae*
Khajuri	*Phoenix sylvestris*	*Palmae*
Khajuri	*Phoenix sylvestris*	*Arecaceae*
Kothu	*Feronia elephantum*	*Rutaceae*
Kusum	*Schleichera oleosa*	*Sapindaceae*
Limdo, Neem	*Azadirachta indica*	*Meliaceae*
Mahuda	*Madhuca indica*	*Sapotaceae*
Medhsingi	*Dolichandrone falcate*	*Bignoniaceae*
Mindhal	*Xeromphis spinosa*	*Rubiaceae*
Moyno, Modad	*Lannea coromandelica*	*Anacardiaceae*
Mokho	*Schrebera swietenioides*	*Oleaceae*

(Contd.)

Local name	*Botanical name*	*Family*
Nana chavdo	*Lagerstroemia lanceolata*	*Lythraceae*
Nilgiri	*Eucalyptus spp*	*Mytraceae (Mysorehy)*
Pongaro	*Erythrina indica*	*Leguminosae*
Panisadad	*Terminalia peniculata*	*Combretaceae*
Passi, Patral/Padri	*Dalbergia paniculata*	*Leguminosae*
Pipal	*Ficus religiosa*	*Urtiaceae*
Ratanjot	*Jatropha curcas*	*Euphorbiaceae*
Rain tree	*Samanea saman*	*Mimosaceae*
Rayan	*Manilkara hexandra*	*Sapotaceae*
Rohan, Royan	*Soymida febrifuga*	*Meliaceae*
Sadad	*Terminalia crenulata*	*Combretaceae*
Sag, sagvan	*Tectona grandis*	*Verbenaceae*
Sargavo	*Moringa oleifera*	*Moringaceae*
Sarasdo, Dholi Siras	*Albizia odoratissima*	*Mimosaceae*
Shamela Gugal	*Gardenia turgida*	*Rubiaceae*
Shisham	*Dalbergia latifolia*	*Leguminosae*
Shivan/Seven	*Gmelina arborea*	*Verbenaceae*
Simal, Semdo	*Bombax ceiba*	*Bombacaceae*
Siras	*Albizzia lebbeck*	*Mimosaceae*
Sissoo	*Dalbergia sissoo*	*Leguminosae*
Sitafal	*Annona squamosa*	*Annonaceae*
Sukhad	*Santalum album*	*Santalaceae*
Tad	*Borassus flabellifer*	*Palmae*
Tanach	*Ougeinia oojeinensis*	*Leguminosae*
Timru	*Diospyros melanoxylon*	*Ebenaceae*
Umberdo	*Ficusracemosa*	*Moraceae*
Umbh, Umbhi	*Miliusa tomentosa*	*Annonaceae*
Vad	*Ficus benghalensis*	*Moraceae*
Shrubs and Herbs		
Ardusi	*Adhatoda vasica*	*Acanthaceae*

(Contd.)

Local name	Botanical name	Family
Aghado	*Achyranthes aspera*	*Amarantaceae*
kdo Moto	*Calotropis gigantea*	*Asclepiadaceae*
Avalor Avar	*Cassia auriculata*	*Caesalpiniaceae*
Dano	*Lantana camara*	*Verbanaceae*
Dhaturo (Dholo)	*Datura metel*	*Solanacece*
Gokhru, Gadar	*Xanthium strumarium*	*Asteraceae*
Kanthar	*Capparis sepiaria*	*Capparidaceae*
Kanksi	*Abutilon indicum*	*Malvaceae*
Kerdo	*Capparis decidua*	*Capparidaceae*
Karoi, Karvi	*Carvia cauosa*	*Acanthaceae*
Karo, Pinjaro	*Cadaba fruticosa*	*Capparidaceae*
Kade, Kudi	*Holarrhena antidysenterica*	*Apocynaceae*
Kini-kherdi	*Dichrostachys cinerea*	*Leguminosae*
Luni	*Suaeda monoica*	*Chenpodiaceae*
Maradasing	*Helicteres isora*	*Sterculiaceae*
Nagad	*Vitex negundo*	*Verbenaceae*
Parijat	*Nyctanthes arbortristis*	*Oleaceae*
Puvad	*Cassia tora*	*Leguminosae*
Thor	*Euphorbia neriifolia*	*Euphorbiaceae*
Vico, Vigo, Vikro	*Maytenus emarginata*	*Cebastraceae*
Yenkdi	*Flacourtia indica*	*Flacourtiaceae*
Zil	*Indigofera oblongifolia*	*Leguminosae*
Climbers		
Amarvel	*Cuscuta reflexa*	*Convolvulaceae*
Asan or Vavdi	*Coculus hirsutus*	*Menispermaceae*
Chairo	*Dioscoria oppositifolia*	*Diascoriaceae*
Chanothi	*Abrus precatorius*	*Leguminoeae*
Chilar, Ganji	*Acacia intsia*	*Leguminoeae*
Chilari	*Caesalpinia sepiaria*	*Leguminosae*
Dodi	*Dragea volubilis*	*Asclopiadaceae*
Fangvel, Fang	*Rivea hypocrateriformis*	*Convolvulaceae*

(Contd.)

Local name	*Botanical name*	*Family*
Galo	*Rinespora cordifolia*	*Menispermaceae*
Karamdi	*Carissa conjesta*	*Apocynaceae*
Kharo Dharm	*Cressa cretica*	*Covolculaceae*
Malkakani, Kangarvel	*Celastrus paniculata*	*Celastraceae*
Moti Khakhi	*Combretum ovalifolium*	*Combretaceae*
Versha Dodi	*Baemia extensa*	*Asclepiadaceae*
Arun	*Cocculus labea*	*Menispermaceae*
Chanoti	*Abrus precatorius* *Demia extensa*	*Caesalpinieae Dodi* *Asclepiadaceae*
Varsha dodi	*Leptadenia reticulate*	*Asclepidaceae*
Jungli Draksh	*Ampelocissus latfolia*	*Vitaceae*
Satavai	*Asparagus racemosus*	*Liliaceae*
Boganvel	*Bongainvillea spectabilis*	*Nyctaginaceae*
Khakharvel	*Butea superba*	*Papilionaceae*
Khakharvel	*Butea parivflora*	*Papilionaceae*
—	*Cayratia auricalata*	*Vitaceae*
Khat-Khatumbo	*Cayratia carnosa*	*Vitaceae*
Venivel	*Cissampelos pareira*	*Menispennaceae*
Ghiloda	*Coccinia grandis*	*Cacurbitaceae*
Vevdi	*Cocculus hirsutus*	*Menispennaceae*
Rubber Vel	*Crypotostegia grandiflora*	*Periplocaceae*
Kakadi	*Cucumis sativus*	*Cucurbitaceae*
Kolu	*Cucurbita maxima*	*Cucurbitaceae*
Nilsoti	*Delbergia volubilis*	*Fabaceae*
Duthle	*Lagenaria leucantha*	*Cacurbitaceae*
Turiya	*Luffa acutangula*	*Cucurbitaceae*
Jungli Turiya	*Luffa acutangula var.amara*	*Cucurbitaceae*
Karela	*Mimordica charantia*	*Cucurbitaceae*
Kankoda	*Mimordica dioca*	*Cucurbitaceae*
Chanak-Chibadi	*Mukia maderaspatana*	*Cacurbitaceae*
Kuvech	*Mucuna pruriens*	*Papilionaceae*
Kuvech	*Mucuna puritsr*	*Papilionaceae*

(Contd.)

Local name	Botanical name	Family
—	*Passiflora foetidti*	*Passifloraceae*
Krishna Kamal	*Passiflora edulis*	*Passifloraceae*
Madhu Malti	*Quisqualis indica*	*Combretaceae*
Gulvel	*Tinospora cordifolia*	*Menispennaceae*
—	*Trichosanthes cucumis*	*Cucurbitaceae*
Khat Khatumba	*Vilis diformis*	*Vitaceae*
Chanothi, Gunja	*Abrus precatorius*	*Fabaceae*
Chilari	*Acacia pinnata*	*Mimosaceae*
Chilari	*Caesalpinia sepiaria*	*Caesalpiniaceae*
Kavach, Kaunch	*Mucuna prurieta*	*Fabilceae*
Madvel	*Combretum ovalifolium*	*Combretaceae*
Nani dodi	*Leptadenia reticulata*	*Asclepiadaceae*
Shikakhai	*Acacia sinnata*	*Minosaceae*
Chilar	*Acacia intsia*	*Minosaceae*
Palasvel	*Butea superba*	*Fabaceae*
Ukshi	*Calcopteris floribunda*	*Combretaceae*
Tanvel	*Cocculus villosus*	*Menispermaceae*
Boadverl, Dhamanvel	*Combretum ovalifolium*	*Combretaceae*
Mendhvel	*Cryptolepis buchanani*	*Ascelpiadaceae*
Kaduvel	*Dioscorea pentaphyila*	*Dioscoreaceae*
Kokharvel	*Ipomea digitata*	*Convovulaceae*
Velabivia	*Millettia racemose*	*Fabaceae*
Ran udid	*Termus labialis*	*Fabaceae*
Charvel	*Tinospora cordifolia*	*Menispermacca*
Asaivel	*Ventilago denticulata*	*Rhamnaceae*
Kangvel	*Vantilago denticulata*	*Rhamnaceae*
Panvivel	*Vitis repanda*	*Vitaceae*
Vaghatvel	*Wagatea spicata*	*Caesalpiniaceae*
Toran	*Zizyphus rugosa*	*Rhamnaceae*
Abvel	*Canavalia gladiata*	*Fabaceae*
Arvel	*Ipomea pes-capre*	*Convolvulaceae*
Achhvel	*Ventilago madraspatana*	*Rharnnaceae*

(Contd.)

Local name	*Botanical name*	*Family*
Akaswel or Amrvel	*Cuscuta reflexa*	*Convolvulaceae*
Alai	*Dalbergia volubilis*	*Fabaceae*
Bamboo and Grasses		
Manvel Vans	*Dendrocalamus strictus*	*Gramineae*
Manvel	*Dendrocalamus strictus*	*Poaceae*
Baru	*Sorghum halepense*	*Gramineae*
Bhatadi	*Themeda quardrivalvis*	*Gramineae*
Bhatadi	*Themeda quardrivalvis*	*Poaceae*
Bhangoru (Karedi)	*Apluda mutica*	*Gramineae*
Bhangoru (Karedi)	*Apluda mutica*	*Poaceae*
Daro or Dub	*Cynodon dactylon*	*Gramineae*
Daro or Durva	*Cynodon dactylon*	*Poaceae*
Dhaman	*Cenchrus ciliaris*	*Gramineae*
Dhaman, Anjan	*Cenchrus ciliaris*	*Poaceae*
Dharamnu	*Cenchrus setigerus*	*Gramineae*
Dhramnu	*Cenchrus setigerus*	*Poaceae*
Dhundu Ghas	*Arundinella pumila*	*Gramineae*
Dhundu Ghas (Bajariu)	*Arundinella pumila*	*Poaceae*
Gandharu	*Cymbopogon jwarancusa*	*Gramineae*
Gandharu	*Cymbopogon jwarancusa*	*Poaceae*
Kakudu, Katusla	*Saccharum spontaneum*	*Gramineae*
Katusla, Katuhal	*Saccharum spontaneum*	*Poaceae*
Khariu	*Dinebra retroflexa*	*Gramineae*
Khariu	*Dinebra retroflexa*	*Poaceae*
Khasi	*Aristida hystrix*	*Gramineae*
Kunchi (Pajala)	*Setaria glauca*	*Gramineae*
Kunchi, Kalvo	*Setaria glauca*	*Poaceae*
Lapdu	*Aristida adscensionis*	*Gramineae*
Lapdu	*Aristida funiculata*	*Gramineae*
Mosi	*Iseilema laxum*	*Gramineae*
Mohti	*Iseilema laxum*	*Poaceae*

(Contd.)

Local name	*Botanical name*	*Family*
Pusha	*Cymbopogon citratus*	*Gramineae*
Bhatdu	*Themeda cymbaria*	*Gramineae*
Bhatedu	*Themeda cymbaria*	*Poaceae*
Rosha	*Cymbopogon martinii*	*Gramineae*
Rosha, Rosdo	*Cymbopogon martinii*	*Poaceae*
Rosha	*Cymbopogon contortus*	*Gramineae*
Sukhli	*Heteropogon contortus*	*Gramineae*
Sukhli	*Heteropogon contortus*	*Poaceae*
Zinzvo	*Dichanthium annulatum*	*Gramineae*
Zinzvo, Rathedo	*Dichanthium annulatum*	*Poaceae*
Bhathdu	*Themeda triandra*	*Gramineae*
Dhudu	*Arundinella pumila*	*Gramineae*
Jinjavo	*Dichanthium annulatum*	*Gramineae*
Katas bamboo	*Bambusa arundinacea*	*Gramineae*
Katas	*Bamboosa arundinaceae*	*Poaceae*
Rathedu	*Themeda quadrivalvis*	*Gramineae*
Rathedu	*Andropogan partusus*	*Poaceae*
Shukli	*Heteropogon contortus*	*Gramineae*
" "	*Panicum antidotale*	*Gramineae*
" "	*Cenchrus ciliaris*	*Gramineae*
—	*Acrachne racemosa*	*Poaceae*
—	*Apluda mutica*	*Poaceae*
Dabholu	*Aristida adscensionis*	*Poaceae*
—	*Arthraxon lancifolius*	*Poaceae*
Zenzvo	*Bothriochloa pertusa*	*Poaceae*
Roicha Ghas	*Cymbopogon martini*	*Poaceae*
—	*Chloris barbata*	*Poaceae*
—	*Chrysopogon fulvus*	*Poaceae*
Kahudo	*Coix lachryma-jobi*	*Poaceae*
Kahudo	*Coix lachryma-jobi*	*Poaceae*
—	*Cymbopogon citratus*	*Poaceae*
Darb	*Cynodon dactylon*	*Poaceae*

(Contd.)

Local name	*Botanical name*	*Family*
Narvans	*Dendrocalamus strictus*	*Poaceae*
—	*Dichanthiunl annulaium*	*Poaceae*
—	*Digitaria adscendens*	*Poaceae*
Adbau, Sarno	*E.crusgalli*	*Poaceae*
—	*E.tenella*	*Poaceae*
—	*E.viscose*	*Poaceae*
Sarno	*Echinochloa colonum*	*Poaceae*
Adhen Nasli	*Eleusine indica*	*Poaceae*
—	*Eragrostis japonica*	*Poaceae*
—	*Hackelochloa granularis*	*Poaceae*
—	*Hemarthria compressa*	*Poaceae*
Dabhsuliu	*Heteropogon contortus*	*Poaceae*
—	*Melanocenchris jacquemontii*	*Poaceae*
Goriu	*Paspalidium flavidum*	*Poaceae*
Sherdi	*Saccharum officinarum*	*Poaceae*
Chano	*Setaria italica*	*Poaceae*
—	*Themeda quadrivalvis*	*Poaceae*
Makai	*Zea mays*	*Poaceae*
Bhoin lampdo	*Aristida histricula*	*Poaceae*
Lampdo, Safed khasli	*Aristida funiculata*	*Poaceae*
Gundan, Dhandani	*Chloris incomplete*	*Poaceae*
Dabdhruvo	*Cynodon dactyion*	*Poaceae*
Bhatkari	*Elyptrophorous articulatus*	*Poaceae*
Kasur, Sukil	*Heteropogon contortas*	*Poaceae*
Bhardi	*Ischoemum aristatum*	*Poaceae*
Tokarband	*Panicum notatum*	*Poaceae*
Dedhya, Dodhu	*Trilobachne cookie*	*Poaceae*
Barn	*Sorghum helepense*	*Poaceae*
Polado	*Spodiopogon xhizophous*	*Poaceae*
Bhatado	*Themada quadrivalvis*	*Poaceae*
Walchond	*Vertiveria zizynoides*	*Poaceae*

(*Contd.*)

Local name	Botanical name	Family
Twinners		
Chanothi	*Abrus precatorius*	*Fabaceae*
Samudrasos	*Argyreia sericea*	*Convolvulaceae*
Amarvel	*C. reflexa*	*Cuscutaceae*
Gharni	*Clitoria ternatea*	*Fcibaceae*
Dhurnmas (Madvel)	*Combretum Ovalifoliam*	*Combretaceae*
Mendvel	*Crypt ole pia buchanani*	*Periplicaceae*
Amarvel	*Cuscuta Chinensis*	*Cuscutaceae*
	Cylista scariosa	*Fabaceae*
Vana Vel (Dhuvasi Kand)	*Dioscorea bulifera*	*Dioscoreaceae*
Bhoi-kand	*Dioscorea hispida*	*Dioscoreaccae*
Kuvel	*Dioscorea pentaphylla*	*Dioscoreaceae*
Jangli Papadi	*Dolichostrilobus*	*Fabaceae*
Dudhvel	*Hemidesmus indicas*	*Periploeaceae*
Photial	*Ipomoca per-tigridis*	*Convolvulaceae*
Kamlata	*Ipomoea quamoclit*	*Convolvulaceae*
Kavach	*Mucunaprurita*	*Fabaceae*
Chamar Ducheli	*Pergularia daemia*	*Asclepiadaccae*
Vidhuari	*Pueraria tuberosa*	*Fabaceae*
Nahni Kamal Vel	*Rhynchosia minima*	*Fabaceae*
Varsha Dodi	*Telosmapollida*	*Asclepiadaceae*
Valia Vela	*Teramnus labialis*	*Fabaceae*
Choli	*Vigna unguiculate*	*Fabaceae*

Source: Government of Gujarat: 2006, Gujarat Forest Statistics.

Annexure-4

Altitude Zone-wise Forest Cover in India

(in Hectare)

States	0-500 meter				500-1000 meter				1000-2000 meter			
	VDF	MDF	OF	TOTAL	VDF	MDF	OF	TOTAL	VDF	MDF	OF	TOTAL
Andhra Pradesh	23600	1771400	1377800	3172800	58400	654000	539200	1251600	0	50300	35500	85800
Arunachal Pradesh	155300	368500	208600	732400	283900	423300	321600	1028800	781200	1029700	450800	2261700
Assam	107100	913200	1213900	2234200	31300	209600	227400	462300	7700	33000	32000	72700
Bihar	22500	310600	319100	652200	600	14200	13400	28200				
Chhattisgarh	187300	1691100	1011600	2890000	227800	1770800	630500	2629100	1100	41900	24900	67900
Delhi	67600	498400	1199800	1765800								
Goa	43100	59300	97500	199900	8000	3100	4100	15200				
Gujarat	33200	490200	878600	1402000	4400	34600	20800	59800	0	100	100	200
Haryana	1600	34400	95200	131200	1100	9900	13400	24400	0	2000	1800	3800
Himachal Pradesh	1300	42400	31100	74800	23700	159400	114800	297900	56900	147900	147000	351800
Jammu & Kashmir	500	18700	70200	89400	14700	133600	217000	365300	68000	252200	213600	533600
Jharkhand	104600	698400	754300	1557300	148300	278500	282800	709600	6100	13000	3400	22500
Karnataka	48600	523200	378900	950700	110100	1321600	972100	2403800	19000	173300	72200	264500
Kerala	21600	471400	425400	918400	59000	319700	135200	513900	60600	144200	82800	287600
Madhya Pradesh	207800	2155300	2513300	4876400	445200	1331100	1082500	2858800	11700	14300	8800	34800

(Contd.)

(*Contd.*)

States	0-500 meter				500-1000 meter				1000-2000 meter			
	VDF	MDF	OF	TOTAL	VDF	MDF	OF	TOTAL	VDF	MDF	OF	TOTAL
Maharashtra	758900	1591400	1565800	3916100	110900	459900	510200	1081000	4100	32100	31700	67900
Manipur	900	60600	252900	314400	2000	166200	434400	602600	38600	300200	415000	753800
Meghalaya	22200	420300	431900	874400	18300	272300	225900	515600	500	257500	83200	341200
Mizoram	100	181300	679100	860500	3400	292100	452000	747500	9800	151600	154400	315800
Nagaland	0	123300	193000	316300	2200	134900	264800	401900	63600	205200	256900	525700
Odisha	358000	1277600	1390800	3026400	339900	830000	629100	1799000	9400	31800	18900	60100
Punjab	0	53000	78500	131500	0	20300	14600	34900				
Rajasthan	1500	268000	887400	1156900	5700	164600	258800	429100	0	12400	5200	17600
Sikkim	200	1600	1500	3300	1600	14100	8000	23700	20600	55200	35400	111200
Tamil Nadu	24500	388200	622100	1034800	140300	425200	305600	871100	106500	180100	83000	369600
Tripura	11100	473600	317000	801700	0	3400	2200	5600				
Uttar Pradesh	162500	435500	794800	1392800	100	20800	20400	41300				
Uttarakhand	52200	177400	78400	308000	95800	216900	85000	397700	156200	555500	267200	978900
West Bengal	233500	409800	465000	1108300	14800	27900	25700	68400	27500	21500	40900	89900
Andaman & Nicobar Islands	375600	240000	49300	664900	600	500	200	1300				
Chandigarh	100	10000	600	1700								
Dadra & Nagar Haveli	0	11400	9700	21100								
Daman & Diu	0	62	50300	56500								
Lakshadweep	0	167100	97700	264800								
Puducherry	0	129400	309300	438700								

VDF = Very Dense Forest **MDF** = Moderately Dense Forest **OF** = Open Forest

Source: State of Forest Report, 2009 (Forest Survey of India).

References

Agro-ecological Sub-regions of India for Planning and Development, (1999), National Bureau of Soil Survey and Land use Planning 1999.

AKRSP, (2008), *Annual Report 2008*, Ahmedabad: Aga Khan Rural Support Programme.

Alam, M., (1991), "Eastern India in the Early Eighteenth Century Crisis: Some Evidence from Bihar", *IESHR*, Vol. XXVIII, p. 66.

Albion, R.G., (1926), *Forest and Sea Power*, Cambridge: Howard University Press, Massachusetts.

Annual Administration Report of the Idar State, 1900-1901.

Annual Administration Report of the Idar State, 1912-13.

Annual Administration Report of the Idar State, 1931-32.

Arnold, J.E.M., (1992), *Community Forestry: Ten Years in Review*. Community Forestry.

Baden-Powell, B.H., (1893), *Forest Laws: A Course of Lectures on the Principles of Civil and Criminal Law and on the Law of the Forest*, London: Kessinger Publishing.

Baillie, W.R., (1951), *Summary of Papers, Relating to Madras and Bombay Forests*, Bengal Secretariat, p. 178.

Bayly, C.A., (1988), *Indian Society and the Making of the British Empire in (The New Cambridge History of India)*, Cambridge: Cambridge University Press.

Bindra, Prerna Singh, (2009), "The Forest Conservation Act is Sacrosanct", *Tehelka*, Vol. 6, No. 25, June 27, p. 56.

Bombay Forest Commission Report, (1887), Vol. I.

Brandis, D., (1897), *Indian Forestry*, Pune: Oriental Institute.

British Administration, (1971), Gandhinagar: Government of Gujarat.

Carney, D. (1998), "Implementing the Sustainable Rural Livelihood Approach" Paper presented to the DfID, Natural resources advisory conference, London.

Forest Survey of India, (2005), *India State of Forest Report 2005*, Dehradun: Forest Survey of India, Ministry of Environment and Forests, Government of India.

Forest Survey of India, (2009), *India State of Forest Report 2009*, Dehradun: Forest Survey of India, Ministry of Environment and Forests, Government of India.

Frank, Ellis, and Biggs, Stephen, (2001), "Evolving Themes in Rural Development: 1950s-2000s", *Development Policy Review*, 19(4), pp. 437-448.

Gadgil, M. and Guha R. (1992), *This Fissured Land: An Ecological History of India*, New Delhi: Oxford University.

Gadgil, M., Prasad, Narendra and Rauf, Adi, (1983), "World Wildlife Fund-India", *Newsletter*, Vol. IV, No. 44, 1. 1. 10, pp. 2-4 and 10.

Grindle, Merilee S. and Thomas, John W., (1991), *Public Choices and Policy Change: The Political Economy of Reform in Developing Countries*, Baltimore: John Hopkins University Press.

Grove, Richard H., (1995), *Green Imperialism: Colonial Expansion, Tropical Island and the Origins of Environmentalism, 1600-1860*, New Delhi: Cambridge University Press, First Indian Edition.

Guha, Ramachandra and Gadgil, M., (1994), "Ecological Conflicts and the Environmental Movements in India", *Development & Change*, 25(1), pp. 101-136.

Government of Gujarat, (1983), *Gujarat Forest Statistics*, Gandhinagar: Principal Chief Conservator of Forests, Gujarat State.

Government of Gujarat, (1995), *Gujarat Forest Statistics*, Gandhinagar: Principal Chief Conservator of Forests, Gujarat State.

Government of Gujarat, (2006), *Gujarat Forest Statistics*, Gandhinagar: Principal Chief Conservator of Forests, Gujarat State.

Government of Gujarat, (2008), Gujarat Sarkare Racheli Uchchadhikar Samitino Aheval (Laheri Report), Gandhinagar: Government of Gujarat.

Government of India, (1988), *National Forest Policy (NFP) 1988*, New Delhi: Ministry of Environment and Forests.

Gujarat State Gazetteers, Dang District, (1971), Government Press, Vadodara.

Gujarat State Gazetteers, Sabarkantha District, (1974), Government Press, Vadodara.

Habib, I., (1999), *The Agrarian Systems of Mughal India 1556-1707*, London: Asia Publishing House (for Aligarh Muslim), p. 1.

Habib, I., (1983), *An Atlas of the Mughal Empire*, Delhi: Oxford University Press. Notes to Sheet 7B (Gujarat, Economic), p. 25.

Habib, I., (1984), *Peasant and Artisan Resistance in Mughal India*, Quebec: McMillon.

Herring, Ronald, (1994a), "State Property Rights in Nature: Beginning Considerations", Paper Prepared for the Conference on Landed Property Rights and Environmental Degradation, organized through SSRC with funding from the National Science Foundation and the Ford Foundation, at Stowe, Vermont, August 17-21, pp. 24.

http://gujaratforest.gov.in/social_forestry/success_story.htm downloaded on September 15, 2009.

http://gujaratforest.gov.in/social_forestry/success_story.htm downloaded on September 15, 2009.

http://m.hardnewsmedia.com/2009/01/2476 retrieved on 21st February, 2012.

http://www.tribal.nic.in downloaded on 6th February, 2012.

http://www.tribal.nic.in downloaded on 6th February, 2012.

http://en.wikipedia.org/wiki/Maurya_Empire retrieved on March 21, 2012.

http://www.guj-tribaldevelopment.nic.in/cms.aspx?content_id=5 retrieved on 12th January, 2012.

http://www.taleemindia.org retrieved on 12th January, 2012.

Imperial Gazetteer of India, Bombay, 1909, Vol. I, pp. 64ff.

Jadhav, S.P. (1959), *Working Plan of the Sabarkantha Forests.*

Paul, John and Panwar, Pramod, (2008), "2 Polo Tribals Killed in Police Firing", *Times of India*, 14.2.2008.

Joshi, Satyakam, (1992), 'Dakshin Gujarat ni Jungle Kamdar Mandalio—Ek Abhyas', PhD. Thesis Submitted to the South Gujarat University, Surat.

Klages, K.H.W., (1958), *Ecological Crop Geography*, New York: MacMillan.

Lal, R.B., (1998), "Tribal Situation in Gujarat", Vidyut Joshi (ed), *Tribal Situation in India*, Jaipur: Rawat Publication, pp. 57-82.

Lobo and Kumar, (2007), Development-Induced Displacement in Gujarat 1947-2004, Vadodara: Centre for Culture & Development, (Mimeo).

Lobo, Lancy and Kumar Shashikant, (2009), *Land Acquisition, Displacement and Resettlement in Gujarat: 1947-2004*, New Delhi: Sage Publications.

Mahapatra, L.K., (1994), *Tribal Development in India: Myth and Reality*, New Delhi: Vikas Publishing House.

Maharasthra State Archives, at Elphinstone College, Mumbai.

Matela, A.G., (1984), "The Agro-Forestry Development Plan and Practices of PICOP", in J.K. Jackson (eds.,), *Social, Economic, and Institutional Aspects of Agro-Forestry*, Tokyo: The United Nations University.

Miles, Col. W., (1884), *The History of the Reign of Tipu Sultan Being a Continuation of the Nishani Hydari*, Trans., London: M.H.A.K. Kirmani.

Moreland, W.H., (1920), *India at the Death of Akbar – An Economic Study*, London: MacMillan.

Muricken, Jose, M.K. George, K.A. Emmanuel, Jose Boban and Prakash Pillai R., (2003), *Development-induced Displacement: Case of Kerala*, Jaipur and New Delhi: Rawat Publications.

Mudrakartha, Srinivas and Kumar, Sujit G., (2001), *Conflict and Conflict Management in Joint Forest Management*, Ahmedabad: VIKSAT Nehru Foundation for Development.

Nadkarni, M.V., Pasha, Syed and Prabhakar, L.S., (1989), *The Political Economy of Forest Use and Management*, New Delhi: Sage Publications.

NAI, PWD, Rev. For., June 1871, nos. 72-3, p.3, "Protection of Fine Trees in Sacred and Temple Groves", Memorandum by Acting IGF, G.F. Pearson, 6 Aug. 1869.

National Commission of Agriculture, (1976), *Report of the Forestry, part EX*, New Delhi: Ministry of Agriculture and Irrigation.

Natural Resources of Gujarat, (2000), *Gujarat Agriculture University and National Bureau of Soil Survey and Land use Planning*, p. 65.

Nayak, D.M., (Retired Chief Conservator of Forest – Government of Gujarat), (1989), "Illicit Felling of Trees—Gujarat Experience", Unpublished Document.

NMSWDF, (2009), *Pictorial Documentation of Horticulture, Floriculture, Vermi Compost and Vegetable Cultivation under Sadguru Foundation Activities in Recent Years*, Dahod: NM Sadguru Water and Development Foundation.

Note 7, Rev. 1, Food and Agriculture Organisation, Rome

Ostrom, Elinor, (1990), *Governing the Commons*, Cambridge, UK: Cambridge University Press.

Patel, Girish, (2009), *Public Interest Litigation and the Poor in Gujarat: Experiences of Lok Adhikar Sangh*, Ahmedabad: Girish Patel Sanman Samiti.

Prabhu, Pradip, (2002), "Land Alienation, Land Reforms and Tribals in Maharashtra" in Ghanshyam Shah and D.C. Shah (eds.), *Land Reforms in India: Performance and Challenges in Gujarat and Maharashtra*, New Delhi: Sage Publication, pp. 247-94.

Rajamani Committee Report, 2005.

Rao, R.K. and Sankaran, S.R., (2003), "Forest Myths, Jungle Laws and Social Justice", *Economic and Political Weekly*, Vol. XXXVIII, No. 46, Nov. 15, pp. 4819-20.

Raychaudhuri, T. and Habib, I. (eds.), (1982), *The Cambridge Economic History of India*, Vol. I, c. 1200-c. 1750, New Delhi: Orient Longman.

Reddy, K.B.R., (1993), "Forests and Forestry in Legal Perspective", *Forest Law Times*, March 1, pp. 26-32.

Reports on the Administration of the Bombay Presidency, 1885-86.

Revenue Department Files, 1894, Vol. 48, pp. 24 and Vol. 151, 1888, p. 65, Bombay: Maharashtra State Archives.

Robbentrop, (1900), *Forestry in British India*, Calcutta: Office of the Superintendent of Government Printing, India.

Roy Burman, B.K. (2006), "Creating Consternation, Draft National Tribal Policy 2006", *Economic and Political Weekly*, Vol. XXIX, No. 26 August, pp. 3645-47.

Sarin, M., (1993), "From Conflicts to Collaboration: Local Institutions to JFM", *Working Paper No. 14*, Society for Promotion of Wasteland Development, New Delhi: Ford Foundation.

Saxena, N.C., (2008), "Tenurial Issues in Forestry in India" – read at http://planningcommission.nic.in/reports/articles/ncsxna/ar_forestry1.htm downloaded on 18th February 2009.

Shah A.M. (2010), *The Structure of Indian Society: then and now*, New Delhi: Routledge.

Shah, S. A. (1996), "Status of Indian Forestry", *Wasteland News*, November 1995-January 1996, pp. 14-31.

Shangpilang, R.M., (2010), *Forest in the Life of the Khasis*, New Delhi: Concept Publishing Company Pvt. Ltd.

Singh & Dhillon, Jasbir, (2006), *Agricultural Geography*, New Delhi: Tata McGraw-Hill.

Singh, C., (1986), *Common Property and Common Poverty: India's Forests and Forest Dwellers and the Law*, New Delhi: Oxford University Press.

Srivastava, Vinay Kumar, (n.d.) "A Critical Reading of the Draft of the National Tribal Policy (A policy for the Scheduled Tribes of India)", (typescript).

Standing Orders of Bombay Presidency, corrected up to 1910, Bombay, 1912.

State of the World's Forest 2007, Food and Agriculture Organization United Nation, Rome 2007.

Stebbing, E.P., (1926), *Forests in India*, Vol. II, London: John Lane.

Sunder, Shyam S. IPS (Retd), "Study of National Forestry Policy of India", mimeo, n.d., pp. 10-40.

Taylor, G.F., (1981), "The Forestry/Agriculture Interface: Some Lessons, from Indian Forest Policy", *Commonwealth Forestry Review*, Vol. 60, No. 1, pp. 45-52.

Times of India, (1993), "The Struggle not yet over for Sardar Sarovar Activists", *Times of India*, April 2.

Tisdell, A. Clement, (2012), "Managing Forests for Sustainable Economic Development: Optimal Use and Conservation of Forest", in Sen, Raj Kumar (ed), *Forest Management and Sustainable Development*, New Delhi: Deep and Deep Publications, Pvt. Ltd., pp. 3-15.

Trautmann, T.R. (2011), *India: Brief History of a Civilization*, New Delhi: Oxford University Press.

Tucker, R., (2012), *A Forest History of India*, New Delhi: Sage Publications.

VIKSAT, (2008), *Towards a Sustainable Future*: Annual Report 2007-08.

Working Plan Report of the North Dangs Range Forests, Surat Agency, (1912-1913), Surat Agency, Surat.

Index